Upsetting Food

Jeffrey Haydu

Upsetting Food

Three Eras of Food Protest
in the United States

TEMPLE UNIVERSITY PRESS
Philadelphia • *Rome* • *Tokyo*

TEMPLE UNIVERSITY PRESS
Philadelphia, Pennsylvania 19122
tupress.temple.edu

Library of Congress Cataloging-in-Publication Data

Names: Haydu, Jeffrey, author.
Title: Upsetting food : three eras of food protest in the United States /
    Jeffrey Haydu.
Description: Philadelphia : Temple University Press, 2021. | Includes
    bibliographical references and index. | Summary: "This book compares
    three food reform movements-Sylvester Graham's diet reform, John
    Harvey Kellogg's push for home economics, and the organic food
    movement of the 1960s and 1970s-to probe continuing consumer
    mistrust over the safety, nutrition, and 'naturalness' of food in the face
    of corporate technology"—Provided by publisher.
Identifiers: LCCN 2020038640 (print) | LCCN 2020038641 (ebook) |
    ISBN 9781439920909 (cloth) | ISBN 9781439920916 (paperback) |
    ISBN 9781439920923 (pdf)
Subjects: LCSH: Kellogg, John Harvey, 1852–1943. | Graham, Sylvester,
    1794–1851. | Food industry and trade—Social aspects—United States. |
    Nutrition—Social aspects—United States—History. | Natural foods—
    Social aspects—United States—History. | Health attitudes—United
    States—History.
Classification: LCC HD9005 .H3595 2021 (print) | LCC HD9005 (ebook) |
    DDC 363.80973—dc23
LC record available at https://lccn.loc.gov/2020038640
LC ebook record available at https://lccn.loc.gov/2020038641

Printed in the United States of America

9 8 7 6 5 4 3 2 1

To Kath and Colin

Contents

Acknowledgments

My previous books examined the social movements of workers and employers. The switch in focus reflected in this book about the social movements of food consumers brought some pleasant surprises. Friends and relatives who asked what I was working on for my next book often wanted to hear *more* about my new research. Colleagues sometimes remarked that the work "must be fun." Although I welcomed these reactions, they're a mixed blessing. The wider interest is gratifying, and the research really was fun. But much like many of the food reformers I studied, for whom something that tastes good must be bad, among academics there's a suspicion that a topic that's fun can't also be serious.

My goal with this study was to have it both ways. I approached my cases of the food movement as a student of social movements and historical methods. I aimed to show how tools from those fields are useful for explaining the character of the food movement and how, in turn, studying food activism over the long run offers lessons for understanding social movements and improving historical sociology. But I hope readers will also share some of the fun I had in doing the research. Food reformers of the past are a decidedly odd bunch. Sometimes they sound uncannily similar to current critics of the food system. Sometimes they sound like kooks from another world. This mix of the strangely familiar and bizarrely different is engaging in its own right. It also offers opportunities to think about recurrent social movements such as "the" food movement differently. That emphasis on a singular food movement, requiring explanation of both consistencies through time and variations from one time to another, led to another change in my work. I have long insisted to colleagues and students that I study only long-dead people. Along with the switch from labor to food, I have made an exception to that rule in this book's concluding chapter.

I thank the colleagues and friends who listened to my ideas, offered suggestions, and read chapter drafts. For helping me make stronger connections among food reform, social movements, and comparative-historical methods, I'm grateful to Amy Binder, Cedric de Leon, Lindsay DePalma, Kevin Gillan, Heather Harper, John Krinsky, Doug McAdam, Chris Rhomberg, and Tad Skotnicki. Valuable feedback on various pieces of the project came from conversations with Charlotte Biltekopf, Michaela DeSoucey, Suzanne Dunai, John Evans, Hanna Garth, John Lang, Kevin Lewis, April Linton, Isaac Martin, Dan Navon, Keith Pezzoli, Belinda Ramirez, Krishnendu Ray, Akos Rona-Tas, and Stacy Williams. Thanks to Brenda Gutierrez and Alexis Navarro for research assistance; to the library staff at the University of California, San Diego, and especially to librarians extraordinaire Alanna Aiko Moore, Harold Colson, and Kelly Smith; and to Steve Siebert at Nota Bene for years of help in my use of this indispensable software for scholarly research and writing.

Michael Haedicke deserves special recognition for his unflagging (if not entirely successful) efforts to set me straight on the organic case. Ryan Mulligan at Temple University Press gave the project a warm reception and continuing support, with an assist from Ashley Petrucci. The reviews Ryan solicited of the whole manuscript provided the perfect mix of support and challenges to do better. And thanks to Susan Deeks for the final round of copy editing.

Finally, but most important, there is Katherine Mooney. I will never meet her high standards for clear argument and graceful prose, but I'm a better writer for trying. That is just one debt among the many I owe her. She and our son Colin (a food professional in the real world) provide my essential sustenance, and I dedicate the book to them.

Upsetting Food

1

Food Politics

One Movement, or Many?

It is not easy to keep up with today's contentious food politics. Consider the following small sample of actors and issues from 2018–2020.

The Center for Science in the Public Interest, Food Corps, the American Heart Association, and the Food Research and Action Center (FRAC), among many others, repeatedly squared off with the Trump administration over school lunch standards. In one recent skirmish, they denounced a new rule that would "simplify" compliance with the National School Lunch Program. The proposed action of the U.S. Department of Agriculture (USDA), FRAC charged, would "weaken nutrition standards, eliminate the guarantee that all children will receive a balanced and healthy school meal regardless of school setting, and diminish the nutritional value of other foods sold in the cafeteria."[1]

Other advocacy groups focused on keeping food safe from harmful contaminants. The spread of food-borne pathogens in 2018–2020 included outbreaks of E. coli in lettuce and flour, salmonella in poultry and ground beef, and listeria in pork and mushrooms. Government oversight, never vigilant, was further weakened in 2019 when the USDA gave meat companies more authority to police the safety of their own operations. The executive director of Food and Water Watch offered a simple equation: "There's no doubt about it: faster line speeds + less inspection = more food contamination."[2]

Despite regular reassurances that no scientific evidence proves genetically engineered food to be harmful to human health, consumers are skeptical. At the least, they support a "right to know." After several years of failed state referenda to require labeling (with food manufacturers outspending proponents by as much as 17:1),[3] action shifted to the federal level in 2018. The law passed that year required labeling—of a sort. Among other things, it exempted ingredients derived from "bioengineered" crops (such as high fructose corn syrup from genetically engineered corn) if no residues could be detected, allowed manufacturers to list information solely through a QR code, and preempted more exacting state initiatives.[4] "No one should be surprised that the most anti-consumer, anti-transparency administration in modern times is denying Americans basic information about what's in their food and how it's grown," lamented the Environmental Working Group's Scott Faber.[5] Nongovernmental organizations have tried to fill the gap left by federal policies. Consumers can look for the Non–GMO Project label, for example, when they do their shopping.

Amid growing concerns over climate change, groups such as the Community Alliance with Family Farmers and the National Sustainable Agriculture Coalition remind us that conventional farming and meat production are big parts of the problem, depleting water resources, reducing carbon sinks, and spewing methane. More sustainable production, they argue, will have to come from smaller farms, using organic alternatives to conventional growing methods, selling to local communities. Proponents of a Green New Deal promise to "reforest riparian areas, invest in conservation practices that rebuild degraded soil, and remove carbon dioxide from the atmosphere to reduce the 9 percent of greenhouse gas pollution from American agriculture to zero."[6] The political obstacles are formidable. Businesses urge an easier solution. Consumers can improve both personal and environmental health by purchasing products with the Eat Real Food label. And for carnivores who are both repentant and affluent, Beyond Meat and Impossible Burgers promise to deliver "the juicy, delicious taste you know and love, while being better for you and the planet."[7]

Healthy, local, and sustainable foods tend to cost more and be hard to find in many neighborhoods. Feeding America is one of the organizations trying to fix that, in part by keeping these inequalities in the public eye. The organization's studies document the scope of food insecurity in an affluent United States and how it disproportionately afflicts African American and Latino families.[8]

Some efforts to remedy the problem take an entrepreneurial tack. Francesca Cheney's Sol Sips is a vegan cafe in Bushwick, Brooklyn, founded with help from a GoFundMe campaign and offering a brunch menu with sliding-scale prices.[9] Other programs work through government channels. At the local level, the Los Angeles Food Policy Council "equips small business owners in economically disadvantaged communities with the support they need to sell the kinds of food that are hard to come by in many neighborhoods."[10] Nationally, a wide range of advocacy groups have tried to fight off restrictions on the food stamp program. Early in 2020, the focus was on President Donald Trump's budget proposal, which "would make steep cuts to the Supplemental Nutrition Assistance Program (SNAP) and other federal safety net programs."[11] Additional activist targets include administration edicts tightening eligibility thresholds, shortening time limits, and toughening work requirements.[12]

These are only a few battlegrounds and combatants in recent food fights. Close up, it is hard to identify common themes or the larger significance of specific goals, such as getting more refrigerated display cases into corner stores. Taking a broader perspective reveals some important commonalities. While the issues and organizational actors are varied, they can be seen as providing different answers to pressing questions about how food is produced, what food is made available to whom, and how best to protect consumers from risky or unhealthy food. There are also efforts to connect the dots among these issues, aiming for "food justice": a food system that is sustainable economically as well as ecologically and equitable for producers as well as consumers, regardless of class, race, and gender.[13] Those aiming for food justice follow different paths, however. The HEAL Food Alliance goes local, aiming to stimulate local economies, protect the environment, and improve conditions for low-wage workers through "cross-community organizing, advocacy for policy solutions, and holding powerful food system actors accountable." Food First keeps the national and global in view. It argues that a Green New Deal can be the starting point for addressing climate change while also democratizing politics and reducing inequality *if* it incorporates the voices and needs of farmers and food system workers.[14] But when goals are at odds—if closer monitoring for food contaminants or higher pay for farmworkers means higher prices for low-income consumers, for example—how should we balance the values of consumer health, environmental sustainability, and equal access? What role can we reasonably expect food fights to play in achieving the larger goals of rebuilding communities, reducing inequality, empowering consumers, and saving the planet? And if we want positive results, how should we divide our energy? Should we guide consumer choices and let markets do the rest, as with the Non–GMO Project? Or pressure governments to take decisive action, such as through the farm bill?

No answers will escape criticism. Market strategies can be faulted for giving in to neoliberalism (or simply for not working). Directing consumers toward better food often neglects class and racial biases in the definition of "better." And most politically practical measures leave control of the food system in the hands of large corporations. Achieving change will surely require broad coalitions among activists. Yet many calls for reform implicitly draw social boundaries: between "corporate" business and small enterprises, between responsible and complacent consumers, between true radicals and mere reformists, and between those with and those without the character and competence to make the right choices.[15]

I. Food Reform and Social Movements

These dilemmas of food reform have been faced many times before.[16] This book resurrects three eras of lively food protest in the United States to show how activists defined food problems, articulated solutions, and mobilized for change. In so doing, the book offers readers historical background to better understand, and important reference points to better evaluate, contemporary food politics.

A. Introducing the Cases

The earliest case features evangelical dietary reformers who gathered around Sylvester Graham in the late 1830s. A former missionary for the cause of temperance, Graham warned that store-bought bread, alcohol, and other "stimulating" foods undermined both health and morality. For Graham and his allies, the products of bakeries, cafes, and spice shops were symptomatic of a commercializing urban society, subverting the appetites and well-being with which natural men and women were endowed by God. Health and piety could be restored with a spare and unadorned vegetarian diet centered on homemade whole-grain bread. Grahamites preached this gospel through public lectures and pamphlets, finding their greatest support among middle-class strivers in the largest northeastern cities. Fifty years later, in the Progressive Era, these arguments were born again among health reformers such as John Harvey Kellogg. This group, too, blamed meat, alcohol, refined flour, and other dietary indulgences for all manner of physical ailments and social problems. But this period also saw more "modern" efforts to combat adulterated and unhealthy products. One campaign, fueled in part by sensational revelations of impure meat, demanded legislative action and helped establish the Food and Drug Administration (1906) to police the industry. Another promoted mandatory home economics classes in public schools to upgrade women's expertise in food preparation and nutrition. More efficient household management, these domestic scientists claimed, would improve health and even solve "the class problem" by teaching poor families how to eat economically. Both Progressive campaigns saw informed consumers and responsible businesses as the keys to safe and healthful family provisioning, with an enlightened state ensuring consumer education and business responsibility. The third era this book covers—the late 1960s and early

1970s—is the heyday of the grassroots movement for organic food. More skeptical of mainstream science and more critical of commercial food production, these activists sought fundamental changes that would ensure that food was grown ecologically, by small farmers, and without the artificial chemical inputs profligately used by "big ag" (the large companies responsible for the lion's share of farm production). Many organic activists went further, calling for a thoroughgoing democratization of the food system through farmer-run certification programs and cooperatively operated retail stores. Ultimately, organized producers turned to the federal government to set and enforce organic standards, creating new opportunities for growers and letting concerned consumers buy with confidence.

This is not an exhaustive collection of historical examples of contentious food politics in the United States. The cases come from the periods before our own with the most intense consumer activism around food issues. The "consumer" part of this claim is important. My focus is on consumers because it is among them that recurrent problems of trust in food arise and because it is among them that cross-fertilization from other social movements is most common. Consumers sometimes allied themselves with producers, and they did not necessarily define themselves with the label of "consumers." Nevertheless, they are the central actors in a coherent, long-running food movement. Accordingly, I set aside the large-scale mobilizations of farmers in the populist movement and during the Great Depression. And even around the time of my chosen periods, there are other "food protests" that I do not include, such as the use of lunch counter sit-ins in the Civil Rights Movement (in which the primary goal had little to do with the production or distribution of food) or the boycotts of lettuce and grapes led by the United Farm Workers (in which consumers were allies but not beneficiaries). One other obvious candidate—temperance—does not figure as a distinct case, but I discuss it as an important tributary to the featured food activists of the 1830s and late nineteenth century.

B. Comparing the Cases

The cases I have chosen offer contemporary readers a mix of the surprisingly familiar and engagingly eccentric. But the book provides more than antiquarian pleasures. It both highlights and seeks to explain long-term continuities (in the problems confronted, the ideals invoked, and some of the tactics used) *and* sharp differences in how these problems have been addressed from one time and case to another. Chapters 2–4 flesh out these similarities and differences. Here, I provide a brief overview. Reformers in each period raised doubts about the healthfulness of particular staples such as white flour and highly processed food. They warned consumers that products such as bread, canned meat, and frozen vegetables, whatever their nutritional value, carried risks from adulterants, pathogens, or chemicals added in production. The quality of such food was thought to suffer because it had been shipped long distances, with the standard for "long" increasing over time. Critics often noted, too, that these hazards were most common in the cheapest food and thus were borne most heavily by the poor. And in each period, those charged with defending consumer well-being—doctors, scientists—were key targets, as villains or saviors, in narratives of public health versus private gain. As we will see, the specifics vary from case to case in important ways, but these general themes of nutritional health, consumer safety, inequality, and the proper role of science run through all three periods, as they do in contemporary conflicts over school lunches, contaminated meat, food security, and genetically engineered ingredients. At a similar level of abstraction, common themes can also be found in the alternatives offered. Reformers in each period anticipated contemporary activists in praising "local" food products, including food made in the home. Most championed some version of "natural" food as superior to the products of commerce and industry. All saw expanding the number of educated consumers as an important lever for change. And all at least dabbled in some kind of certification scheme to help consumers choose healthier and safer products, whether the certifying authority was a civil or a state body. In each era, food activists believed that pursuing the alternatives they championed would contribute to social betterment. Their reforms would improve personal or community morality, reduce the nutritional costs of poverty, and make both the science and governance of food serve the public good.

On the side of these virtues, however, always stood certain kinds of people—respectable or WASP or tutelary or cool, but always solidly middle class. Food, scholars have long noted, is one common tool for marking social differences, from nomads versus agriculturalists and children versus adults to one class or ethnic group versus another.[17] Campaigns to improve food and diet do the same, adding notes of pious superiority.[18] On one side, they name enemies, whether they are small, immigrant-owned bakeries or giant corporations turning out junk food. On the other side, reformers elevate themselves above other consumers who lack the discipline or education or taste to make proper food choices. This relationship between the larger ideals of food reform and the social boundaries they reinforce is another theme running through the case studies I examine.

These striking family resemblances persist over nearly 140 years of food activism. But over the same span, there are similarly striking differences in how activists handled core dilemmas of changing the food system. Some reformers relied more on personal ties (know your farmer!) and others on formal institutions (such as the USDA) to guarantee the integrity of food.

Activists also varied in whether they aimed not just at better food, but also at a more democratic food system. They differed on whether the mainstream science of their day should be treated more as enemy or as potential ally. Campaigns diverged in the degree to which class inequalities, among both consumers and producers, were part of the agenda for change. And over time, the distinction between good and bad food aligned with different social boundaries—pious versus sinful, disciplined versus profligate, native versus foreign, hip versus square, depending on the case.

C. Rethinking the Cases as a Recurrent Social Movement

How can we make sense of this puzzling combination of long-running similarities and sharp contrasts? My answer—this book—amounts to an extended argument for thinking of these cases, and those in our own time, as a single, recurring movement. Social scientists are practiced in devising common labels for discrete objects; for example, from a sufficient analytical distance, many contemporary political movements look like "populism." The argument here is more ambitious: Mobilizations at different times to change the food system are tied together both by systemic causes and by cumulative legacies, even as they conform to the political cultures and models of protest that are distinctive to their eras and allies. In developing this framework, I lean most heavily on sociologists who analyze social movements and on scholars, especially historians and humanistic social scientists, in food studies. The latter have published excellent accounts of particular cases, and they are especially sensitive to the cultural contexts that shape food politics, past and present. It has become easier to marry their work to the sociology of social movements because the latter field has come to include in its bailiwick challenges to cultural as well as to political authority, insurgency that relies more on informal networks than on formal organization, and protest that involves little public and collective action.[19] Social movement theory also offers useful categories of analysis. These highlight (for example) the framing of social problems, the identities underlying participation, and the tactics and forms of organization deployed by activists. This book's case histories are built on this conceptual scaffolding. Last, social movement researchers offer some plausible causal suspects in their explanations for why movements' framing or organization or tactics take the form they do.

I do more than borrow freely from social movement scholarship and food studies. I also stake out different ground. My departures turn on rethinking mobilization around food issues, past and present, as parts of one recurring movement. To begin with, this means organizing the narrative around a single genre of protest over long stretches of time. The analyses published by most social movement researchers focus on short cycles of protest (e.g., the '60s) and on mechanisms of contentious politics (diffusion, scale shift, brokerage) shared by movements of varied types. My work takes a different approach. The general strategy is to ground accounts of protest in an enduring social problem, such as labor exploitation, which both animates and gives coherence to protests scattered over historical time and social place.[20] That focus, in turn, directs attention to the different temporal contexts within which protest unfolds. There is the familiar temporal context of a historical period (the Gilded Age, the New Deal, the neoliberal turn against unionism) within which protest campaigns rise and fall and in which activists are guided both by prevailing understandings of social problems (is the enemy Capital? foreign competition?) and by prevailing constraints on doing so. There is the context of larger trajectories of protest, anchored in the changing character and periodic aggravation of enduring social problems, as in the boom-and-bust cycles of the economy. And there is the context of long-term movement legacies, in which the outcomes of any given struggle (e.g., the triumph of the American Federation of Labor over the Knights of Labor) live on to influence later mobilization.[21]

For all my emphasis on limiting generalization—to specific problems and genres, to temporal contexts—the approach I advocate is a more broadly applicable one, suitable for other recurring movements focused on (for example) human relations with the environment or gender inequality, as well as labor and food. The invitation to generalize, however, is simultaneously a call to unpack temporal contexts. Fleshing out fuller explanatory accounts then requires a deeper dive into each genre of protest. For this book, that means exploring recurrent problems thrown up by a changing food system, the influence of ambient activist cultures in each of the three eras, and the cultural and institutional residues from prior food movements. In the final section of this introductory chapter, I offer an overview of this framework to help situate the case studies that follow.

II. The Food Movement in Three Temporal Dimensions

A. The Long Run of a Capitalist Food System: The Problem of Trust

What makes food activism a genre and gives it continuity is above all its roots in a capitalist food system and, more specifically, in changes in the production of food that regularly threaten consumer trust. My nineteenth-, twentieth-, and twenty-first-century food activists often sound surprisingly alike because they are dealing with similar problems, ones that revolve around trust. All sorts of social interactions are enabled, or at least lubricated, by trust, whether that is based on emotional ties, settled habit, or considered judgment.[22] As consumers, we need some basic assurance that the food we take into our bodies will not harm us. Our sense of confidence may involve nothing more than taken-for-granted familiarity: I have never noticed any problems from eating this stuff, so why think about it? Beyond such personal experience, we also come to trust food by proxy. If I trust the family member, the neighbor, or the well-known shopkeeper, I am likely to trust the food I get from them. Or, moving away from such personal ties, if I trust the brand, the government monitor, the credentialed expert, or the labeling authority, I am unlikely to question the food that bears their stamp of approval.[23]

This fundamental trust in food can break down; doubts can quickly develop about the healthfulness, safety, legibility, or quality of food.[24] Among the reasons for mistrust are innovations in food production, yielding new products (processed cheese, chicken nuggets) or well-known products packaged in new ways (plastic-wrapped, pre-sliced bread). These innovations may temporarily undercut trust based on familiarity. Even if a product is familiar, doubts may be raised if it comes from an untrusted or discredited source, as with some contemporary food imports from China. Or trust may be lost if those who have vouched for a food's safety, such as government agencies or nutritionists, betray consumers' confidence. All of these threats to trust can be expected from the normal operation of a capitalist food system—the background source of the "grievances" that underlie the food movement. There is, to begin with, a relentless process of commodification whereby foods made or food tasks performed in the home are produced for sale on the market. Graham complained about commercial bread in the 1830s (it should instead be made by loving mothers), and Michael Pollan bemoaned the decline of home cooking in the contemporary United States. Moreover, despite the nearly two-hundred-year gap between them, the two men point to a common source of mistrust: a more or less anonymous cash nexus that replaces personal ties and raises the possibility that sellers, unlike loving mothers, will not have your best interests at heart. Over time, newly commercialized foods and food tasks become familiar. But their production tends to move away from local circles—such as the town butcher or dry goods merchant—to more distant sources that can produce more cheaply and distribute more widely. These lengthening commodity chains (delocalization) are also endemic to modern capitalist food systems, whether the distance is down the street to the baker or halfway around the globe. Food businesses also regularly innovate, developing new ways to manufacture products (the animal carcass disassembly line, for example) or entirely new products (e.g., margarine, energy drinks). These will at first be unfamiliar and of uncertain trustworthiness. And a dynamic food system may transform the sources of what we eat in other ways as capital concentrates into large corporations and divides into start-ups seeking niche markets. These sources, too, may at first be suspect.[25]

Commodification, delocalization, and technological change do not operate in a vacuum. Social movement scholars long ago recognized that the grievances that anger us and the opportunities for action that beckon us are filtered by collective beliefs.[26] Similarly, whether developments in the food system undermine trust depends in part on consumer expectations and knowledge; these may change independently of shifts in how food is produced and distributed. Growing doubts about the competence or integrity of government food regulators recruited directly from the ranks of industry, for example, can erode confidence even when the food itself is unchanged.[27] Consumer expectations, however, are themselves influenced by other dynamics of the food system. Food producers and distributors compete, and one way in which they may do so is by casting aspersions on their competitors. Early twentieth-century mass producers such as Heinz made invidious comparisons between their pristine modern facilities and unhygienic small shops. Even earlier, purveyors of "natural" or "pure" food worked to discredit the healthfulness of conventional products.[28] Competitors may also enlist the rival nutritional or safety claims made by scientists, raising consumer skepticism about this important measure of trustworthy food. Advocacy groups have come to use a similar tactic—People for the Ethical Treatment of Animals (PETA) calling consumers' attention to the worst practices of meat production, for example, or the Environmental Working Group calling out "the dirty dozen" fruits and vegetables for their pesticide residues.[29]

A last threat to trust comes from the food scandals that periodically alarm consumers, as with recent cases of pathogens in lettuce, flour, and meat. On one hand, these scares have an "eventful" character: There is an element of serendipity in when and where they occur. On the other hand, such outbreaks are products of the routine operation of the food system. Developments in agriculture and industry, such as concentrated animal feeding operations, raise the odds that, sooner or later, there will be contamination. Food alarms also create opportunities for businesses and advocacy groups to amplify their warnings about competitors' products. Thus, contamination crises are both normal risks of modern food production and occasions to dramatize those risks for consumers who might ordinarily—perhaps deliberately—be unaware of them.

Together, these dynamics of the food system underlie the long-term, recurrent character of "the" food movement. And they go far to explain why contemporary debates over food safety, health, and transparency so clearly echo earlier ones. There are other reasons that food reform campaigns scattered over two centuries show a family resemblance. As Melanie

DuPuis shows, they draw on a relatively stable repertoire of American cultural themes.[30] DuPuis highlights the ideal of pure and disciplined individuals. One could make a similar case for other parts of the repertoire, such as populist skepticism about experts and pervasive doubts about state authority. Another continuity over time involves the consistent gendering of food reform. We will see this in the overrepresentation of women (relative to prevailing norms of public protest) among both the leadership and the rank and file of the reform campaigns discussed in this book. We will see it, as well, in the ways that idealized womanhood serves as one source of trust in food, whether that takes the form of bread-making mothers, expert housekeepers, or Mother Earth herself. My primary emphasis, however, is on those continuities that are rooted in the food system. This focus has the merit of directing attention to the problems that reformers are addressing. It also helps account, as the "constants" of deeply rooted cultural ideals and gender norms cannot, for the timing of mobilization. And it puts in sharp relief the question of why such enduring problems evoked such different responses from one case to another.

B. Short-Term Contexts: Social Movement Piggybacking

Within this long run of food movement activity, reform waxes and wanes on a shorter time scale. And at that scale, there are all sorts of differences, both across periods and, within the Progressive Era, among cases. For example, there are contrasts in how reformers framed their critiques. Does eating the wrong foods endanger your immortal soul, as Graham warned, or does it imperil the environment, as advocates of organic food claimed? Does part of the blame lie with ignorant consumers, as domestic scientists argued, or with corrupt businesses, as some backers of pure food legislation and organic food charged? Differences also appear in how reformers sought to restore consumer trust. Should we rely mainly on educating consumers, the main emphasis of Grahamites and Progressive Era health reformers? On government regulation, such as a pure food law? On voluntary certification, the preferred strategy in the early organic movement? As I noted earlier, standards for good and bad food imply boundaries between good and bad people, but the specific content of these evaluations varies. For Grahamite reformers, the improved diet embraced by good Christians raised a bulwark against the loosening moral standards of an urbanizing society. Sixty years later, the threat was to native Protestants from the immigrant hordes, including their unscientific (and thus unhealthy) food preferences. In the late 1960s, organic-food advocates framed the opposition as one of consumers against avaricious corporations and their government flunkies. In all three eras, food reform is primarily a concern of the middle class. But again, there are variations. What counted as the mark—or the cultural capital—of the virtuous middle? The display of rigorous self-control? Of efficient mothering? Youthful liberation from *old* middle-class norms? Discerning taste?

These marks of virtue reflect general models of middle-class distinction, adapted and applied to food ideals. This is the basic approach I take to explaining differences across the cases. Some of those differences can be tied to the specific problems raised by changing food systems—a theme to which I return when discussing social movements' legacies. For example, one can hardly explain the environmentalist preoccupations of the organic movement without reference to worries over pesticide use, a problem largely without precedent in the earlier periods. But the more pervasive influences on food activism are the prevailing social distinctions and existing models of protest in each era. They provide the lenses through which actors interpreted generic problems such as adulterated or unhealthy food, allocated blame, and thought of appropriate solutions.[31] I especially highlight the ways that food activists piggybacked on other social movements of their day. All of the cases I examine in the following chapters occurred during periods of lively protest: evangelical reform, Progressivism, "the '60s." Leading figures in each case had personal roots in other movements or were part of wider activist networks. Key Grahamites, for example, had backgrounds in evangelical temperance; pure food champions were involved in other Progressive causes; and organic-food advocates often came out of the New Left or environmentalism. For their part, activist organizations commonly overlapped with counterparts in other movements, as with campus ecology clubs in the late 1960s, or they had a hand in other causes, as with reform-minded women's clubs in the early 1900s. There were thus many channels through which wider templates of social reform could travel to activism around food, shaping the critiques voiced, the alternatives offered, the organizational models deployed, the tactics used. Much as social movement scholars speak of the "co-opting" of social networks and institutions for resources to mobilize,[32] I emphasize the co-opting of cultural models for food reform.[33] This transposition is important for another reason. These were, in large part, consumer movements, with little by way of formal organization enlisting rank-and-file participants. The movements on which reform-minded consumers piggybacked provided shared scripts to guide and coordinate choices about which foods to favor and which to shun.

C. The Long Run of Food Reform: Movement Legacies

Cultural piggybacking helps explain differences across cases and adds a more historically grounded layer to my account, rooting the specific characteristics of food activism in particular times and contexts. A third layer of explanation turns back to the long haul, but in a different way. For the Progressive Era and organic-food periods, I show how legacies from prior eras of food activism influence successors.[34] They do so through several paths. Measures to restore consumer trust in food left institutional residues. The most important ones from the Progressive Era are the Food and Drug Administration, university hubs for nutritional research, and formal ties between home economists and food companies. All of these shaped the conflict over organic food in the 1960s. The National Organic Program that came out of the organic movement, in turn, plays a role (often as whipping boy) for contemporary food activists. These institutional legacies may operate by tying the hands of later reformers. One reason that improved conditions for farmworkers could not be incorporated into federal standards for "organic" produce was that labor and agriculture had long been regulated by different government departments. But legacies may also exert their influence by drawing the lines along which trust eventually breaks down. The reliance of pure food advocates and domestic scientists on government regulation and reputable corporations to reassure consumers meant that when these institutions lost credibility in the 1960s, trust in food went down with them.[35]

A second route by which earlier movements may shape later ones involves the languages they use to diagnose problems and valorize alternatives. Historians and historical sociologists often reconstruct how popular understandings of who "we" are and what is at stake take particular forms and how they get reproduced over time.[36] Sidney Tarrow, for example, discusses repertoires of contentious language that, like repertoires of strategy, offer ready-made formulas ("patriot," "revolution") for doing battle and make it hard even to think of alternatives.[37] In the case of food, two important examples are "nature" and "the consumer." The first term has been used in highly flexible ways as a measure of good food (is it "natural"?) and as what needs to be defended in battles against commercial products. These uses of "nature" were not new in the 1830s, but Graham helped make the term a regular touchstone for his successors. "The consumer" as an individual actor with rights and as a collective actor standing chastely apart from self-serving capital and labor was first popularized by Progressive Era reformers.[38] Food activists of that period put it to good use. The category was subsequently institutionalized in government agencies and honored by advocacy organizations, and it saw extensive service in the organic movement.

A third path from past to future movements is, paradoxically, constructed from the future to the past, when activists invoke the examples of earlier insurgencies. Social movement researchers, asking why protest spreads from one place to another, refer to "the attribution of similarity."[39] If actors think of themselves as *like* others who have occupied factories or built protest camps, they are more likely to follow suit as fellow members of the proletariat or the 99 percent. This identification can also be with actors long dead. These individuals may be considered worthy subjects of emulation *or* they may serve as precedents not to be repeated (as too reformist, too violent, too exclusive, or too hierarchical). The influence is activated after the fact, as reformers in the present deem past movements models to follow or oppose. Organic-food advocates sometimes held up Progressive Era champions of scientific agriculture and home economics as part of the problem they faced in the 1960s. Contemporary locavores, in turn, point to the dilution and co-optation of the 1960s movement and cast themselves as a virtuous alternative to an industrialized version of organic food.

Not all of these mechanisms are at work across all the cases in this book. Nor are they the only ways in which earlier periods shape later ones. Plenty of legacies are unrelated to prior activism. A prime example is the long-standing Christian tradition of associating indulgent eating with sin. For the purposes of this book on long-running food politics, however, it is legacies from earlier movements that I call out. How can we trace such legacies? It is all too easy to tell stories about how the past influences the present, and the role of legacies in social movements is no exception. This third layer of explanation becomes more plausible if there is documentation on two points. One consists of identifying mechanisms that transmit residues from a movement over time. Researchers should show how outcomes from earlier campaigns become institutionalized in policies and organizations, for instance, or are reproduced in popular culture and memorial practices.[40] The role of the Seventh-day Adventist Church in carrying Graham's dietary reform into the Progressive Era is one example.[41] Claims about legacies gain credibility in a second way, if we can document actors thinking or acting in ways consistent with constraints laid down by past movements, and even— on a good day in the archives—acknowledging that they are doing so. For instance, proponents of organic food were guided in part by the perceived limitations of agricultural policies and food safety regulations created by Progressive Era reformers.

III. Overview of Chapters

Looking ahead, Chapters 2–4 present the three periods of food activism. Each begins with an overview of major changes in the food system of the day. These changes posed the challenges to consumer trust and the problems with which reformers grappled. The chapters go on to survey the broader social movement environment: evangelical reform (Chapter 2); Progressivism and "social purity" (Chapter 3); and the New Left, environmentalism, and the counterculture (Chapter 4). They then zero in on the critiques and remedies offered by Grahamites and by the early advocates of health food, pure food, domestic science, and organic agriculture. For each, I rely primarily on the writings of leading reformers, on the records of organizations with which they were associated, and on the pamphlets and periodicals that amplified their voices. With each, I relate the reformers and their ideas both to wider movement culture and, in Chapters 3 and 4, to legacies from earlier waves of protest. Chapter 3, on the Progressive Era, carries a heavier load of cases. The quests for pure food legislation and domestic science were in many respects textbook cases of Progressive advocacy, confident in the power of government to solve social problems by applying standards of efficiency and professionalism. The concurrent call from reformers such as Kellogg to improve health through dietary change was—like all the cases in this book—a response to some common problems in the food system. But in this case, those problems were framed more in terms of individual Christian morality than in social uplift through enlightened state policy, a contrast that reflected the era's larger social purity movement (with which Kellogg was allied).

Although such comparisons across movements are sprinkled liberally throughout the case studies, Chapter 5 more systematically sorts through similarities and differences and shows how they can be understood with reference to general food system dynamics, period-specific political cultures, and movement legacies. This concluding chapter goes on to briefly bring the analysis up to date, applying the same logic of explanation to contemporary calls for local and alternative food networks. It reminds readers, too, that my general approach to long-running movements is applicable beyond problems of the food system. But first, American food reformers of the 1830s.

2

Grahamites, 1830s–1840s

Critics of the American food system, and of the average American diet, have found much to complain about. One activist warned consumers away from commercial beef in light of "the various expedients to load the animal speedily with artificial fat." Store-bought bread, another cautioned, is of dubious value because its manufacture, driven by a quest for profits, "destroys much of the virtue of the flour." In place of these suspect foods, a third activist recommended a diet of grains and fresh vegetables, but only if grown in "pure, unadulterated soil." Musty language aside, these sound much like recommendations made by contemporary champions of grass-fed cattle, whole grains, and organic agriculture. They come instead from disciples of Sylvester Graham, writing in 1837.[1] The themes raised in Graham's critique of a commercializing food system are all familiar from our own era of food activism. His concerns about "unnatural" production methods, profit motives undermining the quality and nutritional value of food, and the contamination of soil by fertilizers have their counterparts in current attacks on genetically engineered crops, processed food, and unsustainable agriculture. It is when another acolyte promised to make "a thorough trial of what is now called Grahamism, but it is in fact Bibleism"[2] that we are reminded that these calls for change in 1837 were also part of a larger cycle of evangelical reform, worlds away from contemporary attacks on Food, Inc., by countercultural critics or privileged foodies.

This chapter puts Graham's dietary reform movement in both contexts. On one side, it shows how reformers mobilized in response to changes in the food system—commercialization, technological innovation, lengthening commodity chains—similar in character, if not scale, to changes that would spur later movements. On the other, it shows how reformers' understanding of the problem, the solutions they advocated, and the organization and tactics they deployed all had deep roots in the status boundaries and evangelical activism of the early nineteenth century. Whether driven by recurrent changes in the production and distribution of food or by the specific evangelical and status strivings of the time, however, Graham's nostrums would themselves become influences shaping later movements for food system reform.

In tracing how Grahamites borrowed from a more general model of evangelical reform, I draw on discussions of "diffusion" in the social movement literature.[3] Protest can be infectious. Events—a riot, a sit-down strike, an occupation—in one place often provide the spark for similar action elsewhere. More important for my story, the ways that some activists frame problems, run organizations, or mobilize followers can travel from one place or type of movement to another. They may do so through biographical connections, where individuals move from one cause to another in the course of their activist careers, taking organizational principles or tactical ideas with them. Social movement know-how also travels through network ties among participants in different fields of protest. More formal organizational ties may facilitate diffusion, as when representatives from different movements ally for joint campaigns. These channels for mutual influence tend to be especially lively during cycles of contention when levels of activism are high and widely distributed. Whatever the channels, the upshot is that the character of protest comes to look alike across diverse movements.

I make ample use of this insight in this and subsequent chapters. Thus, I not only highlight similarities between Grahamites' thinking about food problems and wider evangelical scripts. I also document the vehicles through which influence traveled, both personal (such as key figures' involvement in multiple causes) and organizational (such as the way that Graham boarding houses served as hubs where diverse reformers mingled). But I also extend the notion of diffusion and put it to a different explanatory use. One extension, which appears in later chapters in the guise of social movement legacies, is to trace diffusion over time periods well beyond individual cycles of protest. *Within* those cycles, another extension is to look beyond other social movements for sources of diffusion. Grahamites, as we will see, also transposed to their reform agenda the assumptions and anxieties of the emerging urban status order (reminding us how porous the boundary is between movement and mainstream). The difference in explanatory use lies in where I locate causal influence. Theorists of contentious politics have teased out an impressive list of social mechanisms—including attribution of threat, brokerage, scale shift—which, in varying combinations, carry the burden of explaining individual cases.[4] Diffusion is also on that list. But in my view, it has little explanatory value in itself. The causal work is instead done by the specific models of protest and the particular social boundaries on which activists draw. These are what produce particular responses to recurring problems in the food system. To understand the Grahamites, let us start with those problems.

I. A Commercializing Food System

Today, alarm over the safety, healthfulness, and sustainability of conventional food is often expressed through calls to "know where your food comes from" or even to "know your farmer." Americans in the early nineteenth century might be expected to have had fewer concerns, because a majority *were* farmers. With rapid economic and urban growth, however, came changes in how food was produced and procured. Some economic statistics suggest the pace of change. Between 1810 and 1840, manufacturing employment increased by more than six times; farm output nearly tripled; and circulating currency grew by a factor of about seven.[5] Cities, too, boomed. The 1820s and 1830s brought waves of migrants from rural areas to northeastern cities. (Foreign immigrants would not outnumber them until the 1840s.) New York grew from 125,000 people in 1820 to 800,000 by 1850; Philadelphia, from 81,000 in 1800 to 408,000 fifty years later.[6] City dwellers had little choice but to purchase more of their food in the market; farming families thus had many more mouths to feed than their own. That changing trade relationship had profound implications for both agricultural production and urban distribution.

On the farm, production for market sale rather than for home use was not new in the 1830s: commercialization was well underway by the last decades of the eighteenth century. With improvements in the reach and speed of transportation and with increases in the sheer size of urban markets, however, it became profitable for farmers to change production strategies in other ways.[7] Rather than grow a variety of crops and sell the surplus, farmers in the early nineteenth century increasingly specialized in a few crops, using the profits to meet their own household needs. Some "agricultural" operations moved off the farm altogether. Pig slaughtering, brining, and packing began to be done on a more large-scale, factory-like basis in centers such as Cincinnati. Thanks to improved roads and new canals, some products that until recently had been produced and consumed locally could be shipped longer distances—a trend reinforced by increasing regional specialization. The latter included, in addition to Cincinnati's salt pork, Ohio's wheat, with flour milled to slow spoilage. And to maximize yield without leaving land fallow, farmers increased the use of animal manure to restore fertility.[8]

As for urban consumers, having to purchase food as a commodity rather than grow or slaughter it themselves had its benefits.[9] As in our own time, longer commodity chains made for greater variety in what shoppers could find in urban markets.[10] But greater dependence on markets also meant greater vulnerability to market swings, which were probably greater at a time when longer-distance and more specialized supply chains were still new. Price spikes for flour, for example, were serious enough in 1837 to spark old-fashioned food "riots" in New York.[11] Concerns went beyond the cost to the integrity of food. Food produced in cities rather than on the farm caused the greatest anxieties. Those anxieties focused on three indispensable staples: milk, meat, and bread. The interplay of commodification, longer supply chains, technological changes, and eager muckraking (professional and commercial) all fueled consumers' concerns.

The 1830s saw the first public outcry over "swill milk" in northeastern cities.[12] A growing urban population attracted larger dairies, with cows concentrated in squalid barns and fed, for reasons of economy, the spent grain from breweries and distilleries. The scale of production and new technology developed together. Visitors to New York City dairies might find hundreds of cows fed by an ingenious system of troughs carrying swill from nearby breweries, the animals "inhumanely condemned to subsist on this most unnatural and disgusting food."[13] Writing in 1835, the health reformer William Alcott insisted that good milk could come only from cows "in perfect health, [fed] from the first on pure and perfect grass.... [They] should also roam the pasture freely, and breathe pure air."[14] Public concern, however, focused more on human health than animal welfare. In letters to newspapers and in public petitions, physicians warned of the risks, especially for children. Swill milk "contains too little nutrient for the purposes of food, [and] appears to possess unhealthy properties; owing in part . . . to the confinement of cows, and the bad air which they consequently have to breathe, as well as the unnatural and pernicious nature of the slops on which they are fed." Unscrupulous dairymen compounded the problem by disguising the pale blue color of swill milk with added starch, flour, or plaster of paris. The "beautiful white color" produced by these artificial means then allowed them to "dilute with an equal quantity of water."[15] Rival dairies seconded physicians' warnings, taking out ads to promote the superiority of their own "pure milk" by invidious comparison. "As a man and a Christian," the dairyman Thomas Martin promised readers of the *New York Evangelist* that "nothing of the swill kind is . . . given to [my] cows."[16] "The time has come," concluded the *Graham Journal of Health and Longevity,* "in which 'still slop' should [share] the fate of diseased meat, and be thrown into our rivers."[17]

Graham's *Journal* may have been too optimistic about that meat. Like milk, it spoils quickly without refrigeration. The solution for larger cities was bigger slaughterhouses in town, exposing residents to the sights, sounds, and smells of the carnage. (In the 1840s, New York City finally relocated the slaughterhouses to city outskirts, keeping them out of sight and out of mind.[18]) In early nineteenth-century cities, the *sale* of this meat was at least regulated as a matter of public health, sold only through city markets by licensed butchers. Municipal inspection, public scrutiny, and the professional reputation of individual butchers all served to safeguard quality. These safeguards eroded as unlicensed butchers increasingly catered to consumers wanting cheaper meat and more conveniently located shops. Licensed butchers, fearful of losing trade protection, publicly warned of unsafe meat from competitors. Consumers registered their complaints with municipal authorities, but the trend was to loosen rather than tighten market regulation.[19]

The story for bread begins, naturally, with flour. In a pattern that would become familiar with other foods, technological innovations and improved transportation favored larger-scale, more geographically concentrated flour production. The technical side included elevators that allowed firms to handle grain in bulk and milling improvements that, by removing the oily bran, made a pleasingly white and longer-lasting flour. The expansion of America's canal system, including the opening of the Erie Canal in 1825, lowered transportation costs. Together, these developments allowed bigger producers to supply more distant markets and drive the local small fry out of business.[20] One New York newspaper voiced concerns about grain "heaped up in larger masses when [still] damp, in . . . granaries or store-houses, where . . . highly pernicious gases are generated." How could urban consumers trust the flour on sale? Their vulnerability is suggested by the newspaper's impractical recommendations for checking quality: "Select your own grains, and be careful that they are fresh and pure. . . . Have them ground in a coarse manner, under your own inspection."[21] But city residents increasingly were not even making their own bread, much less monitoring their flour, and here were more grounds for worry.[22] What was going on in urban bakeries? In answer, popular newspapers offered plenty of horror stories about both ingredients and sanitary conditions. "In no article can fraud be more dexterously practised [*sic*] than in that of flour," with bakers adulterating it with "calcined plaster of Paris, or sulphate of lime."[23] By contrast to the "well baked, wholesome loaves" made at home, one could expect only "wretched, insipid stuff [from] some of the city bakers."[24] Higher standards for bread might have been upheld out of craft pride, but in city bakeries less skilled labor increasingly took the place of craftsmen.[25] That shift was hardly limited to baking, and it points to the wider social and political context of 1830s food problems.

II. The Context of Middle-Class Boundary Work and Evangelical Reform

Organized food politics has generally been the work of middle-class consumers.[26] Among the influences on the middle-class men and women who rallied behind Sylvester Graham were the rapid economic growth and emerging national markets of early nineteenth-century America.[27] Labor historians highlight the boom in production of consumer goods in larger shops that employed wage labor and that, wherever possible, divided work tasks and substituted less-skilled employees to speed output and cut costs.[28] Those trends spurred widespread mobilization of skilled workers to protest declining opportunities, growing social inequality, and the betraying of republican ideals. But many of these same changes created new opportunities—and anxieties—for an emerging middle class of retailers, small manufacturers, and clerical workers.[29] Expanding urban industry allowed a fortunate minority of artisans to make the transition from skilled hand to small-scale employer; increasing specialization of production and distribution added opportunities for aspiring shopkeepers; and the heady growth of manufacturing, finance, and trade multiplied positions for office workers to keep track of it all. These men and women could look down on manual workers: they earned more, they had a measure of independence, and they kept their hands clean. But looking up, they had nothing like the wealth and recognized status of merchants and established professionals. And no less than manual wage earners, these new middle-class strivers were subject to the still-unfamiliar cycles of boom and bust.[30]

Booming cities promised freedom as well as fortune, but they also surrounded newcomers with uncertain mores, anonymous throngs, and preying confidence men, all dramatized in cautionary popular writings.[31] It was in the city, too, that new clerks and small tradesmen were most exposed to the political turbulence of the time. From the late 1820s, workingmen turned traditions of artisan republicanism into industrial and electoral weapons against economic and political elites.[32] Even the Jacksonian insurgency, hardly anticapitalist, challenged the authority of merchants, lawyers, and financiers in the name of "the people." The proposed national bank was dubbed the "Monster Bank" by opponents and made to symbolize the concentrated power, aristocratic privilege, and parasitical occupations arrayed against productive citizens.[33]

This new environment for new men and women—novel job opportunities and unstable markets, enticing and alarming cities, the prospect of enhanced status above a threatening working class—fostered two responses of particular importance for food politics. The first was a cultural quest for recognition as a distinct, respectable middle class. The second was involvement in the era's evangelical revival and its reformist offshoots.

The quest for recognition combined a developing class consciousness with pervasive boundary work vis-à-vis the lower ranks. At the heart of middle-class consciousness by the 1830s and 1840s was a commitment to gentility, evident in an exacting code of self-discipline and good manners in private and public life.[34] The code had practical value for securing one's reputation with prospective creditors and employers. But in urban settings where rules of conduct were less anchored in interpersonal ties and "ruin" was less remote, strict conformity to etiquette books, advice manuals, and formal standards of deportment offered a stable identity and a recognized place in society. It offered, too, clear grounds on which to distinguish the respectable middle class from lesser sorts. The key occupational dividing line became that between nonmanual and manual labor, those who worked with their heads versus those who labored with their hands.[35] The former was associated with intelligence, cleanliness, and refinement, in contrast with the dimmer minds, dirtier clothes, and rougher ways of even skilled manual workers.

These collective standards, and the class identity that went with them, were marked and reinforced in a wide range of settings. At work, manual and nonmanual employees increasingly occupied separate physical spaces (floors of an establishment, buildings in a city) with different expectations of cleanliness and ornamentation.[36] At home, middle-class consumption practices, increasingly a feminine responsibility, set higher standards of refinement, with their pianos, decorative touches, and separate parlors for entertaining.[37] A greatly expanded array of voluntary associations, from fraternal orders to literary societies and music clubs, allowed clerks and shopkeepers to display their gentility in settings with people like themselves.[38] Nor did it require social historians to notice these developments. They were widely remarked at the time in endorsements by journalists and etiquette guides and in criticisms by spokesmen for resentful "hands."[39]

The Second Great Awakening was another important arena in which an emerging middle class both defined itself and sought to impose order on others. The evangelical revival of the 1820s and 1830s had doctrinal roots within the competitive leadership of Protestant denominations.[40] But it brought a more populist style to religious life, questioning the authority of the credentialed clergy, supporting the spiritual enthusiasm of members, and encouraging the rank and file to embrace a more direct relationship with their God. The revival mobilized middle-class believers in a wide variety of Bible societies, missionary organizations, and Sunday schools,[41] making piety another important marker of respectability and self-control.[42] For more substantial manufacturers, it had another value: Evangelizing their employees promised (if it did not necessarily deliver) a more disciplined workforce.[43] The more direct relevance of the revival to Grahamites lies in the way it became a powerful engine of reform movements.[44] The 1820s and 1830s saw a remarkable cycle of protest targeting a wide range of issues, from slavery and intemperance to violations of the Sabbath and of sexual propriety. This explosion of activism on a national scale had many sources, including a newly improved infrastructure of transportation (roads, canals, steamboats) and communication (cheaper printing, improved postal system). But its deepest roots were in religious life.

Those roots were of several kinds. One involved institutional resources and leadership of the sort familiar to all social movement scholars. Over the first three decades of the century, the elite Protestant churches (Presbyterian, Congregationalist) developed a "benevolent empire" of societies to deal with social problems—establishing colonies for freed slaves, fighting violations of the Sabbath, supporting the deaf and dumb, encouraging temperance, and (above all) doing missionary work. The 1830s brought a shift in this religious base from elite churches to more populist ones (Baptists, Methodists) and from established clerics and their gentlemen supporters to lay leaders and enthusiasts. That shift involved a tremendous infusion of grassroots energy, but the energy continued to draw on the "co-optable institutions" of religious life.[45]

Abolitionism, temperance, Sabbatarianism, moral purity: These movements had more cultural roots in evangelical revival. Missionary techniques such as the revival meeting, the distribution of tracts, and the simplification of doctrine for popular audiences were all readily applied to social movement mobilization. Evangelicals also embraced a doctrine of perfectibility, believing that individuals and the nation, far from being condemned to sin, could be saved—*now*. Indeed, as Michael Young has emphasized, the evangelical revival offered a general script linking personal conversion with national salvation. By coming together to publicly renounce their sins (their drinking, their Sabbath-day work, their tolerance for slavery), believers could at once win individual redemption and solve the nation's ills. It was a formula well suited to solving social movements' collective action problem and one widely applicable to problems of the day. Moreover, because evangelicals had an obligation to bring the Good News to others, reform movements got an additional religious boost. Finally, evangelicals linked the personal and the political through gender. They shared in the emerging doctrine of separate spheres, which made women and domesticity the locus of moral virtue, particularly because they were insulated from the corrupting influence of markets and politics. Evangelical women had to bring that moral influence to bear on others. They assumed new roles as agents of change, turning their parlors into meeting places and participating in more public efforts to save the souls of individuals and the nation.[46]

The temperance movement both illustrates these patterns and is the most important immediate precursor to Graham's dietary reform.[47] In the 1820s, temperance was the subject of elite church benevolence. Most cities had a Society for the Promotion of Temperance headed by local clerics and notables. By the 1830s, however, the movement had become more popular, more emotionally charged, and more absolutist: Fighting the demon of drink was a matter of lay missionary work, and salvation required not moderation but the complete renunciation of alcohol. Much of the crusade fell to Christian women, both in their own families and in their communities. Further, renouncing drink, like embracing Christ, was an individual choice; it was also a key to social betterment, saving homes from discord, careers from ruin, and neighborhoods from squalor.

For all its ties to religious institutions and religious worldviews, however, temperance was also bound up with class identities and interests. Sobriety became the most important outward sign of piety and Christian self-control, and Christian self-control "was the moral imperative around which the northern middle class became a class."[48] That identity drew social boundaries on both sides: against the intemperate working class and the self-indulgent rich. It also proved useful to manufacturers and master craftsmen as a tool for social control. Sober workers were more worthy of their hire, and employers (and their wives) made that message clear.[49] Temperance had much more than instrumental importance, though. Repudiating or consuming alcohol meant the difference between respectability and ruin—and, eventually, heaven and hell. Graham would make similar claims about certain foods.

III. Graham and the Movement for Dietary Reform

Proponents as well as critics of dietary reform in the 1830s, together with historians of the movement, identify the cause with Sylvester Graham (1794–1851).[50] He was the most active and popular lecturer, and one of the most widely read writers, to warn audiences of their dietary sins and advocate alternatives that could save their health and their morals. Graham first gained prominence in 1830 as an agent for the Pennsylvania Society for Discouraging the Use of Ardent Spirits, giving lectures and organizing auxiliary societies in local communities. Drawing on both his ministerial and his medical training, Graham went on to lecture on physiology, diet, and health in Philadelphia, New York City, Boston, and many smaller cities across the Northeast. He attracted particular attention in 1832 during a cholera outbreak, claiming that his dietary regime provided immunity, and his reputation grew through his controversial lectures on the physical and spiritual perils of masturbation. In addition to a demanding schedule of public speaking, Graham published several popular tracts and collections of testimonials, along with weightier books on bread and "the science of human life," among other topics. He mostly withdrew from public activism at the end of the decade, but dietary reform was not a one-man show. William Alcott, active from the early 1830s through the 1840s, was an important ally and an even more prolific writer of popular books and journals on health, diet, and good living. Other prominent Grahamites included David Cambell, publisher and editor of the *Graham Journal of Health and Longevity*, and Mary Gove, proprietor of the Graham Boarding School in Lynn, Massachusetts, editor of a successor to Cambell's journal, and a popular writer and lecturer in her own right.

In the following account, I draw most heavily on texts written by or to Graham; he was the center of the movement. But selections from other sources show that the main themes in Graham's approach were shared by other reformers. And because this was a reform *movement*, I highlight key features of all movements: What problems did Grahamites identify? What solutions did they propose? How did they organize their efforts to promote change? And who supported those efforts? Answering these questions makes it possible to then step back and consider the movement's relationship to the food system, to class boundaries, and to evangelical revival.

A. Framing the Problem

1. Bad Bread, Depraved Appetites

Graham is best known today as a champion of whole-grain bread—the precursor to Graham crackers—and his critique of commercial bread is a good starting point for understanding his broader diagnosis of what ailed Jacksonian America. The first objection was on nutritional grounds. Refining flour to make it whiter and less prone to spoiling during shipment stripped it of nutritional value. Bakers compounded the problem: "Their mode of manufacturing bread . . . destroys much of the virtue of the flour."[51] These are familiar charges today; the theory underlying them, less so. Graham argued that all foods contain a mix of "stimulating" and unstimulating components. Foods with excessive "stimulating power," such as flour without the whole grain (or coffee, spices, and alcohol), led to inflammation and exhaustion. "Proper alimentary substances [are those] whose stimulating power is barely sufficient to excite a full and healthy performance of the functions of the digestive organs, in the appropriation of their nourishment to . . . the vital welfare of the body."[52] A second objection to commercial bread traced the problem back to profit-driven bread making. Bakers making bread on a commercial basis "have always had recourse to various expedients in order to increase the lucrativeness of their business," including chemicals to lighten bread and adulterants to disguise its defects.[53] Whether on the farm or in the urban bakery, the underlying problem was the commodification of food. "So important an article" as bread, Graham's fellow reformer William Alcott concluded, "should never be made by hirelings."[54]

Bad bread, then, is symptomatic of a commercializing food system. It also illustrates a larger perversion in the relationship between men and women's "appetites" and their health. In his public lectures on the science of human life, Graham described a natural state in which our desires, our resources, and our well-being are aligned. In this Eden, the foods we want, in the amounts we crave, are readily available and perfectly suited to our bodies' needs. This natural balance ensured lives of Old Testament length, free from disease. It remains true that foods "adapted to the constitutional nature of man" bring good health. "The more entirely man subsists on them, the more perfectly he fulfills the laws of his nature, and secures his highest interests."[55] Such perfect harmony reflects God's creation, but there is nothing arbitrary in God's control: one can discern through scientific study, and choose to follow, these "fixed laws of life."[56] No less clear, Graham told his audiences, is evidence of a steady deterioration in this harmonious relationship. Civilization has perverted our appetites. As society offered more variety and abundance in our food (a particular curse of city life), we developed a taste for more stimulating foods, in excessive quantity: "The artificial wants of man become so numerous and so imperious that a large proportion of the time and powers of every member of society are employed in supplying them."[57] An ally of Graham's sounded the same alarm. "The accumulation in large cities, the noxious effects of impure air, sedentary habits, and unwholesome employments; *the excesses in diet, the luxurious food, the heating drinks, the monstrous mixtures,* and the *pernicious seasonings* which *stimulate* and *oppress* the organs,—the unnatural activity of the great cerebral circulation, excited by the *double* impulse of our *luxurious habits* and undue *mental exertions,* of the *violent passions* which agitate and exhaust us," these are curses of civilization.[58] And for this woeful state, socialized appetites and the products of industry share the blame. Bakers, for reasons of their own, make light bread from refined flour, but we develop a taste for the stuff. Farms, slaughterhouses, medical advice, and unnatural tastes for flesh combine to make meat a large part of the modern diet. And "artificial" foods, larded with spices and often with alcohol, both foster and cater to our increasingly depraved appetites. In Graham's summary of this culinary fall from grace, "Man's superior intellectual and voluntary powers not only increase his ability to supply his bodily wants . . . but also increase his power of multiplying those wants, by his artificial modes of supplying them, and by the artificial circumstances of social and civic life." Those "thousand artificial wants . . . become engrafted upon his body and exert their influence upon his intellectual and voluntary powers in precisely the same manner as his original instinctive wants do, and always with a more despotic and imperious energy; and with a continual and powerful tendency to excess."[59]

The consequences for our health are everywhere to see, Graham argued. Much as perfect health follows from the balance between natural appetites and nature's food, "civilized" appetites and commercial food lead to unnatural disease and early death.[60] The diseases begin with poor digestion—inflammation, loss of appetite, constipation—but extend throughout the body to produce all manner of physical and mental pathology, including irritability, exhaustion, and headaches. These ailments are the central narrative threads in letters from Graham's followers. A "grateful friend," writing from Philadelphia in 1831, is typical. "It is more than five years since my health began to fail, and although I was not attacked with any definite disease, yet I gradually declined: Suffering first a loss of appetite—then a general languor and debility, and sense of weariness, and occasional depression of spirits,— pains in my head, chest, side, &c."[61] These symptoms recur throughout other accounts, blending physical and mental ills: headaches, pains, feebleness, coughs, irregular bowels, nervousness, despondency, indigestion, inability to concentrate. The litany goes on. The afflicted often link their deteriorating health to moves from country to city. "I was brought up in the country, and had excellent health until I arrived at the period of manhood," wrote one rueful New Yorker. Since then, "I have resided in this city, being a period of about ten years, with health gradually declining."[62] Illness and debility followed in short order, temporarily relieved only by a brief return to the country. Letter writers also regularly note another dire consequence of their deteriorating health: an inability to work, whether men at their businesses or women in their homes.

For these dietary reformers, the pernicious effects of artificial appetites and foods went beyond the medical to the moral. The connection was in part physiological. An overly stimulating diet inflamed, among other organs, the sexual ones. In his "Lecture to Young Men," delivered throughout the Northeast in 1838, Graham warned that "all kinds of stimulating and heating substances, high-seasoned food, rich dishes, the free use of flesh, and even the excess of aliment, all, more or less—and some to a very great degree—increase the concupiscent excitability and sensibility of the genital organs, and augment their influence on the functions of organic life, and on the intellectual and moral faculties."[63] Nor did the trouble stop down there.

Comparative anatomy demonstrated that over time a stimulating diet gave a neurological boost to immoral behavior. Put the flesh eater in a city, and the moral peril only gets worse. "A thousand other causes besides flesh-eating, and the use of intoxicating substances, are continually operating in civic life, to excite unlovely and injurious passions in man: and for that very reason, flesh-eating is a far more powerful cause of these effects, in civilized than in savage life."[64] Ultimately, poor diet undermined the morals of whole communities. Directing his criticism especially to carnivores, Graham offered this summary:

> Flesh-meat is more stimulating, more heating than vegetable food, and its immediate effect on those who eat it, is to increase the energy of the more exclusively selfish propensities and the violence of the more turbulent, ferocious and mischievous passions. Its permanent effects, from generation to generation as a general fact, are to increase the relative proportion of the lower and back part of the brain, and to cause the animal, to predominate over the intellectual and moral man: and when the numerous exciting, irritating, debilitating and depraving causes which abound in civic life, co-operate with this, their combined efficiency of evil is tremendous.[65]

The Grahamite Arthur Foote offered a political application of this theory. "Had the populace of Paris satisfied their hunger at the ever-furnished table of vegetable nature," they would never have "lent their brutal suffrage to . . . Robespierre."[66] A less charitable contemporary scoffed at Graham's promise to "revolutionize the world with johnny-cake and boiled beans,"[67] but there is no doubt that Graham saw just such redemptive power in dietary reform.

2. What Is to Be Done? Returning to God's Nature

What was the recipe for restoring individual and social health? The main recommendation from Graham and the main "activism" of his followers was to return to a "natural" diet of simple and plain food. "By simple food I mean that which is not compounded and complicated by culinary processes; by plain food I mean that which is not dressed with pungent stimulants, seasonings or condiments; by natural food I mean that which the Creator has designed for men."[68] Pride of place in a reformed diet went to bread made from whole-grain flour. Ideally, the grain should be grown in "new soil, in its virgin purity, before it becomes exhausted by tillage, and debauched by the means which man uses to enrich and stimulate it."[69] Ideally, too, this wholesome flour would be made into bread by the loving hands of wives and mothers. This recommendation comports with Graham's general aversion to commercial food and his nostalgia for a simpler time of rural calm:

"Who that can look back thirty or forty years to those blessed days of New England's prosperity and happiness, when our good mothers used to make the family bread, but can well remember how long and how patiently those excellent matrons stood over their bread troughs, kneading and moulding their dough? and who with such recollections cannot also well remember the delicious bread that those mothers used invariably to set before them?"[70]

But Graham claimed a more scientific rationale that pays respect to "nature" in another way. Yeast-risen bread is finicky, requiring close observation and mature judgment.

> Are we to look for such a sensibility in public bakers? Can we expect that they will feel so lively and so strong an interest for our enjoyment and for our physical and intellectual and moral well-being, that they will exercise all that care and attention and patience, and watch with that untiring vigilance and solicitude in all the progress of their operations, which are indispensably necessary in order to secure us the best of bread? Or can we reasonably expect to find these qualifications in domestics—in those who serve us for hire? . . . No;—it is the wife, the mother only—she who loves her husband and her children as woman ought to love, and who rightly perceives the relations between the dietetic habits and physical and moral condition of her loved ones, and justly appreciates the importance of good bread to their physical and moral welfare,—she alone it is, who will be ever inspired by that cordial and unremitting affection and solicitude which will excite the vigilance, secure the attention, and prompt the action requisite to success, and essential to the attainment of that maturity of judgment and skilfulness [sic] of operation, which are the indispensable attributes of a perfect bread-maker. And could wives and mothers fully comprehend the importance of good bread, in relation to all the bodily and intellectual and moral interests of their husbands and children, and in relation to the domestic and social and civil welfare of mankind, and to their religious prosperity, both for time and eternity, they would estimate the art and duty of bread-making far, very far more highly than they now do.[71]

Homemade, whole-grain bread epitomizes the more general dietary reforms championed by Graham. Foods close to their natural state are best adapted to our constitution. Those that are stimulating should be shunned, a category that includes alcoholic beverages, coffee, tea, spices, refined flour, sweets, and meat. Although Graham advocated a vegetarian diet, those unable to go that far should at least eat *wild* meat, from animals "which live after nature's intention" rather than from domestic cattle.[72] Such food, eaten in small quantities, chewed thoroughly, accompanied by cold water, guaranteed sound health, long life, and good morals. Graham even argued for the benefits of "natural" clothing (meaning none at all) on the grounds that this allowed for pure air to circulate and movement to be unfettered. He assured readers that this would not lead to vice, because natural health means that "the sensual appetites would be more purely instinctive, and exert a less energetic and despotic influence on the mental and moral faculties, and the imagination would be deprived of its greatest power to do evil."[73] Graham did not push the point, but he joined fellow reformers in making fresh air, exercise, loose clothes (rather than constricting fashions), and hard beds part of an encompassing regimen to restore physical and moral health.[74] Their followers got the message. Testimonials focus on diet but cover a wider range of bodily reforms to return men and women to their natural health. "I adopted the Graham System quite strictly," one convert wrote, "avoiding all artificial stimuli of every kind." The result: improved health, diminished headache, and, most important, a renewed ability to work.[75]

B. Pursuing Change: Individual Responsibility and Movement Strategies

The goals of improving individual health and community morality through better diet are clear. Graham and Alcott were no less clear about strategies for reaching these goals. These strategies involved educating and persuading individuals to make the right choices rather than pursuing change in social policy through collective action. Proponents realized that winning hearts and minds would not be easy. Change would require enormous self-discipline on the part of converts, both to conquer their artificial appetites and to defy prevailing medical views of diet and health. But leading Grahamites also pioneered a variety of supporting institutions to make it easier for individuals to mend their ways.

Because our natural appetites have long since been corrupted by artificial and overstimulating foods, individuals cannot consult their instincts to eat the right things in the right quantities. In effect, people have become addicted to bad food, and they resist Graham's recommendations because they are "given . . . up to the control of factitious appetites."[76] In choosing how much to eat, too, our bodies lead us astray: "There cannot be a blinder guide, in regard to quantity of food, than appetite."[77] Dietary penitents, accordingly, will at first have to exercise exacting self-control, turning away from what they crave (coffee, spices, a full stomach) and contenting themselves with what will seem to be small, insipid meals.[78] Only when natural health is restored and perverted appetites purged will the body come to *want* exactly what it *needs.* "The more simple our diet and the more conformable it is to the constitutional laws of our nature, the more we not only promote health and healthful enjoyment generally, but also, gustatory enjoyment of the purest and highest kind. . . . Even pure soft water, which most men consider tasteless . . . has a deliciousness to such a pure organ of taste, wholly unknown and inconceivable to those whose gustatory powers have become depraved by artificial habits."[79] Until that time, self-discipline is essential. The corollary is a familiar American one. Once educated about the path to health and morality, it is a matter of the individual's own choice whether or not to take it. The causes of disease, Graham reminded his audiences, "are almost universally to be found within the precincts of our voluntary conduct."[80] And as in body, so in morals. Whenever "men are induced to adopt and perseveringly observe a simple and restricted regimen, their bodily health and longevity are as much improved and increased as their virtue and piety."[81]

There is, however, an obstacle to dietary reform that has less to do with internal individual appetites than with external social pressures. Medical professionals of the day recommended meat as the centerpiece of a nutritious diet; they saw disease as something to be cured with drugs rather than prevented with good food; and they often prescribed drugs that contained the very substance that was poisoning many patients—namely, alcohol. Small wonder that, according to Alcott, "in those countries . . . where no physicians have ever been in vogue . . . the health of the people is quite as good, and the longevity quite as great, all other things being equal, as in those countries where physicians and medicine have obtained a strong foothold."[82] Characteristically, Graham went further. Precisely because medical science's focus was on curing rather than preventing, it was unable to grasp that—much less study why—disease is an *un*natural human state: "Such a delusion necessarily has led to the deeper and more fatal error, that there is in medicine an intrinsic health-giving virtue. . . . And thus has led the way to that wide-sweeping evil . . . the eternal and suicidal drugging! drugging! drugging! of mankind."[83] Medical professionals returned the compliment, dismissing Graham as a quack and his American Physiological Society (APS) as the "bran bread and sawdust pathological society."[84]

In the face of orthodoxy and derision, then, it took some gumption to stick with Graham's prescribed regimen. The collected testimonials to that regimen regularly recount the authors' struggles against tempting food ("the delicious chicken pie, who could withstand?"[85]). But they also regularly recount their struggles with medical professionals. In their myriad sufferings, these men and women first consulted doctors and followed their prescriptions. The results, through rounds of treatment, often with a series of physicians? Deepening misery. Nor were their initial trials of Graham's system well received by others. "When they saw how I was living, they were much alarmed, and gave me no peace till I consented to abandon my new regimen," an accommodation the writer would soon regret.[86] "My friends all declared that I was destroying my life and continually remonstrated against the course which I was pursuing," wrote a Mr. Wheeler in 1833. "And I confess, that my dreadful distress and their importunities, often shook my resolution." The narratives, however, always end well. In Mr. Wheeler's case, "I thought to myself, shall I prove faint hearted? Shall I throw down my cross before I have fairly tried its virtues? No! I will persevere."[87] Through such personal effort and self-discipline, misinformed doctors and friends are defied, and Graham's unorthodox diet restores health. One larger lesson drawn by Graham himself affirms the power of individual initiative in dietary reform. Thanks in no small part to his own lectures and writing, individuals can learn for themselves the underlying science of nutrition. Doing so not only allows them to choose health. It also helps break doctors' exclusive hold on medical expertise: "Knowledge of *Human* physiology—the science of *Human* life—has been principally confined to the members of a single profession. And if we cannot justly say that medical men have intentionally monopolized this species of knowledge, is it not most true that they have taken very little pains to diffuse it?"[88]

Grahamites assumed that change would come through disciplined individual choice, but they also worked to enable those choices. The main strategies for reaching potential converts, typical of the time, were public lectures and popular publications. Graham himself maintained a heavy schedule of public appearances, including a lecture series on the science of human life and his "lecture to young men" on sexual restraint, both later published as books.[89] In 1837 alone, Graham could be found in Portland, Maine; New Bedford, Massachusetts; Providence, Rhode Island; New York City; Newark, New Jersey; Philadelphia; and Boston, with the Boston visit including three general talks on diet, four talks to young men, four addressed to mothers, and his long-running course on physiology.[90] No wonder one critic deemed Graham "that Prince of . . . Locomotive Humbugs."[91] Alcott had an even more prodigious output of advice books on diet, vegetarianism, cooking, and health. Followers could also subscribe to journals that offered diet advice and testimonials, including the *Graham Journal of Health and Longevity* (edited by its publisher, the Grahamite David Cambell), Alcott's *The Moral Reformer and Teacher on the Human Constitution*, and Mary Gove's *Health Journal and Advocate of Physiological Reform*. One hub of organizational activism was the APS, cofounded by Alcott in 1837.[92] The society hosted meetings and lectures, where its roughly three hundred male and female members could meet kindred spirits from around the Northeast and

> GRAHAM HOUSE IN ROCHESTER N. Y.
>
> It must be gratifying to all the friends of dietetic reform to learn, that the demand for boarding houses kept on the most rational temperance principles is steadily increasing. A Graham house has been established for some time past, in Rochester, N. Y. in Fitzhugh street.
>
> Mr Graham is about lecturing in Rochester for the first time.
>
> A similar house is very much needed in Philadelphia, and if some enterprising friend of "Temperance in all things" will undertake it, they would receive essential aid from that philanthropic gentleman, DAVID F. NEWTON, the well known teacher in the "Institute for the cure of Impediments of Speech."

Figure 2.1. Notice for the Rochester Graham House. (*Graham Journal of Health and Longevity*, October 12, 1839.)

receive further education in dietary science. But its officers also encouraged the formation of local chapters throughout the country "for the purpose of diffusing physiological knowledge."[93] The *Graham Journal of Health and Longevity*, for its part, claimed to have 141 agents in towns across sixteen states, doing their part to advance the cause of dietary reform.[94]

These were all useful means to popularize Graham's message. Actually following his advice, however, required more than knowing what foods to eat. It also meant finding those foods and learning how to prepare them. For a time, students at Oberlin College in Ohio had no choice. The dining hall steward was Cambell, who enforced strict Graham principles until protesters unseated him for banning pepper.[95] Connecticut's Wesleyan College took a less heavy-handed approach. Its Graham Club used an off-campus house to prepare proper meals for members. Older adherents had other options. The APS helped establish boardinghouses where Graham's disciples could get satisfactorily bland meals while away from home (see Figure 2.1).[96] For city dwellers cooking their own food, the APS worked to establish stores where members could find "a supply of the very best of those articles which enter into their diet," and it may have solicited farmers to present samples of their produce for approval.[97] If in doubt about how to cook sound meals from these ingredients, Grahamites could consult cookbooks prepared by the boardinghouse operator Asenath Nicolson (*Nature's Own Book*) and by Mary Mann (*Christianity in the Kitchen*).[98]

C. The Grahamite Rank and File

Who subscribed to this vision of alternative, health-giving, natural food? Graham's followers appear to have been typical of the constituency for reform movements of the period. The best source is the membership of the APS. Stephen Nissenbaum tracked down eighty-four of them, all middling in class and Protestant in religion. At least eighty were small businessmen or skilled artisans of modest wealth; neither unskilled laborers nor professionals make any appearances.[99] This finding matches more impressionistic evidence from letters to Graham collected in the *Aesculapian Tablets of the Nineteenth Century*, where writers occasionally identify themselves as businessmen and more frequently focus on their ability to attend to their business, suggesting a discretionary relationship to work that would hardly fit manual labor. Graham's supporters also included substantial numbers of women—one-third of the membership of the APS and about one-third of contributors to the *Aesculapian Tablets* for whom the sex is clear.[100] As with class background, the role of women among Grahamites is consistent with patterns in other reform movements of the time. It is consistent, too, with the prominence of women in food activism that extends back to earlier food riots and forward to our own locavores.[101]

IV. Graham's Reform Movement in Three Temporal Contexts

A. Generic Problems

The story of the Grahamites is in part a backlash against changes in the food system. A variety of innovations in the production and distribution of staple foods came in for criticism by Graham and his allies. They included, as we have seen, new ways of fertilizing soil, fattening cattle, refining flour, baking bread, and running dairies. Graham's followers do not go on the historical record with their views on these specific issues. They do make clear, however, that they had turned to alternative "experts" to guide them in what to eat—that they had come to doubt the conventional wisdom. These doubts, and Graham's and Alcott's explicit criticisms, reflected more than the sheer novelty of particular food practices. New practices were suspect because they were no longer embedded in traditional social relationships. For city dwellers, grain no longer came from local farms, milk from rural dairies, bread from the loving hands of mothers and wives. The particular social relationships that had anchored trust in food—familial, gendered, face-to-face—may set this period apart from later eras of food activism. But the underlying dynamics of commercialization, delocalization, and (early) industrialization of food production, together with the tendency to outstrip relations of trust, are recurrent ones.

B. Particular Solutions

If the changes in the food system that motivated Graham's protest remain familiar today, the form this protest took was very much a creature of its time. The movement reflected historically specific conditions in three important ways. The untrustworthy character of food became a metaphor for other anxieties; the invidious contrast between good food and bad mapped onto prevailing status distinctions; and Grahamites piggybacked on and adopted the character of other movements in this cycle of protest.

1. Diet and Urban Anxieties

The other anxieties were bound up with the rapid growth of markets and cities in Jacksonian America. Historians have seen this as the dominant force behind a wide range of social and political developments in the period.[102] Graham's support came primarily from men and women living in rapidly growing urban centers, and Graham's analysis of food and diet channeled their concerns. As Nissenbaum points out, the very language Graham used to describe the effects of "stimulating" food—engorging organs, inflaming digestive tracks, bursting blood vessels—makes the body a mirror of excess and loss of control in urban commerce. Graham's corresponding calls to rein in the appetites that now enslave us and to moderate consumption of food add up to "a declaration of physical independence from the capitalist marketplace."[103] The critique of unhealthy food as "artificial" similarly makes it both exemplar and metaphor. Much as recent arrivals in the city worried about being deceived by con men and painted women,[104] so they mistrusted their bread and milk.

2. Diet and Status Distinctions

While Graham's vision of food was partly about rampant markets and hustling cities, it was also about different kinds of people. All food reformers make invidious comparisons between good food and bad. One way in which they are rooted in particular times and places is in how they map good and bad food onto prevailing social distinctions. Among Grahamites, these distinctions included that between the virtuous country and the corrupting city. A resolution in praise of Graham from supporters in Providence declared his lectures "of great and general interest to the human race; and more especially to the inhabitants of populous cities in which the prevalence of luxury, connected with the sedentary habits of most of the population, induces inevitable disease."[105] Alcott, too, saw his regimen of natural food and clean living as antidote to the debasing influence of cities.[106]

Good and bad food also mirrored emerging social distinctions between middle-class men and women. They were increasingly consigned to separate spheres. On one side was the masculine world of commerce and politics, with its sharp-elbowed competition. On the other was the feminine haven of the home, with its nurturant family and moral purity. Here was a beneficent division of labor. Men's work world paid the bills, while women's caring offered moral refreshment. According to one 1830 *Ladies Magazine* tribute to the well-bred woman, when a man returns home after the day's struggle to get ahead, he "not only feels safe but is actually renovated."[107] For Grahamites, women played a similar purifying role vis-à-vis food. It was not just that commercial and homemade bread corresponded to gendered separate spheres. At a time of doubt about commercial food, pious women offered—or Graham offered them up as—a source of trust. Their bread bore the imprimatur of their inherent moral natures. Indeed, according to an APS resolution, there could be only one greater stamp of approval: "Woman in the character of wife and mother, is only second to the Deity in the influence which she exerts."[108]

It is within cities that we see food practices associated with status distinctions of the day. A diet of vegetarian food and cold water in small amounts marked Grahamites as men and women of moderation and control, in contrast both to the rougher sorts below and the self-indulgent fashionable set above. Both extremes were intemperate. Drinking, for example, undermined the ability and commitment to work for laborers and businessmen alike, and it served as a sign of ruin, current or impending.[109] But other foods mark similar distinctions of social standing and worth. For Graham, of course, proper bread set the caring middle-class family off from the frivolous rich. He complains that it is thought "not only perfectly respectable, but highly genteel for a young lady to be employed in making cake" when she should be learning to bake sound Graham bread.[110] As for restaurant meals, the worst culprits were establishments catering to the upper crust. The *Graham Journal of Health and Longevity* printed one offensive menu from 1839 with the label "Bill of Fare—Not Nature's, but at the Astor House."[111] For a contributor to Alcott's *Library of Health*, the moral hierarchy is measured in dumplings. "A person's fondness for dumplings may . . . be considered a pretty sure test of his disposition. . . . When we see men devour balls of thick, clammy dough, anointed with grease, and filled with *suet, pork,* or *lard,* can we help believing that those who relish such food are either physically or morally impure?" And that impurity can be found at the top as well as the bottom of the social ladder: "Wherever I go, I see continual proofs of depravity and brutal appetite, that to a temperate man are torture. I have no doubt that I suffer more agony in looking upon a dinner party, and seeing the ravenous propensities of *ladies* and *gentlemen,* than I should from an application of the thumb-screw."[112] In between these depraved extremes is the middle-class striver, embodying respectability and self-control and demonstrating those virtues with his diet as with his parlor piano.[113] Proper food did not merely signal respectability. It was a means to achieve it, disciplining rapacious appetites and restoring the ability to work.

3. Diet and Evangelical Revival

Graham's movement also piggybacked on the larger evangelical revival of the early nineteenth century, and that relationship gave the movement's approach to food and diet a distinct character. The piggybacking can be seen in Grahamites' social base, in their ideology, and in their organization and strategies.

There were several channels through which evangelical religion influenced Graham and his followers. As noted earlier, the two drew on much the same constituency of small businessmen, clerks, and artisans, together with large (for the time) numbers of middle-class women. Evangelical and dietary reformers also moved in the same circles, both over their careers and at any given time. Graham himself trained as a minister and agitated for temperance before taking up the cause of proper food. Alcott began to speak and write on dietary reform at the time of his own evangelical conversion.[114] Cambell moved back and forth between dietary and temperance advocacy.[115] And Grahamites and other religious activists regularly crossed paths in churches, on the lecture circuit, and at temperance houses—a pattern of overlap typical of the multitasking reformers of the time.[116]

One could use the language of social movement scholarship and point out that for Grahamites, churches were co-optable institutions, a source of clerical allies and of forums for lectures. But this would miss how evangelical religion was not only a supporting institution but also a cultural model. The modeling is clear in most aspects of Grahamite thinking about food as a dietary and social problem. To begin with, food and health are matters of sin and salvation. In the long view, the arc from a state of harmony between appetites and natural food to corrupted appetites and artificial food echoes the biblical fall from grace. In the personal view, Grahamites' own narratives closely follow the script of personal sin (poor diet) and suffering (disease, fatigue, etc.), followed by revelation (hearing of Graham's principles) and salvation (a return to health, with occasional, instructive episodes of temptation and backsliding). Even the language of these narratives makes regular use of evangelical keywords, with Graham in the role of personal savior. "I was a hearty proselyte, before seeing him," wrote one convert. "But when I traced him through his reasonings, comparing them with . . . my own sad pilgrimage, truth in all its splendor burst upon me. . . . I went from the Hall, making the firm resolve, to tear the last idol from my lips, and bade a final adieu to my beloved coffee."[117] Others made the point more directly, including a female acolyte reporting that "the change in my body was as great as it was in my soul when I was converted to the Lord."[118]

Grahamites' approach to food further echoed evangelicals in emphasizing individual responsibility for their dietary redemption. Much as evangelicals determined that they could *choose* salvation, so Grahamites believed they could choose health, physical and moral. And much as evangelicals expressed faith in the perfectibility of man and his works, so Grahamites argued that the right dietary choices would produce perfect health—freedom from disease, mental clarity, long lives. What Grahamites relentlessly stressed was the tight link between spiritual and physical perfectibility. "They who would make the highest attainments in spiritual things," wrote one follower, "must learn to . . . keep [their body] in subjection, and crucify its improper passions and appetites."[119] And as with other versions of this American faith in personal responsibility, if Graham's diet appeared not to work, the failure was one's own: "Many cheat themselves out of great benefits, and unjustly reproach your System, in consequence of their own fickleness."[120]

Even Grahamites' relentless criticism of doctors and their "drugging! drugging!" follows an evangelical script. Historians have noted that the revival's challenge to the doctrines and authority of Protestant clerical elites spilled over into a wider populist challenge to leaders in other institutions, including government, law, and medicine.[121] Graham and his supporters were quick to contest the knowledge—and even the good faith—of doctors when it came to health and diet. "The people are beginning to enquire" into diet, one contributor to the *Graham Journal of Health and Longevity* wrote. "It is idle for any man or for any profession to attempt to screen their opinions or their actions from this scrutiny. Dogmas have ceased to be lawful tender; prerogatives receive but little reverence from the 'democracy of numbers.'"[122]

Michael Young argues for a more general role of evangelicalism in Jacksonian reform. A key task of mobilization in any social movement is to connect the personal to the political, to persuade individuals that their own personal grievances are social problems requiring collective action. Arguably this occurred on a national scale for the first time in the early nineteenth century. Young finds the key development to be the link evangelicals constructed between personal sin and national salvation. Whether in the temperance, abolitionist, or moral purity campaigns, evangelicals internalized social problems as matters of individual sin and saw individuals' public repentance as the key step toward social reform.[123] That dynamic fits Graham's movement as well, with the twist that repentance was, in the first instance, a matter of bodily self-discipline; spiritual and civic betterment followed.

The emphasis on personal transformation as the initial step toward reform suggests how Grahamites borrowed from evangelical reformers fundamental tactics for social change. The organizational strategies largely mimic the temperance crusade: conduct public lectures, distribute pamphlets, set up local auxiliary societies to carry the torch once Graham or Alcott moves on. Grahamites probably took from temperance the idea of boardinghouses where travelers would not be tempted by alcohol or stimulating food. The larger pattern here is a nonstatist strategy for pursuing movement goals. Like most evangelical reform crusades through the 1830s, Grahamites did not make government policies—even at the local level—a tool for improving the supply of food or the character of diet.[124] That strategy rested on the bedrock evangelical belief that change would come through individual rebirth. Those individual transformations could be supported with certain institutional initiatives. Grahamites joined temperance advocates and free-cotton abolitionists in trying to build alternative supply chains: Graham groceries, temperance boardinghouses, stores for slave-free clothing and sugar.[125] But these strategies still eschewed any role for the state. Formal politics and policy are not even topics of discussion in Graham's lectures and writing. At least at the national level, using the government to reform food supplies and dietary choices would not come until the next wave of activism, in the Progressive Era.

C. Legacies for Later Cases

Although a creature of his time, Graham was also the heir to religious ideas about diet and morality that long predated the Second Great Awakening.[126] As the first case of a U.S. *movement* around dietary reform, however, it is the legacies Graham and his allies left to later eras of food activism that take center stage in my account. Graham's responses to commercialization, lengthening commodity chains, and industrial food were, as the next two chapters show, carried forward to later eras of food activism. One such legacy was Graham's valorization of "natural" food as both rhetorical foil for conventional offerings and active cure for what ails us. In effect, he took an older romantic ideal of nature, in contrast to civilization and artifice, and applied it specifically to food. Moreover, he rooted that celebration of natural food in a physiological account of the debilitating and restorative effects of conventional versus natural food. That contrast reappears in subsequent food reform movements. And while it was not uniquely Graham's, for many later reformers the debt to Graham is explicit.

Graham's specific dietary recommendations to restore our natural health are also echoed regularly by later generations of food activists. The endorsement of whole-grain bread; the disavowal of meat, spices, and stimulants such as coffee; and the insistence on plainness and moderation in eating all became staples of dietary reformers in the late nineteenth century and beyond. More distinctive to Graham, and reappearing more selectively in later periods, is the tight connection drawn between diet and morality: It was not just that what you ate and how you ate it marked your social worth, although this is certainly a recurrent view. Diet was an actual causal agent for Graham. To overstate only slightly, good and bad foods produce good and bad people. Further, he put this contrast in food and moral character into a larger, longer context of social change. Graham maintained that over time, appetites are corrupted by man's culinary achievements and become wholly unreliable guides to consumption. These connections between food and morality also make many appearances in later eras of American food activism.

The corruption of our appetites, finally, means that we have to turn to more reliable guides. Here, too, Graham was not the first to dispense dietary advice. But he was the first important dietary expert in nineteenth-century America to present his advice as based on science rather than God's word[127]—and, indeed, as guidance *more* scientific and trustworthy than what was on offer from the credentialed authorities of the day. That model of the counter-expert on food, speaking scientific truth to power, is also taken up by later activists, often with a nod to Graham. Chapters 3 and 4 explore *how* these achievements of Graham carried forward to influence subsequent waves of food reform.

3

Food Progressives,
1890–1906

Six decades after Sylvester Graham called his followers to dietary redemption, organizers of the National Pure Food and Drug Congress once again warned of unwholesome food and its moral dangers—but they also took those warnings in new directions. "Adulteration, mishandling . . . [and] substitutions . . . undoubtedly exist to an alarming extent, to the detriment of health, legitimate business, and sound morals, and it will be needful to secure legislation that will check this growing evil and permit an honest man to do an honest business."[1] Women had a key role to play in this campaign because "the state will do nothing till there is a demand for pure food. . . . The pathway of the missionary in America lies through the kitchen."[2] In this missionary work, women had a powerful ally. In place of outmoded tradition, "all science and engineering stands ready to help," including with the correct identification of foods that are adulterated or unhealthy.[3]

Many of these concerns reflected changes in food production that Graham would have found familiar in character, if not scale. Wholesome wheat was still defiled by processing and long-distance transport; animals were still artificially fattened and confined; mothers were still shirking their responsibilities by purchasing bread rather than making it from scratch. Other developments would have been unrecognizable to Graham, including entirely new manufactured foods, assembly-line slaughtering of beef, and such commercial alternatives to homemade food as canned vegetables and soup. Familiar or not, goods such as these reflect the normal operation of our food system as it cheapens production of established commodities and tempts the consumer with new ones. And although commercialization, technical innovation, and delocalization are features of capitalism in general, they also raise more distinctive problems of trust when applied to the food we eat.

It is the recurrent activism around an enduring social problem that warrants analysis of "the" food movement as a genre with features that set it apart from other movements. This analytical move—lumping food-related protests together as a movement but splitting them off from other fields of activism—complements an approach common among students of contentious politics. Scholars in this tradition more often aim to generalize across movements, including when tracking long-term trends. In Charles Tilly's canonical story of the rise of modern social movements, for example, the development of capitalism and the consolidation of state power favored national organization and a new, more modular strategic repertoire across fields of activism. One standard method for studying such changes takes the same tack: collect data on all manner of individual protest events (what sort of claims were made? addressed to whom? backed by what tactic?) to discover aggregate changes in the character of protest.[4] New social movement theorists contrast themselves to the school of contentious politics both in their initial assumptions and in their research methods. Yet they, too, proceed from large-scale social changes associated with postindustrial societies to outcomes, such as participatory organization and post-material concerns with identity, shared across a wide range of movements.[5] These are valuable intellectual goals and empirical insights. But they necessarily strip away characteristics, continuities, and causes that are distinctive to important genres of protest. One could not adequately tell the story of the labor movement without reference to the dynamics of the labor process. No more can one tell the story of the food movement without attention to long-running, systemic challenges to trust in food.

Collective responses to these challenges reflect other influences, including those operating along a shorter time scale. In the Progressive Era, these responses both echoed Graham and left him behind. Some advocates for healthy eating—notably, John Harvey Kellogg—focused on the individual and social evils of processed food, alcohol, and meat. These Grahamian concerns were revived in the Progressive Era's wider "social purity" movement. But the period also introduced three new themes to food activism, themes that largely define Progressivism. Many reformers demanded that the federal government enforce food standards and restore "honest" business practices to the industry. Consumers were called on to choose and prepare food following nutritional science and norms of efficiency. And those good wives and mothers who Graham hoped would make bread in their homes were now themselves prominent food activists in the public sphere, agitating for state regulation and scientific eating. These new directions in food reform were clearest in the push for a pure food law and in the calls for "domestic science." In different ways, the two movements sought to restore trust and reassert control over a compromised food system. But they also reflected standard templates for Progressive reform and for women's new roles in an emerging consumer society. And like other Progressives, advocates for pure food laws and domestic science drew moral boundaries along lines that differed from both their Grahamite predecessors and their social purity contemporaries: less between the virtuous and corrupt individuals pictured in those movements than between natives and immigrants and between a civic-minded middle class and the benighted poor. To understand these movements, accordingly, we should look first at ambient changes in the food system (Section I) and in the period's progressive and social purity politics (Section II). We can then take up each movement (Section III), their similarities and differences (Section IV), and their legacies (Section V).

I. New Techniques, New Foods, New Anxieties

Many of the hallmarks of our contemporary food system took form in the Progressive Era. Some developments were certainly anticipated in Graham's lifetime, but by the early 1900s they operated on a vastly expanded scale. To begin with, rationalized production methods that we associate with the manufacturing sector also were applied to food. The change is particularly well documented for meat.[6] Pork processing led the way, with *dis*assembly lines predating Ford's system by six decades. By the time of Upton Sinclair's exposé, *The Jungle*, similar methods turned out trimmed beef for a national market. Several innovations fit together to make this possible. An extreme division of labor and less-skilled workers in the slaughterhouses enabled meatpackers to increase output and cut costs. The development of refrigerated railroad cars and a nationwide distribution network, in turn, made it possible for a small number of Chicago-based firms to supply retailers around the country. In the case of bread, both home production and local bakeries lost ground to factory production. Automatic machinery turned out vast numbers of standardized loaves—15,000 daily in the largest factories around 1900 and 100,000 (pre-sliced) by the late 1920s—for distribution throughout regional markets. In 1890, 90 percent of America's bread was baked at home; by 1930, that figure had dwindled to 6 percent.[7] Similar stories can be told for many other "traditional" foods, from beer to cheese and pasta.[8]

Large-volume production and national distribution depended in part on new techniques of preservation: Food that would otherwise rot could be shipped long distances and sit on shelves awaiting purchase. Chilling vegetables and putting up fruit were nothing new, but widespread use of refrigerated transport and industrial canning were. For consumers, canning represented the most visible change. The underlying technology dates back to Napoleonic France; later, it helped feed, and sometimes poison, Civil War soldiers. But as a way to supply a large consumer market, canning took off in the late nineteenth century. A workshop of the late 1860s, employing skilled metalworkers, might turn out a few hundred cans of food in a day; in 1883, a day's output from a Chicago factory with twelve unskilled boys reached thirty thousand.[9] One key to success was the advent of machinery to fill and seal cans. Another, more clearly visible by the 1910s, was effective national marketing to reassure customers that eating food from cans was safe and socially acceptable.[10] And a third was the increasing use of chemical preservatives such as benzoate of soda and boric acid.[11] For manufacturers, this created a virtuous circle: new technologies made centralized production and distribution possible, and economies of scale favored large firms that commanded the resources to invest in automatic machinery and national marketing. Canning also contributed to another hallmark of modern food production—namely, that it makes available a wide range of fruit and vegetables (although not necessarily fresh ones) in and out of season. And if manufacturers could can tomatoes, a next step was to add value by cooking the tomatoes into soup and canning that. It was in this period that Campbell's (soup), Heinz (condiments), Kraft (prepackaged cheese), and Borden (canned milk, juice) mastered the formula of mass production, mass advertising and branding, and national distribution to bring affordable prefabricated foods to consumers.[12]

Canned tomato soup, spaghetti, and relish may not have matched homemade for quality, but they could at least be recognized as tomato soup, spaghetti, and relish.[13] Another major step toward our modern food system during the Progressive Era was the increasing sale of edible substances produced more by science than nature. Oleomargarine was the most controversial example (see Figure 3.1). Its ingredients varied over time. Early versions used animal fats (lard, beef fat); later versions relied on one or another vegetable oil. All included water, colorings, and assorted flavorings to increase the product's resemblance to butter. That masquerading, together with margarine's lower price and convenient longevity, led to a long-running regulatory battle with the dairy industry.[14] Other testimonials to the innovative spirit and technical prowess of American food businesses included jam with no fruit, ice cream with no milk, and meat with no flesh.[15] *Good Housekeeping* marked the trend by using the term "synthetic food" in 1907, although the magazine's definition understated the ingenuity of American chemists in creating entirely new compounds for use in food: "The term synthetic food as herein used is applied to a food product made of a mixture of various other food products and not of itself possessed of any of the characteristics of a natural . . . food."[16]

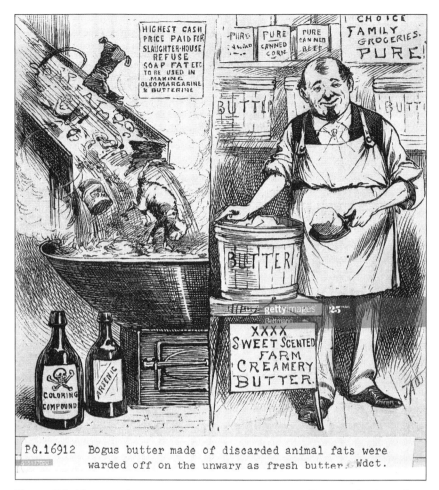

Figure 3.1. Nineteenth-century anti-margarine cartoon. (Accessed at http://uploads.neatorama.com/images/posts/928/70/70928/1396843751-1.jpg. Original source unknown.)

The obvious corollary to factory food was commodified food. Graham had inveighed against women buying bread rather than baking it themselves. By the end of the nineteenth century, far more of women's food labor was being outsourced to commercial purveyors. "The chief difference in our food supplies," wrote *New England Kitchen* in 1894, "consist[s] in their preparation outside the home."[17] Working-class women, short on time and cooking space, were the most likely to rely on food from small-scale local vendors such as bakeries, delis, and carts.[18] Middle-class families were the earlier adopters of canned and nationally branded products. A report to members of the General Federation of Women's Clubs (GFWC) in 1906 observed that "the time of drying apples, and pickling, preserving, canning, preparing and storing the winter supply of food is within the memory of most of us. The factory has gradually taken this from the home, until to-day, the housewife may, if she will, provide her family with all kinds of canned fruits, meats and preserves without any effort other than ordering them from her grocer."[19] For women of this class, the turn to commercial foods also helped them cope with the dreaded "servant problem."[20] Owing to improving employment opportunities for working-class and immigrant women, and to the stigma attached to "service" in the land of the free, the nineteenth-century norm of household help for middle-class families moved out of reach: Hired hands to do the cooking were expensive, hard to find, and insufficiently deferential. Aided by cookbooks that made far fewer assumptions about readers' competence, middle-class women took up the slack, but these new demands made commercial alternatives to home cooking especially welcome.[21] That shift raised other concerns. Kitchen magazines of the 1890s began to issue warnings about a slippage in the quality of home-cooked meals. "Has the housewife become not less domestic but less given over to drudgery? Has she with these changes sacrificed the quality of her food for the ease with which it may be provided?"[22]

In all of these respects—standardized products, national distribution, mass advertising, widespread commercialization—the food system was a crucial ingredient in an emerging consumer society in which buying rather than making became a major part of middle-class women's activities and identities.[23] Much as department stores added convenience to commodification by offering one-stop shopping for clothing and home furnishings,[24] so did "combination stores" and (beginning in the 1920s) supermarkets for food. The shift can be seen in advice to homemakers. Where they once learned how to raise a pig, they now got tips on finding a trustworthy butcher; over successive editions of her manual of household management, Catherine Beecher added guidance on how to choose ripe fruit and recognize fresh fish.[25] Women clearly perceived the need for new expertise under new conditions. "When the preparation of food is passed from the walls of her own home," the GFWC advised members, "she seems to have given up all responsibility in regard to it. . . . This is one of the problems that must be solved socially, that we all together must take hold of and insist that the food which is necessary to a greater part of the people must be pure and wholesome. Law and labels are as much needed for effective work in this direction as they are in . . . our muslin underwear."[26]

"The problems that must be solved socially" included the exploitation of labor hidden in commodities, but they also involved a fundamental breakdown of trust. Progressive Era changes in the food system jeopardized trust in ways that were widely discussed at the time.[27] Some anxieties can be traced to the unfamiliarity of new food production methods and, in some cases, well-documented risks associated with new products. Canned food again offers a prominent example. Inadequately sterilized ingredients might allow anaerobic bacteria to thrive, with explosive results; improper application of lead solder could contaminate contents; and incomplete sealing left customers with spoiled goods.[28] Reliability was much improved by the 1890s, but popular magazines still offered cautionary advice.

> It is admitted that canned goods are not necessarily unhealthful per se, and their great convenience and comparative cheapness render them very popular. Moreover, greater care is exercised by the canners than ever before, so that the real danger which attended the use of goods put up in tin cans has been in a great measure eliminated. Nevertheless some caution should be exercised by consumers. Decomposition in animal products often develops poisonous alkaloids, like the tyrotoxicon which is sometimes the cause of illness to persons eating milk products or cheese, and cases of illness from eating canned goods are usually to be traced to this source. There is also an element of danger in salts that may be formed by the action of the contents on the metal of the can. Both these sources of danger have been reduced to a minimum by improved methods of canning, but it is idle to deny that they exist, and they demand reasonable precaution in purchasing and using canned goods.[29]

With such faint praise and evocative warnings, readers could not rest easy. Margarine, too, was regularly denounced as unnatural (and, perhaps worse, French). Its promoters might sing "the praises of the product of the French patent," a congressman argued in 1882, but the consumer "longs for the fruits of God's patent, the pure spring water, the sweet grasses, and the lowing herd."[30] This suspicion of unnatural foods extended well beyond margarine. *Good Housekeeping* lamented in 1913:

> Unfortunately, there is a growing tendency to do away with the work which looks to the preparation of food products for eating purposes. The ready-to-eat vegetable, the soup which needs only hot water, the pudding which is only to be warmed in the can before opening, the beans which are already baked, the coffee which is already extracted, and the breakfast foods which are already cooked and partly predigested, are coming into greater and greater vogue. I am not blaming the manufacturers who supply these wants, especially when they do it well, as most of them do. At the same time I realize the grave dangers from the point of view of domestic economy which such

processes entail. I would be glad, if foods which keep best in their natural form could be sold to the consumer as such and prepared by him [sic] for consumption.[31]

Even when a food item was not new, it might have lost legibility for consumers—perhaps because it came from far away, beyond local circles of familiarity and reputation. The town butchers and bakers could not convincingly vouch for meat from Chicago slaughterhouses or plastic-wrapped bread from a New Jersey factory. The packaging of mass-produced foods also limited the ability of buyers to use old metrics of smell, feel, and appearance to judge the contents—or even to be sure that they were getting what they expected. "Mary had a little lamb," ran one late nineteenth-century ditty, "and when she saw it sicken, she shipped it off to Packingtown, and now it's labeled chicken."[32] These suspicions created a ready market for advice in recipe books, kitchen magazines, and cooking classes on how to discriminate between sound and unsound food.[33]

The need for revised rules of thumb came, as well, from changing household responsibilities. Even had little altered in the foods on offer and in how they were produced, the new responsibilities of middle-class women for provisioning and cooking raised anxieties. They had to learn on the fly, without help from more experienced servants, at a time when old methods for verifying food safety and nutritional adequacy were becoming obsolete but before new ones had become conventional wisdom.[34] As Ellen Richards wrote in 1898,

> The methods of their mothers and grandmothers will no longer answer. [The older generation] had no trouble with their soap, for they superintended its making and knew its properties. They knew how colored fabrics should be washed, for they had the coloring done under their own eyes. We buy everything, and have no idea of the processes by which the articles are produced, and have no means of knowing beforehand what the quality may be. Relatively, we are in a state of barbarous ignorance, as compared with our grandmothers, about the common articles of daily use.[35]

Times now seemed to require that "the modern housewife [become] her own chemist."[36] Knowing too much could be as alarming as not knowing enough. As Nancy Tomes shows, this was a period in which scientific discoveries of bacteria and its role in disease were coming to wider public attention.[37] Awareness that invisible, potentially harmful germs lurked in everyday foods made shopping and cooking treacherous (see Figure 3.2).

Figure 3.2. Frederick Burr Opper, "Look before You Eat." (*Puck Magazine*, vol. 15, no. 366, March 12, 1884. From Prints and Photographs Division, Library of Congress, https://www.loc.gov/resource/ppmsca.28300.)

Should consumers waver in their focus on these risks, periodic scandals commanded their attention anew. Kitchen magazines and newspapers of the day regularly printed horror stories, from trichinosis in pork to botulism in canned food.[38] Canned meat got especially wide coverage during the Spanish-American War as inedible "embalmed beef" served to the nation's patriotic young soldiers.[39] Sinclair's revelations in *The Jungle* added gruesome detail to warnings already issued in *Good Health* about the "killing establishment" for animals.[40]

Unfamiliar food, food made in new ways, food coming from long distances, contaminated food, and food scandals all eroded consumers' trust. To these should be added social actors who found it profitable to highlight food risks. Chief among them were food manufacturers themselves, although only if they could associate the risks with their competitors. Advertisements for white sugar used microscope images to help consumers visualize the impurities of brown sugar; representatives of the dairy industry alerted consumers to margarine's dangers; sellers of factory-made foods raised the alarm over unsanitary conditions at small-scale producers; and marketers promoting "modern" packaged foods, safe from contaminants, made invidious comparisons with unsealed and bulk goods.[41] Other actors had other motives. Newly minted nutritionists could gain professional standing by emphasizing the perils of shopping and preparing food without expert guidance. Advocates for food safety laws used dramatic examples of adulteration to win support for their cause. Even their opponents played the game. Eager to discredit calls for "pure food," the trade journal *National Provisioner* reminded readers of meat going bad and crawling with maggots in the absence of "modern improved methods" such as the application of antiseptics.[42] What was to be done?

II. The Political Context of Food Reform

What was to be done depended in part on what other reformers were doing, and troubles with food joined a much larger set of social problems in the late nineteenth century.[43] Some of these problems paralleled those in Graham's time, but on a bigger scale. Cities became home to a majority of the nation's population, packed in more tightly, with more concentrated poverty than in the urban centers of the 1830s. Immigrants came in far larger numbers and from parts of the world (southern and eastern Europe, China) that, in the view of established residents, made them poor candidates for Americanization. Other social challenges were associated with an industrial capitalism unimaginable to Graham's contemporaries. The Gilded Age brought extremes of economic inequality that would not be matched until our own time, with the destitution of those at the bottom compounded by a severe economic depression from 1893 to 1897. Financial insecurities, changes in the organization of production that undercut the position of skilled workers, and an uncompromising attack on unions by employers in key industries all contributed to a sharp spike in class conflict. Major battles—Haymarket (1886) for the eight-hour day, Homestead (1892) over union rights in steel, Pullman (1894) against railroad wage cuts—received wide publicity for their scope and violence.

A. Progressivism

"Progressivism" is the label that historians have used to summarize a remarkable mobilization of collective responses to these challenges. The period, conventionally dated from the early 1890s, was one in which "fiddlers were tuning up all over America."[44] They never played a common tune. Many of the calls for change accord with what we now consider "progressive." Some aimed to rein in big business, whether through antitrust laws and regulatory commissions to curb their economic power or provisions for popular initiatives and referenda to offset their political clout. To contain industrial violence and even the playing field, a group of reformers sought to protect union rights and encourage peaceful collective bargaining. Activists established settlement houses to provide services to the urban poor and educate new immigrants; other Progressives lobbied for public parks to both beautify the city and provide wholesome recreational opportunities. They sought changes in public education to foster social mobility, called for improved sanitation to protect public health, demanded the vote for women and an end to child labor, and much more.

Is there a unifying thread running through these diverse initiatives? Increasingly, historians answer "no." Important scholarly work from the 1970s into the 1990s had claimed to find such a thread in the status anxieties of a besieged traditional elite, in the enlightened self-interest of a capitalist class, in the search for order by businessmen and professionals, and in the transposition of maternal care to the body politic.[45] More recent interpretations, by contrast, are more likely to speak of progressivism*s*.[46] But the habit of synthesis dies hard, and even these later scholars identify some common denominators.

Perhaps the most obvious one is a new willingness to treat the state, from municipal to federal governments, as a necessary instrument of change, whatever the specific goals. Progressives generally concluded that laissez-faire had been found wanting. They further agreed, without necessarily putting it this way, that many goods—the environment, transportation, health, sex, labor—should not be treated as mere commodities. This resistance to unrestricted market capitalism in the United States echoed similar moves in most other industrial nations.[47]

In their quest for change, Progressives of many stripes also treated science as the proper means and efficiency as the proper end of social reform. Whatever the problem, a first step should be systematic study, and whatever the institution or service, it could be improved through more efficient administration. The workplace received special scrutiny. There, Frederick Taylor and his acolytes developed new methods for the scientific analysis of production and new techniques for managing workers.[48] But this logic of efficiency was both older and more generally applicable than Taylorism, particularly in demands for government reform. Urban elites after the Civil War, alarmed by immigrant voters and machine politics that enlisted them, were already calling for civil service reform to make municipal administration more efficient and less prone to corruption.[49] Young Progressives took up the call and directed it to a range of city services, from education to public transportation and street cleaning.[50] It was an agenda that was both associated with and promised benefits to new cadres of professionals. Engineers, management consultants, social workers, nutritionists, even sociologists were the men and women with the requisite training to analyze and solve problems in their domains and who deserved corresponding jobs and status.[51]

A third characteristic of many Progressive movements was a vastly expanded role for women. Excluded from electoral politics, increasingly educated and engaged in the public sphere, middle-class women formed the rank and file of most (and the leadership of some) of the period's reform campaigns.[52] They commonly acted through local clubs and leagues, such as affiliates of the GFWC and the National Consumers League (NCL). And they spoke a language of "maternalism" that both motivated and legitimated their efforts. Women's maternal roles, in this view, sensitized them to the plight of the poor and the exploitation of women and children at work. Against critics of their public activism, women replied that they were merely exercising their familial responsibilities for a larger family: "The world has ever looked to woman as the home-maker and the home-keeper. Can she not become the regenerator and keeper of the nation?"[53]

Fourth and finally, even while recognizing pervasive class conflict, most Progressive reformers believed that society should (and they themselves could) transcend narrow and partisan class interests. Statism, science, and maternalism all helped them stand above class. The liberal ideal of using government to solve social problems conjured the state as a representative of the public interest and an antidote to class partisanship.[54] The commitment to scientific analysis and efficiency freed reformers from class bias.[55]

And women, by virtue of their moral character rather than their scientific objectivity, stood above the partisan fray.[56] Reviewing "The Relation of the Woman's Club to Civic Life," Clara Bourland set an ambitious agenda: the need to separate municipal administration from politics, to clean streets, to expand schooling, to give the poor "breathing space," to protect abandoned women and children, and to suppress gambling. In all this, club women must "sacrifice, if need be, their private interests as well as their personal tastes and comforts to secure independence for the citizen, and an honest distribution of the public funds."[57]

B. Social Purification

The Progressive agenda overlapped with a different genre of activism in the late nineteenth century, described generally as a quest for social purity.[58] Compared with Progressives, purity advocates focused on a somewhat different set of outrages from the larger menu of urban social ills. Many involved sex. The movement got its start in the 1870s fighting prostitution, showing particular horror at proposals to regulate, rather than abolish, the vice. From there it widened the field of battle to combat the erosion of sexual morals and restore traditional controls. The agenda included purging "obscene" material from museums, newspapers, and the mail; raising the age of consent for girls; improving the moral education of boys and girls; promoting chastity, including through the distribution of "purity pledges"; curbing or abolishing alcohol consumption; and preventing "racial degeneration." For the ministers and "purity elite" who dominated the movement, these were all connected.[59] Alcohol fostered unchaste thoughts and behavior; "sexual drunkenness" fueled venereal disease; masturbation led to mental illness; and all contributed to a weakening of the Anglo-Saxon racial stock.

Although never singularly focused on social purity, the Woman's Christian Temperance Union (WCTU), the largest women's organization of the day, was one hub of the movement. Founded in 1874, the WCTU took up the already long-running temperance campaign. But under the formidable leadership of Frances Willard, president from 1879 to 1897, the organization broadened its mandate to, as Willard put it, "do everything." Everything included a variety of purity goals, loosely coordinated by the WCTU's Social Purity Committee. What tied temperance to these campaigns was the common theme of "home protection."[60] Still subscribing to the ideology of separate spheres, WCTU activists saw women and the household as bastions of morality in an increasingly corrupt urban society. Accordingly, women had a special responsibility for reform. Donning their white ribbons of virtue, WCTU members marched into battle against all that threatened pure homes and pious families, whether drunken husbands, masturbating sons, philandering con men, vice-ridden saloons, or pornographic art.[61] Under Willard, too, the battle called for unconventional tactics, including women's suffrage. But the larger goal remained a restoration of traditional pious living, as embodied in women's special domain.

The social purity movement generally has been interpreted as a form of backlash politics in which middle- and upper-class WASPs rallied to defend their families and their moral standards from perceived assault.[62] And at least in the last two decades of the nineteenth century, purity campaigns clearly differed from Progressive responses to urban social problems. Groups such as the White Cross Society, the American Purity Alliance, and the WCTU put their strategic emphasis not on remedial action by the state but on individual redemption. Christian morality would be restored by winning hearts and minds through educational campaigns to purge alcohol, promote chastity, eliminate the moral double standard, and reclaim fallen women. These groups also framed problems and posed solutions differently from most Progressive reformers. Prostitution, promiscuity, masturbation, and other vices were not treated as the products of social causes, to be studied with scientific dispassion.[63] Instead, they were hateful affronts to traditional morality and religious values. "Purity reform drew its social ideal from Protestantism. Reformers were . . . moral individualists crusading against an immoral society . . . [with] faith in the perfectibility of the social world through applied Christianity."[64]

After 1900, these two categories of activism began to blur. The purity movement's leadership shifted from ministers toward doctors and social workers. With that shift came a change in language, from social purity to the science of social hygiene—albeit a science whose laws governed both physical health and moral behavior.[65] Purity activists also came to place more emphasis on the reform of municipal government (high on the agenda of Progressives), the better to combat urban vices. But the relative weight of individual moral reform and collective political action and between religious and scientific standards persisted. These distinctions reappear among the variants of Progressive Era food reform.

III. Food Movements

A. *Progressive Food Reform*

1. Pure Food

The most storied Progressive Era food activism advocated government action to ensure that food was neither unsafe nor deceptive. Such efforts date back at least to the 1830s, focusing on municipal regulation of public markets and milk supplies.[66] State legislation followed, and in 1879 the first national law was proposed. Congress would first consider and then reject nearly 190 more such bills before finally passing laws in 1906 to curb adulteration and deceptive advertising of food and to ensure a safer meat supply.[67] Social movement scholars will recognize this fight as conventional contentious politics. It enlisted a wide range of organizations and tactics, including those of both insiders and outsiders. This ad hoc coalition aimed to educate the public and make claims on Congress. By conventional standards, the coalition's efforts were a clear success.

Much of the credit for that success goes to Harvey Wiley (1844–1930), head of the Bureau of Chemistry in the U.S. Department of Agriculture (USDA).[68] Wiley grew up in rural Indiana, the son of a farmer and occasional schoolteacher. He must have liked his home state, staying local for college and for a subsequent medical apprenticeship, then returning to teach chemistry at Purdue University after graduate work at Harvard and further study in Germany. In the early 1880s, he pursued interests in sugar. One line of work was to develop commercially viable methods for extracting sugar from sorghum. Another, undertaken on behalf of the Indiana Board of Health, tested retail honey and molasses for adulteration with glucose syrup. His connections in the sugar trade served him well. A business leader in the state's industry successfully lobbied for Wiley's appointment to head the USDA's Division (later Bureau) of Chemistry in 1883. He stayed there until 1912.

From his position at the USDA, Wiley focused on what he regarded as two key problems in the food system: adulteration and unsafe additives. Until the 1880s, he argued, "there was little need for protection of the people from impure, adulterated and misbranded food and drugs." But with industrial growth, larger cities, and the corresponding boom in mass-produced preserved and canned food, "manufacturers of food products sprang up on every hand [sic]. They turned naturally to the cheapest and most convenient methods of preserving their products, and adulteration and misbranding of foods were the natural consequences."[69] Wiley used his lab to document that adulteration. He issued a series of technical publications on specific foods (Bulletin no. 13, 1887–1902) and wrote a more accessible booklet, *Popular Treatise on the Extent and Character of Food Adulteration* (1890), in which he made a public call for national legislation. He applied a similarly populist touch to food additives. The safety of increasingly common preservatives such as benzoate of soda, Wiley argued, should be subject to careful scientific evaluation. To do so, he recruited twelve healthy young male government employees for a series of experiments, carefully standardizing their diets and assessing their health before and after consumption of the preservative. Dubbed "the poison squad" by a fascinated newspaper corps, the experiments gave Wiley seemingly clear evidence, widely publicized, of the health hazards of this and other additives.

Wiley did not limit his advocacy to scientific reports. He also made his expertise available through extensive public testimony and movement networking. He frequently appeared at congressional hearings on food adulteration, held as part of one unsuccessful legislative effort after another. Perhaps more important to the eventual passage of the Food and Drug Law, he cultivated ties with professional and civic organizations to marshal support. The professional groups included the Association of Official Agricultural Chemists (of which Wiley was a past president) and the American Medical Association; the civic groups included the GFWC, the WCTU, and the NCL. Key contacts in each got regular bulletins and alarming news flashes from Wiley, and they could count on him as a reliable inside ally in public attacks on the unholy alliance of self-interested canners, fake whiskey producers, and unscrupulous labelers.

a. Impure Food as a Market Problem: It was a diverse coalition that Wiley helped assemble, and there was much for them to criticize in the food supply. Even while agreeing on the need for state action to restore trust, different factions offered different rationales for change. One focus, of course, was safety. Activists other than Wiley tended to express general fears on this score rather than making specific claims about particular health risks. The omnibus call to action issued by the 1898 National Pure Food and Drug Congress ticked off safety in a much longer list: "adulteration, misbranding, . . . substitution and imitation undoubtedly exist to an alarming extent."[70] The litany of affronts to the consumer that were said to arise from the nation's food supply was lengthy but vague. The absence of detail is understandable and was itself a cause for concern. Lacking reliable information about what was in their food or how it had been processed, consumers could only worry that it *might* be harmful. Critics considered that lack of knowledge itself a grievance against food purveyors. Adulteration, one congressman charged in 1898, violated every consumer's "right to know what he is eating and drinking."[71] (For one representation of popular suspicions of meat, see Figure 3.3.)

Women involved in the campaign were most likely to highlight this need for accurate information, and they often framed the issue in terms of their maternal duties. Marion McBride, representing the WCTU, proclaimed impure food to be "a home question" with high stakes. "The welfare of the family is the welfare of state and nation," she warned, and a pure food bill was needed to help the homemaker discharge that responsibility.[72] "What can be within the proper sphere of woman and of women's clubs," the Reverend Caroline Crane asked delegates to the 1906 Convention of the

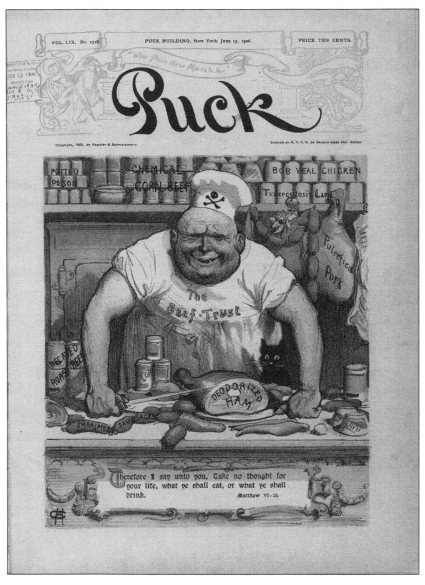

Figure 3.3. Carl Hassmann, "The Meat Market." (*Puck Magazine*, vol. 59, no. 1528, June 13, 1906. From Prints and Photographs Division, Library of Congress, https://loc.gov/pictures/resource/ppmsca.26067.)

GFWC, if not "the wholesomeness and cleanliness of the food which daily a woman sets before her family?"[73]

Other critics put little emphasis on the safety of adulterated food. Instead, they complained about "dishonesty." Wiley was particularly voluble on this theme. Bowing to American libertarianism, he insisted that the federal government had no business telling consumers what to eat. But it should ensure that consumers were not deceived—that when they bought jam or cheese or whiskey, they got the real thing. Any added ingredients not normally part of jam, cheese, or whiskey should be clearly listed on the package. "Anything under heaven that I may be pleased to do I want the privilege of doing, even if it is eating limburger cheese. What I don't want, and what the ethics of pure food demands shall not be, is that foods can be sold for what they are not."[74] Businessmen as well as consumers needed protection from dishonesty. Purveyors of adulterated food seized an unfair advantage over their competitors; worse, they forced the honest businessman to take the same shortcuts, use the same fillers, and add the same chemicals in order to survive. A pure food bill would "permit an honest man to do an honest business."[75] *Good Housekeeping* reminded readers that they were partly responsible. "It's really the consumer who is to blame for food adulteration, because they demand the lowest possible prices," with each producer able to claim that "he simply put on the market what the trade demands. . . . In this condition of affairs the state must step in to regulate the traffic."[76] Such regulations would remedy the grievances of consumers and producers alike: "What we want is that the farmers may get an honest market and the innocent consumer may get what he thinks he is buying. . . . The object of this bill is to secure honesty."[77]

For the most part, Progressive Era advocates of a pure food law no longer talked, as Graham did, about the food created by God for man's consumption. Nor did those most active in the legislative campaign connect impure food to the moral degeneration of individual consumers. Instead, what many of them inherited from Graham was the use of "nature" as a metric for trustworthy food, and a corresponding suspicion of "man's attempt in his conceit to make a better food than nature provides."[78] The less a food had been modified from its natural state, the less suspect it was. Pure food advocates were also no less explicit than Graham in linking food reform and moral uplift, although they did so in different ways. For maternalists, legislation would support women in their mission to keep the nation's households uncorrupted.[79] This is a mission Graham would have blessed. For more business-minded advocates, the legislation promised to end the "demoralizing" of the market.[80] And for both camps, in contrast to Graham, government action was an indispensable part of reforming the food supply.

A third, less prominent theme that runs through pure food advocacy is the need to protect the poor rather than women's families and businessmen's honesty. Reformers noted that the problem of adulterated food fell most heavily on consumers for whom low price trumped all other considerations and for whom the presumably more reputable branded goods were too expensive. One appeal to the U.S. Senate in 1898 emphasized how fraudulent representation of food was "menacing the health and purses of the poorer classes especially."[81] "Club women," who could afford better ingredients and might have kitchen help to prepare meals, had a special obligation: "It is [their] privilege to demand necessary legislation."[82] Much less often, supporters of a pure food law reminded their audiences that poor workers as well as poor consumers needed help. The NCL, in particular, resolved to investigate "the working condition[s] of the employees who prepare" food products, with the league's General Secretary Florence Kelley noting that, "while the Shredded Wheat Factory was clean, its employees were poorly paid and unhappy and so often on strike."[83] Frustrated by repeated congressional defeats, pure food advocates sometimes even saw the struggle as symptomatic of larger inequalities in wealth and power. Charlotte Smith, a delegate to the 1899 National Pure Food and Drug Congress, bemoaned "the tendency of the times to accumulate wealth, regardless of the injury inflicted upon others, [and] the present laws being inefficient, manufacturers and dealers had no fear of punishment."[84] "Is this no longer a Government by the people, for the people, and of the people," asked Alice Lakey of the NCL, "but of the corporations for the corporations?"[85] But as with other Progressive reformers, class analysis did not come easily. Pure food activists were more likely to depict businessmen as aspiring to honesty but helpless in the face of unscrupulous competitors. Club women, in turn, were not so much allies of the working class as civic-minded patrons of the needy. One member added that the only reason to get involved to begin with—rather than leaving matters to city government, as in France—was the necessity of overcoming class partisanship in the United States.[86] And even when criticizing the dishonest businessman, pure food reformers sounded more like populist insurgents than class critics. Who should be blamed for ruining the virtuous dairyman or farmer? According to Congressman Hugh Price, it was "the scalpers of the city . . . fat, sleek, kid gloved gentry who manipulate boards of trade. . . . I would sooner trust a Winnebago Indian with a jug of whiskey as trust the Chicago Board of Trade."[87]

b. Pure Food's Social and Organizational Base: These varied political claims reflected a remarkably broad coalition calling for pure food legislation. Some business groups were early supporters, for the usual mix of reasons: to ensure uniformity rather than a patchwork of state regulations (as with the National Board of Trade), to use the federal government's imprimatur to reassure consumers (as with the National Retail Grocers' Association), or to win a competitive advantage over trade rivals (as with the National Association of Dairy and Food Departments, eyeing the margarine threat). The roster of business organizations at the National Pure Food and Drug Congresses of 1898 and 1899 includes, as well, many more-specialized trade associations, from confectioners and brewers to beekeepers.[88] Western farmers had their own business interests in supporting legislation that would protect the reputation and markets for wheat and dairy and lard, interests reinforced by continuing populist resentment of eastern "moneyed interests" conspiring against the yeoman farmer.[89] Professional groups were also among the early backers of a law, particularly chemists. They were often involved in state-level programs for evaluating food ingredients and monitoring purity, and they stood to gain further professional recognition, influence, and employment from a federal system. The American Medical Association came to the campaign later, focusing particularly on the drug side of food and drug legislation, but it lent significant support during the final five years of lobbying. Chemists and doctors were an especially eager audience for Wiley's somewhat showman-like appeals to scientific investigation as the basis for government action.[90] Reform-minded middle-class women emerged as important backers of legislative action in the late 1890s. They quickly gained national traction, and in 1906 a triumphant Wiley—not usually shy about claiming credit for himself—declared the law's passage "the victory of the women of this country, whose influence was felt as irresistible."[91] The coalition was much less diverse in class background. The Women's National Industrial League did urge cities to "protect working-class homes from debased food."[92] But there is little additional evidence for labor backing the pure food bill and some evidence that, for working-class households with limited money and time, newer manufactured foods were more a convenience than a threat.[93]

Each of these constituencies spoke through its own sets of organizations (with agenda that extended well beyond pure food). Businessmen had their trade groups; farmers their Grange and commodity-specific associations. Representing chemical analysts employed in state government, the Association of Official Agricultural Chemists brought both scientific legitimacy and experience with state food regulation to the fight and helped give the campaign a mix of insider politics and outsider insurgency.[94] And for middle-class women, the main vehicles were the WCTU, the NCL, and the GFWC. Most of these had a federated structure of local, state, and national bodies mirroring the structure of American government, a particularly effective model.[95] Loosely coordinating their efforts were yet more peak organizations and Harvey Wiley. The National Pure Food and Drug Congress brought together representatives of chemical societies, pharmaceutical groups, retail grocers, and Granges from thirty-two states. For his part, Wiley showed boundless energy in circulating damning analytical reports on adulterated foods to potential allies and presenting the case through correspondence with, or talks to, many of them.[96] The combination of sectoral organization and national coordination also had its advantages. It enabled supporters to mobilize outsider public meetings and petitions, yet also use insider strategies such as picking favorable witnesses at congressional hearings. And it made it possible for officials of constituent organizations (including grocers, chemists, and temperance women) to frame the issue of pure food in distinctive ways that appealed to their members even while national leaders pieced together a reasonably united lobbying campaign.[97]

In the end, it worked. Industry lobbyists and southern defenders of states' rights had long managed to defeat pure food bills. Success finally came in 1906, with Congress passing and Theodore Roosevelt signing both the Meat Inspection Act and the Food and Drugs Act. The first required the USDA to check slaughterhouses for diseased animals and unsafe meat. The second banned interstate commerce in food deemed to be misbranded, mislabeled as to weight, or containing unlisted additives. It also empowered the USDA's Bureau of Chemistry (Wiley's fiefdom) to test sample goods for compliance, to define the "standard" content of basic foods (thus specifying the criteria for identifying counterfeits), and to evaluate for safety suspect ingredients such as preservatives. Historians generally attribute the eventual passage of the law to three developments. First, organized women's groups increasingly mobilized around the issue from the turn of the century. Second, the publication of *The Jungle* in 1906 commanded the public's attention by turning their stomachs. Third, and partly for these reasons, Roosevelt signed on to the cause and made it one of his administration's priorities.[98] International emulation may have helped. Between 1890 and 1905, Germany, Japan, France, and Switzerland adopted comparable food safety laws.[99] Enforcement was another matter. Pure food advocates continued to struggle against business efforts to dilute government standards. And many food reformers argued that state action was not enough: Consumers needed to take matters into their own hands.

2. Domestic Science

The pure food movement's weapon of choice against untrustworthy food was government regulation. The domestic science movement's primary strategy was instead to upgrade the scientific literacy of women as both producers and consumers of food. As early as the mid-1880s, cooking schools and magazines such as *Table Talk* called for a more systematic approach to food selection and preparation, one that put greater emphasis on efficiency than on tradition. The movement gained momentum through the 1890s, fueled by the burgeoning fields of nutritional and hygienic research and coming to wider public notice with exhibits at the 1893 World's Fair in Chicago. Leading figures included Ellen Richards, an instructor of "sanitary chemistry" at the Massachusetts Institute of Technology (MIT); Caroline Hunt, from 1903 a professor of Home Economics at the University of Wisconsin; and Mary Abel, a prolific writer on nutrition. They shared a basic goal: "the application of [the] various sciences to the labor of the household."[100] In 1899, organizers settled on the label "home economics" to represent their work.[101] By World War I, they had succeeded in making home economics a recognized profession and a standard part of school curricula.[102]

Ellen Richards (née Swallow, 1842–1911) rejected stereotypes and broke barriers along the way to enshrining home economics as women's expertise. Recognizing his "tomboy" daughter's intellectual gifts, Richards's father (a farmer, teacher, and storekeeper) moved the family from rural Massachusetts to a larger town with superior educational opportunities. The teenage Ellen then moved herself to Worcester to better prepare for college. She entered Vassar in 1868, studying sciences and complaining in her diary of "the delicate little dolls [and] silly fools who make up the bulk of American women."[103] From Vassar it was on to MIT to become the first woman admitted (albeit as a "special student"). Richards studied chemistry and helped support herself by conducting analyses of water quality in the state. She remained at MIT for the rest of her life, first as founding director of a lab to train other women in chemistry, then, from 1884, as an instructor of Sanitary Chemistry. Along the way, she married an MIT mining engineer.

Using her skills as an analytical chemist, Richards took on food issues as an academic, a consultant, and, eventually, the country's leading advocate for domestic science. In addition to her work on water quality, she used her laboratory to assess adulteration in food. She conducted similar analyses for the Massachusetts Board of Health. That work led, in 1885, to the publication of "Food Materials and Their Adulteration." But unlike Wiley, she also investigated the nutritional properties of different foods. And drawing on the pioneering research of Wilbur Atwater and the cooking tools invented by Edward Atkinson, Richards developed guidelines for meeting dietary needs at the lowest possible cost. Beginning in the early 1880s, she also worked to make such knowledge available to more women through public school "manual training" programs (the precursors to home economics classes). As if that were not enough, Richards played a leading role in projects to bring sound food and cooking knowledge to poor and immigrant communities in Boston. (By and large, immigrants showed little interest in these efforts.) Together with her colleague Caroline Hunt, she reached a national audience at the 1893 Chicago World's Fair with exhibits showcasing scientific cooking and housekeeping methods. Richards's role as the personal hub of a domestic science movement took more formal shape in 1899, when she founded the Lake Placid Conference on Home Economics. The conference evolved into the American Home Economics Association (1908), with Richards as its first president.

a. Feeding the Family with Science: Other home economists joined Richards in embracing science as both a tool to combat problems of adulteration and food safety and as a strategy to realign consumers—especially women—with an increasingly commodified food system.

At a time of growing concern about the integrity and healthfulness of food, domestic scientists argued that food choices should be guided by the emerging science of nutrition. They quickly enlisted the findings of Atwater, citing his studies of calories and of the functional components of different foods to help consumers calculate what foods, in what quantities, were needed to correctly nourish family members.[104] The guidance also allowed for science-based customizing so that older and younger family members, males and females, the physically active and the sedentary would be properly fed. By invidious contrast, homemakers were warned not to be misled by tradition, cultural prejudices, or even taste. Food is fuel, to be calibrated to the human machine: "Knowing what to eat should be almost as exact a science for every intelligent adult in this age as for an engineer to know what to feed his engine to secure from it the most effective service."[105] New cookbooks, including the first from Fannie Farmer of the Boston Cooking School (1897), offered help. Readers could find the nutritional content of different foods and combine them in precise amounts to yield the necessary doses of protein, nitrogen, fat, and so on. For the less bookish, a 1902 Home Economics exhibit offered the "dietary computer," a "clever invention to aid the uninstructed in dietetics to compute the food value of selected menus, and compare the result with the standard for required nutrition."[106] We can also see the growing emphasis on scientific research in the changing sources of dietary authority. Although *Good Housekeeping* clearly stressed the need for cooks to be better informed about nutrition, as late as 1887 the solution was still to solicit tips from readers. Tell us what you have learned from experience, the editors asked, and we will pass that guidance along to readers. Two years later, the magazine instead invoked research by Atwater to advise readers on what to eat.[107]

Science-based education of women as both shoppers and cooks would also meet the challenge of food adulteration. "The practices which have savored of dishonesty on the part of some dealers," according to *New England Kitchen,* "have had their origin through the ignorance of the consumer."

The GFWC offered the same advice: "The only way to get pure food laws and protection from base imitations of all kinds, is to provide an education which will enable the purchaser to know when 'things are not what they seem.'"[108] Better education would further help women make informed choices between the useful and sound "patent foods" (manufactured substances sometimes referred to as artificial foods) and the useless or dangerous varieties.[109]

In making more intelligent choices, women could draw on the expert advice of kitchen magazines to make "simple tests for the purity of food," such as using iodine to see if sausage is adulterated with starch.[110] Branches of the GFWC boasted committees dedicated to home economics, making reading materials, demonstrations, and lectures available to members.[111] The NCL's Food Committee prepared educational materials "designed to spread the doctrine of not only pure food, but clean food," and it made these leaflets available in Italian and Yiddish, as well as English, for distribution in New York City grammar schools. The same committee came up with a set of "Sanitary Maxims" to send out to settlement houses, churches, and branches of the National Congress of Mothers' Clubs.[112] And these local groups, in cooperation with national organizations such as the American Home Economics Association, helped set up displays at food exhibitions. There women could see educational demonstrations and try out new products. Madison Square Garden hosted a Domestic Science and Pure Food Exposition in 1910, sponsored by *National Food Magazine* and the Associated Clubs of Domestic Science. Products were carefully screened for "purity and integrity"; booths displayed the use of food scales to avoid scams, demonstrated chemical analysis to detect adulteration, and offered pamphlets on "What Every Housewife Should Know" to ensure sound food at home.[113]

Domestic scientists had another rule of thumb to guide consumers in distinguishing between reliable and suspect foods: Modern is better. In this we can see another sort of legacy from Graham's era. His approach identified "pure" food as that closest to nature and produced by traditional methods. Domestic scientists held up this model as one to be repudiated. Bread making and canning, for example, could be done more economically by machinery, in high volume. Home economists argued that, far from being threatened by industrialized food, consumers should take advantage of it. "Worn-out traditions and relics of past conditions," Richards opined, just stood in the way. "Why cannot bread made by the yard and pies by the hundred, be . . . accepted? It may be argued there is more individuality about the food than about the furniture. I grant that each family has a weakness for the flavor produced by its own kitchen bacteria, but that is prejudice due to lack of education. The cleanliness which can be obtained in a large, well-conducted factory is far beyond that which is possible in an ordinary kitchen, and the evenness of product due to skilled labor will in time commend itself."[114] "Pure" food, in this view, was the product neither of nature nor of loving mothers following traditional recipes. Rather, it was produced under hygienic conditions by reputable manufacturers. One way to avoid adulterated foods, *American Kitchen* counseled readers, was to "buy groceries bearing the name of firms known for honesty."[115]

This counsel to women had a larger purpose than guiding them toward healthy food choices. Domestic scientists also recognized (as pure food advocates generally did not) larger dilemmas in the changing relationship between women and the food system. The widespread commercialization of food made women both a problem and a potential solution. They were increasingly responsible for buying rather than producing food and thus faced the problem of what to buy. Moreover, owing to their diminished roles in producing food, they had less firsthand knowledge to apply in making choices. "The status of the household as an economic factor has changed radically in the last fifty years," *American Kitchen* observed. "Many of its former industries have been relegated to the factory where we see the work simplified by use of machinery and by the specialization of labor."[116] That radical change left women, as consumers, ignorant. The solution also lay with women: They needed access to scientifically grounded education.

In an increasingly complex food economy, however, different women would occupy different roles, each requiring more specialized training than pamphlets and exhibitions could afford. Accordingly, home economists devoted much energy to devising and lobbying for changes in formal educational institutions. Domestic science periodicals and conferences regularly featured papers detailing curricular changes to better train women in the sciences of household management. The changes applied to every level of education, from elementary schools to universities, and the movement was remarkably successful. A survey of eighty-nine colleges conducted in 1901 found fifty-eight with some home economics instruction, twelve with more advanced domestic science courses, and four more with such classes in the works.[117] New curricular materials were to be science-based at every level, with variations among educational tiers corresponding to different classes of women, as well as to advancing levels of knowledge.[118] Many women would never finish high school. They should still be trained to more expertly prepare meals and maintain hygiene, major parts of what would become the standard home economics classes of public schools. Women preparing for "service" would need more extensive grounding in how to provision, cook, and clean, for which purpose domestic scientists supported the expansion of manual training centers. If these programs helped solve "the servant problem," so much the better. College-going middle-class women would benefit from more exposure to the theories that guided successful household management, including chemistry, bacteriology, physiology, even sociology (for understanding "the home as [an] organized social unity").[119] Colleges should not abandon the general education courses needed by cultured young ladies, however. "No greater danger can threaten our homes than to have a large body of women specifically educated for the home without a sufficient number of women broadly educated for life with all its manifold complexity of interests."[120] In addition to hired domestic help, that larger body of women for whom broader cultural literacy was extraneous might include women planning careers as professional cooks, cooking instructors, or managers of cafeterias in hospitals and schools. They would need more thorough training than future servants. For these more elevated positions, public or private trade schools could provide appropriate education. And at the top, a few women had the interest and capacity to undertake graduate training and equip themselves as professors and researchers in the component sciences of home economics.[121] Ideally, these different types of education would work together to make women the vehicles for more scientific domestic labor. (For one vision of the system as a whole, see Figure 3.4.) According to the director of Boston's School of Housekeeping,

> The Kitchen Garden, . . . Manual Training in the Grammar Grades, the Manual Training High School, the Agricultural School, the Normal School for Domestic Science, the Course in Sanitation in College or University—are they not all varying expressions of the same conviction: that the home is the organic unit of society, that to raise the standard of living and of life in the home is to elevate the whole social system? A lecture on the economics of consumption, and a lesson on the making of bread, are they not phases of the same whole? Both stand for a bettering of home conditions; the one by reading into it laws of science, the other by translating scientific law into practical action.[122]

Domestic scientists highlighted one additional problem associated with the broader commodification of food: Many people could not afford the commodities. Here, too, science came to the rescue, neutralizing class inequality. The underlying issue was not low wages but ignorance in buying and preparing food. "Scientific research," Atwater announced, "indicates that we make a fourfold mistake in our food economy. First, we purchase needlessly expensive kinds of food. . . . Secondly, our diet is apt to be one-sided. It often does not contain the different nutritive ingredients in the proper proportions. . . . Thirdly, we use excessive quantities of food. . . . Fourthly and finally, we are guilty of serious errors in our cooking. We waste a great deal of fuel in the preparation of our food, and even then

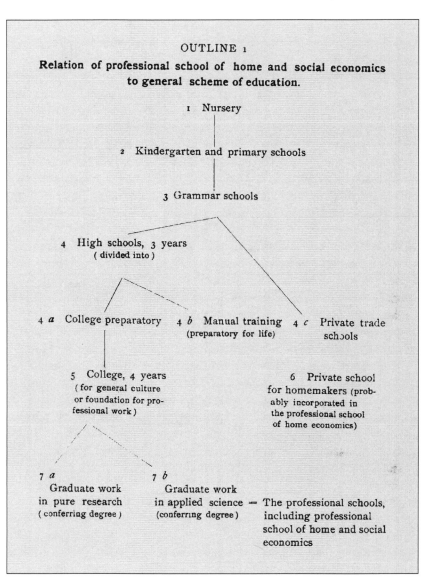

Figure 3.4. "Suggestions for a Professional School of Home and Social Economics," by Henrietta I. Goodrich, director, School of Housekeeping, Boston. (Lake Placid Conference on Home Economics, *Proceedings of the Annual Conference*, 1900, 28.)

a great deal of the food is very badly cooked."[123] Proper nutrition, geared to the specific needs of each diner, would maximize his or her ability to grow, to work hard, to think clearly. And nutritional expertise would make women better shoppers, choosing ingredients that met all family members' physical needs at the lowest cost. Helping them in this task, Atwater and his followers published tables giving the nutritional content *and* average cost of different foods so that readers could calculate the cheapest way to get the requisite quantities of protein or carbohydrates. In preparing sound food, women could make use of mechanical aids such as a special oven developed by Atkinson to minimize consumption of cooking fuel. Domestic scientists often made the more general point that a household should be run like a business. A contributor to *Good Housekeeping* elaborated the analogy:

> The machine-shops of the nation have been systematized and stan-
> dardized; but our homes—factories whose products are the men
> and women of tomorrow—are managed after no methods at all or
> the methods our wives and mothers have inherited. The man of the
> house goes off to a shop where every machine and every human unit
> is measured by the one rule—efficiency, and never gives a thought
> to the establishment his wife is running. Which is wrong—and un-
> economical. Money made in the mill should not be wasted at home;
> neither should a wife's time be held of less moment than a stenog-
> rapher's. . . . The success or failure of a matrimonial firm depends
> upon the product it turns out, and the product is of three kinds,
> happiness, public service, and children of the right sort. That firm
> is most successful which turns out the largest and best product in
> the shortest time for the least cost in muscle, money and brains.[124]

b. Domestic Science's Social and Organizational Base: Marching be-
hind this movement agenda was a constituency similar to pure food's in its middle-class character, but even more feminized. At the first Lake Placid Conference, in 1899, women outnumbered men 19 to 1; at the last, in 1908, the membership roster tilted 185 to 16.[125]

But like the pure food movement, domestic science had characteristics of both insider and outsider politics. It included some government sponsor-ship and had some members working at USDA experiment stations, where (usually male) employees conducted nutrition research. As historians of the movement have emphasized, home economists had growing ties to food businesses by World War I. These firms supported domestic science exhibi-tions and marketed products using the language of nutritional science and household economy. Leading domestic scientists, in turn, endorsed prod-ucts and made national branding and factory production into markers of trustworthy food.[126] "The up-to-date domestic science expert . . . spreads the gospel of cooking with a can opener," according to *Table Talk*. "She fully realizes how important it is that the housewife should make the acquaintance of the prepared foods which mean efficiency in cooking."[127]

The structure of the domestic science and pure food movements also was similar, but domestic scientists' organization proved more durable. The founding of a National Household Economics Association came in 1893, bringing with it specialized committees, including those for sanitation, food supplies, cooking schools, sewing, and housekeepers' clubs.[128] For nine years, the Lake Placid Conference offered activists an annual opportunity to caucus, deliver papers, and plan for the coming year. The conference reconstituted itself in 1908 as the American Home Economics Association. That organization lives on today as the American Association of Family and Consumer Services, a conjoining of family obligations and consumer choice that the domestic science movement helped construct. These home economics associations had state-level counterparts. But the movement probably had its broadest roots not in dedicated organizations but in women's clubs. Like the GFWC as a whole, many of these clubs had home economics committees that aimed to advance the cause locally. Unlike pure food advocates, domestic scientists also had footholds in the organized *practice* of home economics, whether local cooking schools or periodicals such as *New England Kitchen* and its successor, *American Kitchen*.

3. Framing, Strategy, and the Progressive Template in Pure Food and Domestic Science

The pure food and domestic science movements mobilized in response to some common problems in the food system, and they framed those problems in broadly similar and typically Progressive ways. The resemblance is clearest in the two campaigns' moral distinctions between good and bad food products, consumption choices, and preparation methods. The moral distinctions did not run along the lines of sin and salvation, as they did with Graham. Instead, Progressive food activists framed the threats to good food and healthy eating in terms of partisan self-interest corrupting markets and scientific ignorance spoiling diets. In the campaign for a food and drug law, partisan interest took the form of unscrupulous businessmen padding their profits and undercutting their honest competitors by adulterating food. The main solution was a government regulatory role, using scientific standards and monitoring to safeguard the public interest. Home economists had a similar critique of dishonest purveyors of food. But their larger concern was with those who selected and prepared food following obsolete traditions and ignorant tastes rather than nutritional and hygienic science. Once enlightened, the individual consumer could detect adulterated food and maintain a healthy and economical diet. And far from following Graham's preference for food in its natural state, prepared by women following traditional methods, domestic science became a champion of manufactured food. This food you could trust because it was made efficiently, under hygienic conditions (ideally, untouched by human hands), by reputable corporations.

For both movements, self-interest and scientific ignorance were bound up with larger social inequalities. Pure food advocates emphasized that the poor were the primary victims of food adulteration and the ones most in need of state protection. Home economists also saw laborers and immigrants as at the greatest risk. In their case, poverty was part of the problem, but so were nutritional ignorance and blind adherence to culinary traditions. The poor, to be sure, had no monopoly on poor dietary judgment. Middle-class women could be as frivolous in their choice of foods and as unenlightened in cooking it. Still, the problem had a class tilt, and so did the solutions. Education, domestic scientists insisted, should be improved for all but customized to the occupational trajectories of women (and to the languages of benighted immigrants).[129]

In these diagnoses of and solutions for problems of food supply and consumption, activists on both the political and domestic fronts appear as model Progressives. They recognized that bad food and diet are the products of social circumstances—unregulated markets, poverty, lack of education—rather than individual choice. They saw an indispensable role for government in setting things right, whether through legal controls or government-sponsored research and education. And these controls and curricula should be based on such modern sciences as analytical chemistry and nutrition. Like other Progressives, they both acknowledged and denied class. They argued that food risks were bound up with poverty. But they tied neither the problems nor the solutions to class relations. For pure food advocates, the problem was not capital. It was dishonest businessmen. Once the U.S. Food and Drug Administration (FDA) put the public interest first, honesty would return to food markets. For domestic scientists, laborers and immigrants ate poorly more out of ignorance than poverty. With suitable educational reforms and outreach, they could be taught how to eat well and within their means. Food reforms could also reduce class conflict. Better-fed workers would be more satisfied with their wages and resistant to the insidious lure of union demagogues.[130] Both sets of food reformers, finally, made use of a general maternalist script. Food and drug laws and more scientifically managed households were needed so that women could better fulfill their roles as protectors of the family and parents of future good citizens. Domestic scientists gave this script an additional plot twist. Other Progressives invoked women's maternal responsibilities to justify their active public roles in fighting urban social problems and pushing for suffrage.

Domestic scientists continued to focus on women's roles in the private sphere, as cooks and, increasingly, as shoppers. But they also sought to elevate those roles in dignity and importance by making them the work of well-educated, scientifically literate women—professionalized housewives. The warrant for trusting women in the kitchen was their expertise, not (as it was for social purity reformers) their piety.

In terms of strategy, by contrast, the two movements might appear to favor nearly opposite, although not incompatible, approaches to food problems. Pure food advocates viewed federal regulation as the best way to combat unsafe and adulterated foods. They put most of their energy into overcoming congressional resistance to that regulation. Domestic scientists regarded ignorant or backward housewives as the bigger problem. Upgrading their skills would enable them, as individuals, to identify bad food and, as a group of educated consumers, exercise market leverage in favor of good food. More broadly, pure food and domestic science represent contrasting approaches to restoring trust in the food system. The Food and Drugs Act and the Meat Inspection Act promised to restore trust in at least two ways. Consumers would know that (most) food available for purchase conformed to government rules.[131] But the laws also relieved buyers of having to make judgments on their own. Was this beefsteak sound? Were the additives in canned peaches safe? Was this jar of honey actually honey? For such questions, the government empowered experts, such as meat inspectors and chemists, to make decisions on behalf of consumers. Domestic science, by contrast, sought to lodge that expertise among individual consumers rather than the state. Women needed to be better informed so as to judge food purity for themselves; armed with that knowledge, they could then pressure merchants to sell only pure food. They would learn partly from popular magazines such as *Table Talk* and *Good Housekeeping* and from educational displays at food exhibits.[132] But the more systematic teaching and learning of housekeeping sciences would come through formal educational programs in public schools, training centers, and colleges.

Ultimately, however, the two movements' strategies differed only in the relative weight that they assigned to state-centered as against consumer-based tactics. Pure food advocates also urged women to demand safe and unadulterated products from merchants, and they sponsored educational displays at expositions that allowed consumers to visualize dangers in food production and home preparation. California's State Board of Health joined forces with Stanford University; the University of California, Berkeley; and the Women's Public Health Association to organize a touring "hygienic exhibit," complete with a special railroad car showing how upstairs tenements could spread tuberculosis and typhoid to butcher shops below. Expositions aimed to do more than shock visitors into caring. Attendees could learn safe techniques for preserving and handling food; marvel at new methods for testing food and detecting adulterants; and purchase items from an array of wholesome products on display. Thus, "the public generally will be taught to discriminate between pure and doctored foods."[133] On the other side, domestic scientists not only agreed on the need for a pure food law. They made use of other state-centered strategies. They demanded change in curricula of public schools, agricultural colleges, and state universities. And they lobbied to expand the role of state and federal governments in research on nutrition and food safety—notably, through the USDA's experiment stations and, beginning in 1923, a dedicated Bureau of Domestic Science within the USDA.[134] On both fronts, domestic science women and organizations were vigorous lobbyists.[135]

The pure food and domestic science movements converged, moreover, in urging women to bring *collective* market pressure to bear on offending food producers. Informed women could be strategic consumers. "One can easily imagine," Alice Lakey warned, "what would happen to any manufacturer if the hundreds of thousands of women belonging to the . . . Federation of Women's Clubs should decide to boycott his goods."[136] The GFWC's Pure Food Committee went further. In anticipation of its exhibit at the 1905 St. Louis Expo, the committee prepared "a 'white list' of canned foods guaranteed pure and honestly labeled."[137] On the home economics side, *Good Housekeeping* offered its readers a similar service on a still more ambitious scale. Using its own test facilities and closely scrutinizing advertisers, the magazine developed a "Roll of Honor of Pure Foods." The regularly updated roster would meet "the great need . . . for some responsible authority to give positive information as to what foods and Brands are all right."[138]

Still, these consumer strategies did not take the place of political action for either movement. The GFWC's Pure Food Committee and *Good Housekeeping* both emphatically supported a pure food law. Pure food and domestic science activists also recognized (as their counterparts today sometimes do not) that it was unrealistic to expect the poor to wield the power of the purse. Making sure you bought only wholesome meat took time and money, a 1906 GFWC report acknowledged: "It would be folly to suppose that any large proportion of the general public is going to take any such precautions. . . . The general public will continue to buy what is cheap."[139] However, state regulation and market pressure could work together to improve the food supply, and women's groups continued to advocate consumer vigilance well after the passage of the Food and Drugs Act. To be effective, moreover, that vigilance required expertise on the part of women in the market, as well as chemists at the USDA.

Pure food and domestic science reformers thus followed a Progressive script. Social problems had to be addressed through the application of science, with the aid of government powers, and with special attention to the poor, even while regulators, scientists, and crusading women stood above class. It is hardly surprising to find them applying this template. They lived and worked in an ambient Progressive political culture. They also belonged to organizations and professional networks that were active in a much broader range of causes. Advocates for a food law or for home economics education commonly had dedicated committees within local, state, and national units of the GFWC, alongside similar committees for civil service reform, child protection, city beautification, and much more. And many women, as individuals, crisscrossed the Progressive reform scene and its constituent organizations—Marion McBride, for example, was a domestic science instructor, WCTU member, and participant in the National Pure Food Congress; Lakey belonged to the GFWC and NCL and worked with Wiley in support of pure food legislation.[140] Such close organizational and personal ties fuel rapid diffusion of movement ideas and tactics within a cycle of contention like that of the Progressive era.[141]

B. Social Purity through Healthy Food

Pure food and domestic science advocacy offered explicit critiques of contemporary food risks and proposed both government policies and consumer strategies to restore trust. A third form of Progressive Era food activism focused more narrowly on the relationship between diet and health. Loosely affiliated institutions and gurus, including certain cooking schools, health magazines, and John Harvey Kellogg's Battle Creek Sanitarium, dispensed detailed advice on what to eat. But they also traced some of the perils of modern eating to foods they defined as adulterated and artificial, and they made ambitious claims regarding the beneficent effects of a proper diet on personal morality and social betterment, as well as physical health. For these reasons, health food advocacy deserves consideration as one of the Progressive Era's food movements. Its central tenets both echo Graham's and belong to a larger, religiously grounded "social purity" movement that included campaigns to fight sexual license, pornography, and (above all) intemperance.[142]

Progressive Era health reform lacked a preeminent political strategist like Harvey Wiley or a commanding agenda setter like Ellen Richards. John Harvey Kellogg (1852–1943) came close.[143] A prolific author and, in his trademark white suit, a striking figure, Kellogg was both representative of and influential in this branch of turn-of-the-twentieth-century food reform, including its eventual straying from religious orthodoxy.

Kellogg grew up in Battle Creek, Michigan, in an intensely religious household. Both parents had close ties with the Seventh-day Adventist Church elders and zealously promoted the faith with financial contributions and evangelical efforts. Kellogg followed their example. He also inherited from his parents a suspicion of conventional medicine and an early enthusiasm for the alternative water cure. Kellogg absorbed Adventist orthodoxy in another way: as an apprentice printer for the church's press, typesetting the dietary revelations of the prophetess Ellen White and the Adventist journal *Health Reformer*. At the urging of church leaders, Kellogg studied at the leading college of "Hygieo Therapy" before completing his medical education in 1875, at the mainstream Bellevue Hospital Medical School in New York. He returned to the Seventh-day Adventist Church's Western Health Reform Institute as its physician-in-chief, became superintendent of the facility (rechristened Battle Creek Sanitarium), and ascended to its board chairmanship in 1885. Kellogg remained in control until "the San" entered receivership in 1932.

Under Kellogg's leadership, the San became a prominent health resort, offering curative diet and other treatments (some typical of professional medicine of the day; others, such as yogurt enemas, less so) for whatever ailed visiting businessmen and celebrities.[144] That was only a small part of the institution's work. There was a publishing operation, with Kellogg editing the *Good Health* journal and issuing a stream of books and pamphlets. At different times, the San operated training schools for nurses, hygienists, home economists, and medical missionaries. Most famously, it launched commercial ventures for the production and sale of healthful breakfast cereals and meat substitutes.[145] Kellogg added to these enterprises a prodigious output of his own articles, books, and lectures. Some of them were written in collaboration with his wife, Ella, herself a formidable WCTU activist for temperance and social purity.

Kellogg's embrace of commercial activities and his drift away from doctrinaire Adventist health principles led to increasing tensions with church leaders after 1900. He succeeded in taking both the Sanitarium and its food businesses away from church control; the church retaliated by expelling him in 1906. Excommunication did not slow Kellogg down. He joined forces with "the great masticator" Horace Fletcher to launch the Health and Efficiency League (1909), and he put a lasting stain on his reputation by founding the eugenicist Race Betterment Foundation (1906). But despite these detours in matters of religious faith and racial politics, Kellogg's basic diagnosis of American dietary ills remained largely consistent from the 1880s on.

1. Conventional Food versus God's and Nature's Dietary Laws

Kellogg and like-minded health reformers called out many of the same problems with the food system as did other Progressive Era critics. To begin with, they joined the hue and cry over adulterated food, their newspapers printing regular warnings about such adulterants as glucose syrup, sulfur, and artificial coloring. As advocates of a vegetarian diet, they had extra incentive to warn of hazardous meat. Writers for *Good Health* seized on reports of trichinosis in pork and "embalmed" beef to win new converts.[146] By 1891, the paper was running a regular "Detective Bureau," with tips on identifying adulterants, quack cures, and unsafe food. And like some pure food advocates, health reformers expressed doubts about "artificial" foods produced in the factory rather than on the farm.[147] *Good Health* assured its readers in 1893 that "the most sanguine experimenters have at last been brought to confess that there is no possible hope that man will ever be able to duplicate in the chemical laboratory the marvelous alchemy of the vegetable kingdom."[148] On this point domestic scientists, not *Good Health*, had a clearer view of the future.

Even unadulterated food of unimpeachable rural provenance, however, could be "unnatural" and harmful if at odds with the laws of God and science. Here the views of Kellogg and his colleagues closely followed Graham. Once again, men and women put themselves at grave peril if they deviated from a natural diet of plain, unstimulating food. "Three-fourths of all our bodily ailments or diseases, and many of our immoral acts," by the rough count of *American Kitchen*'s Reverend Clymer, "are the legitimate results of improper dietetic habits."[149] The dietary improprieties, as with Graham, covered most of what make eating a pleasure, including spices, coffee, sugar, meat, and alcohol. These were all "stimulating" foods that caused inflammation and overtaxed the digestive system. From there, most bodily ailments followed. Individuals compounded their miseries by consulting doctors: "The chief agency that has caused these well-nigh general unnatural conditions in the physical man of today, is the eating of unnatural foods, and what is still worse, millions of people are spending millions of their hardearned dollars for proprietary medicines to cure, or rather palliate, the effects of eating unnatural foods."[150] Nor should men and women of the 1890s, any more than those of the 1830s, be guided in their food choices by taste and appetite. For most, these guides were corrupted by long addiction to stimulating foods. Unthinking pleasure led even the young astray. "At a very early age, the child should be taught that the appetite is to be controlled, that its palate must not be the sole judge respecting its food, but that reason must wield the controlling influence; that it should eat what is best for it, rather than what it likes best. . . . The aim should be to preserve natural simplicity of taste, unexaggerated by morbid excitation of the bodily appetites."[151] As with Graham, on these points nature's and God's laws concurred: "The science of life teaches the importance of self-denial; so does the religion of the Bible."[152]

The real cure would come from following neither doctors' advice nor personal tastes but a Graham-like regimen of unadorned natural food, with a special place for whole wheat bread. ("The scourge of all civilized countries," a health reformer advised GFWC members, "is white bread."[153]) And the benefits went well beyond restoring physical health; indeed, there "is no question of social economics as important as that of bread reform."[154] For individuals, proper diet fed proper morals. After summarizing the shocking spread of moral corruption, John and Ella Kellogg's popular address on social purity advised listeners that "nothing tends so powerfully to keep the animal impulses in abeyance as a simple, unstimulating dietary."[155] Sexual impulses aroused special concern and followed directly from misguided eating. Here again, science confirmed divine dietary advice. "Physiology teaches that our very thoughts are born of what we eat. A man that lives on pork, fine-flour bread, rich pies and cakes, and condiments, drinks tea and coffee and uses tobacco, might as well try to fly as to be chaste in thought."[156]

Activists with the WCTU agreed with both Kellogg and Graham: "stimulating" foods (including white bread) aroused a craving for alcohol and thus paved the way to sinful lives.[157] Curing corruption in individuals through temperance and dietary reform, in turn, would add up to a wider social uplift. "If a bloated, pimpled moral degenerate, sorely afflicted with intestinal diseases, can be brought to normal weight, purified in complexion, cured of a craving for drink and put in possession of natural manhood without the use of medicine, but only with proper attention to diet, and all within three months, what may not be the possibilities involved?"[158] The possibilities included labor peace, but not achieved the way domestic scientists envisioned. It was not so much that workers would live more efficiently, at their current wages, through proper diet. It was that they were wasting their money on the types of food that stirred up trouble. What they should have been doing was struggling for a better diet, not striking: "If the working men would organize for the purpose of suppressing the traffic in, and the use of, narcotics and stimulants, they would accomplish much more for the amelioration of their condition than they can possibly do by any other means."[159]

More broadly, dietary uplift was the key to social purity, and here the boundary work of health reformers such as Kellogg was painfully clear. Domestic scientists, to be sure, drew sharp distinctions between those with and without nutritional knowledge, and they targeted immigrants in particular as needing instruction. Kellogg and writers for *Good Health* took this boundary work several unsavory steps further, from immigrants as ignorant and unhealthy to immigrants as morally degraded by their diets and lifestyles. Natives were starting to follow their bad example. Like other champions of social purity, dietary reformers lamented what they saw as a general moral decline in American society. Adding a racial twist, they argued that the diminished "viability of the race" could be traced "simply and wholly [to] the departure from the divine order established by the Creator for man, in the cultivation of habits detrimental to health, physical, mental, and moral, in the use of the body as an instrument of pleasure."[160] The boundaries between the saints and sinners were starker for Kellogg and his colleagues in part because they believed in a more direct biological relationship between poor diet (including alcohol) and moral depravity. Dietary and moral failings, in turn, were concentrated among immigrants and poor slum dwellers, giving rise to most urban ills. Tenements, Kellogg warned, were "a veritable Pandora's box, out of which continually arise evils innumerable, social, moral, political, physical: the ranks of lunatics, idiots, imbeciles, drunkards, epileptics, thieves, prostitutes, criminals of all sorts, and defectives of all classes." The slums' reformation would come only through "the entire science of wholesome living."[161] And while domestic scientists also hoped to improve "the race" through proper diet—what they called "euthenics"[162]—Kellogg took a darker turn, raising the alarm over race degradation and supporting eugenics measures. As early as 1892, *Good Health* envisioned an "aristocracy of health" uniting brides and grooms from "families that for many generations have been free from the slightest taint" of unhealthy living.[163] By the 1910s, Battle Creek had its own Race Betterment Foundation, and *Table Talk* and *Good Health* regularly ran articles by leading eugenicists denouncing racial degenerates and proposing measures to stop the rot.[164] They included a Eugenics Registry, health certificates for marriage, and enforced segregation of male and female "imbeciles."[165] The underlying assumptions were that unhealthy living, including "a perversion of nutrition," corrupted morality, and these corruptions were inherited. "Poverty, crime, physical ills, and a blunted or perverted moral sense are the penalties we may be called upon to pay for the disobedience to Nature's laws; penalties which not only we may have to pay, but which may be passed down to succeeding generations."[166] Graham had attributed a long-term decline in human health and morality to poor diet. Kellogg worried most about the decline of "the white race."[167]

In this view of the power of diet to improve or degrade society, health reformers were creatures both of their time and of times past. "The Battle Creek idea" is part of the larger social purity movement, both in its religious ethos and its approach to reform. *Good Health* proudly acknowledged the connection, linking its dietary program to a "great moral reform movement" that also featured the YMCA and the WCTU.[168] The religious template is clear even in the names first given to healthful Battle Creek cereals, such as Food of Eden and Elijah's Manna.[169] And Kellogg's brand of health reform dovetailed with the *Christian* temperance movement, whose activists made many of the same dietary recommendations.[170] The ideological affinities were reinforced by organizational and personal ties. John and Ella Kellogg qualified, in the historian David Pivar's account, as part of "the purity elite." Both were founding board members of the American Purity Alliance (1895); Ella ran the Social Purity Department within the WCTU; and the couple funded a center for the dissemination of purity knowledge at Chautauqua, New York.[171]

But Kellogg's approach was also a direct descendant of Graham's, with multiple vehicles carrying ideas from the 1840s to the 1890s. The most important was the Seventh-day Adventist Church, whose prophetess Ellen White took Graham's precepts as holy writ and whose Western Health Reform Institute (1866) made them institutional practice.[172] The Adventists' *Health Reformer* also regularly introduced readers to Graham and his divine science of human life. The continuities even ran through families—not just from the Graham acolyte John Preston Kellogg to his son John Harvey, but also from William Alcott senior to junior, a regular contributor to *Good Health* in the late 1890s. Contemporary influences and legacies from Graham thus combined to provide a particular, religiously inflected model for interpreting "adulterated" food and advocating dietary reform in the Progressive Era.

In the WCTU, too, we find a bridge both from the past and across fields of Progressive Era activism. The organization carried forward a tradition of temperance that specifically connected spicy and "stimulating" foods to the devil of drink, calling women to virtuous battle against each.[173] And within the WCTU, particularly as it followed Frances Willard's call to "do everything," participation in common campaigns and coordination among different WCTU departments linked dietary reform to the wider cause of social purity.

2. Strategy: The Business of Dietary Salvation

How were these reforms to be achieved? Not primarily by the standard Progressive approach of state action to ameliorate social environments, but by reclaiming individual souls. Although leading health reformers and allied newspapers did support a pure food law, their strategic focus lay much more with educating individual consumers about the requirements and benefits of proper diet. Indeed, they expressed some skepticism about the value of government mandates. "The only way to bring about a general reformation of any kind is to begin with individuals," Kellogg's *Good Health* emphasized. "When the individual men and women who compose society are made good, society will take care of itself."[174] As with salvation, so with health: "The Battle Creek idea" is that "there is no healing power, as far as the individual is concerned, outside of himself."[175] How to reach and redeem these men and women? Some movement figures spread the word by way of influential cooking schools (Henry Perky's Oread Institute, Harriet Higbee's New Era Cooking School) and cooking magazines (*What to Eat*, as well as *Good Health*). Acolytes also worked through WCTU locals (the WCTU hosted a Bread Reform League in 1895[176]) and could practice what they preached in pure food restaurants, health-oriented college dining halls, and even company cafeterias at firms owned by Battle Creek alumni.[177] Kellogg himself, recognizing the value of networking, offered opinion makers— prominent businessmen, clergymen—discounts to visit the San in the hope that they would convey the salutary results back to their communities.[178] Battle Creek's own publishing arm spread dietary advice through news- papers, pamphlets, and cookbooks. And Kellogg was an energetic public speaker. Over the course of his career, he gave an estimated five thousand public lectures to church groups, temperance meetings, and professional associations.[179] The Health and Efficiency League's outreach efforts included waiving membership fees for college students, women's clubs, YMCAs, and medical associations; forming local clubs with free lending libraries and free courses in nutrition and hygiene; and organizing lectures by dietary reformers around the country on such uplifting topics as social hygiene, food adulteration, diet and health, and racial vigor.[180] Although Kellogg and his allies did not press local governments to incorporate their ideas into public school curricula, they did provide schooling in cooking and domestic economy through the Battle Creek Sanitarium, expecting graduates to carry the San's lessons on to their jobs in cafeterias, hospitals, and clubs.[181] Un- like advocates for pure food and domestic science, though, health reformers did not try to marshal educated shoppers as a collective force for change. Pure food would be chosen by purified individuals, not won in the market through the coordinated purchases of consumers.

These individual choices would get a powerful boost from marketing, however. The Kelloggs added to the tactical repertoire of dietary reform by developing alternative foods on a commercial basis. Other food companies certainly took advantage of popular enthusiasm for pure food and domestic science in selling their products. John Harvey Kellogg, and especially his brother Will, managed the commodification of reform themselves. They created and marketed whole-grain cereals and nut-based meat alternatives in part as conveniences, saving shoppers the cooking time and know-how needed to meet dietary requirements. Those products were also marketed as cures. Most Americans suffered from diseased appetites owing to years of meat, spices, coffee, and booze. The San's food could help, including, above all, "dry cereal . . . better prepared for quick digestion in stomachs crippled by disease."[182] This fusion of food prophesy and profiteering was further marked by the increasing appearance of recipes in *Good Health* that incorporated branded products, such as "Tasty Dishes Prepared from

Battle Creek Sanitarium Health Foods and Sanitas Nut Foods."[183] By tying together commercial food products, modern marketing, and dietary advice, the Kelloggs developed a powerful engine for educating consumers in what was good to eat.[184]

IV. Variations in Progressive Era Food Politics

Pure food, domestic science, and health reform activists had plenty of common ground. They shared a concern with adulteration in the food supply. They worried that readily available foods and typical food choices posed risks to individual health. They offered new principles by which consumers could more confidently decide what to eat. And they connected food risks to larger social problems and more trustworthy food to larger social improvements. The differences are in the details. Even here, the three cases sometimes blur at the edges. There were supporters of a pure food law who framed the problem in a religious language more characteristic of Kellogg's *Good Health*, as when Joseph Blackburn, president of the National Pure Food and Drug Congress, linked adulteration to original sin: "What myriad of evils would have been avoided had not the first of all pure food laws been violated?"[185] Kellogg urged improvements in culinary training that overlapped with domestic science's education reforms; along with his wife, Kellogg was a member of the Lake Placid Conference.[186] Wiley lent his authority to the domestic science agenda as a paid columnist for *Good Housekeeping*. This reformist multitasking was, of course, typical of the Progressive Era, as it is of other periods of upsurge in social movement activity.

But key distinctions exist. The different reformers assigned quite different meanings to "adulteration" and "purity," and they attached them to different social ills. For organizers of the pure food campaign such as Wiley, those differences were a strategic asset: The fact that varied groups could diagnose problems and interpret goals to suit themselves made it possible to bring a diverse coalition together into a potent political force. For scholars, the variations offer the analytical opportunity of exploring how and why concurrent social movement responses to similar problems took divergent forms.

Consider, to begin with, the meaning of "purity." Domestic scientists and leading supporters of the food bill (including Wiley) deemed "pure" those foods that were safe and contained what they said they contained. Kellogg set the bar higher: Pure food was that intended by God for human health. Both sorts of pure food packed an additional moral punch, but of different kinds. Pure food for Wiley was uncorrupted by selfish commercial interests, whereas for Kellogg it was uncorrupt*ing* of the consumer. In effect, the moral stain ran in opposite directions, from corrupt people (business-men) to tainted food, in one case, and from improper food to corrupt people (eaters) in the other. There are corresponding differences in the invocation of "natural" to legitimate alternatives. Some pure food lobbyists still used the term to refer to foods unsullied by human artifice and manufacturing—butter fresh from the milk of grazing cows rather than from the urban dairy, much less the margarine factory. Wiley, himself a chemist rather than a Grahamite, doubted that any "chemist [could] ever imitate nature's combinations. . . . Of everything made by man, almost nothing has the hy-gienic value of that made by nature."[187] But for Kellogg, even pasture-raised pork was unnatural because it violated the divine science of human life. By contrast, granose, protose, and shredded wheat, all products of Battle Creek industrial ingenuity, fully qualified as "natural." Domestic scientists made little use of the term. They treated the nutritional value and pristine production of a food to be the main standards of evaluation, standards that welcomed many synthetic foods of modern manufacture.

Whatever its specific meanings, the goal was pure food. Pure food, in turn, led to larger social benefits. The benefit envisioned by Wiley and most of his business allies was a more ethical marketplace. Requiring ac-curate labeling ensured honest competition and protected both the hon-orable businessman and the naive consumer. Domestic scientists raised the ante by going to work on that consumer, equipping her to shop and cook more knowledgeably and efficiently. Doing so would certainly weed out dishonest products in the market. But it would also reduce poverty because scientifically designed and prepared meals allowed the poor to eat well at less expense. It would lessen class conflict, in part because thrifty workers would not need to be paid more, but also because well-fed workers "are not going to be the prey of the . . . political partisan, or the walking delegate."[188] And it would advance the nation because a science-based diet improved health, and "national virility . . . depends upon individual health."[189] "The work of improving food conditions," in short, "will make all the other reforms . . . easier of accomplishment and should, therefore, have first place."[190] Health reformers had a no less ambitious, but different, vision. Dietary change was the key to reversing America's moral decline, reducing drunkenness, prostitution, masturbation, and racial degenera-tion. Healthy food would achieve these goals by different mechanisms from those advanced by domestic scientists. The latter did not share Kellogg's view that an individual's diet directly affected his morals. Proper diet did its good work instead by improving nutritional efficiency and household economy. The contrast reappears even where Atwater and Kellogg appear to agree, that food choices should not be guided by "appetites." For At-water, appetites are poor guides not because they are corrupted but because they are uninformed, and they should be reined in by experiment rather than scripture. "We need to observe our diet and its effects more carefully, and regulate appetite by reason."[191] Accordingly, even while championing the same whole-grain bread as Kellogg, domestic scientists spoke of digestive efficiency and nutritional value,[192] not the alarming contributions of lesser bread to "concupiscent excitability."

The different framing of dietary vices and virtues by health reformers and domestic scientists appeared, as well, in their quite different versions of maternalism. The two campaigns were highly gendered. Most obviously, women played disproportionate roles among the rank and file. Even by the standards of the Progressive Era, they helped lead the troops, as with Ellen Richards at Lake Placid or Ella Kellogg in the WCTU. But these movements were also gendered in the ways they sought to reconstruct trust in food. Both vested special authority in women. Wives and mothers had primary responsibility for choosing and preparing proper food for families, and their good judgment in this area had wide-ranging benefits for individual health and social order. Their authority, however, rested on different foundations in the two campaigns. Echoing older notions of women's essential moral natures, the WCTU called on women to renounce stimulating food and drink and thereby lead their families to more pious lives. In domestic science, women assumed greater responsibility for proper dietary choices for a different reason. They had become chiefly consumers rather than producers of food. Health reformers and domestic scientists also might have agreed that food offered up to the family by a woman's hand was thereby elevated. But for health reformers, that gendered sanctification was bound up with women's responsibilities as moral guardians of the home, charged with protecting family members from corrupting food and drink. Domestic scientists put no faith in women's moral nature, much less their traditional know-how. Wives and mothers could be trusted to properly feed their families only if they became experts, trained to apply new scientific knowledge of nutrition and chemistry.

The strategies chosen to achieve these goals differed sharply, as well. Champions of a food and drug law certainly encouraged consumers to take matters into their own hands, but the indispensable prerequisite for honest competition was federal regulation. Restoring moral purity, by contrast, was a matter of reeducating individuals, not changing government policy. Domestic scientists split the difference. They hoped to improve the nutritional expertise and domestic efficiency of individual women, but that also meant reforming public education. And while for Kellogg social purity would come through reformed individuals, domestic scientists included in their tactical repertoire the strategy of coordinating the purchasing behavior of educated consumers in order to change food business practices.

Ultimately, these different responses to untrustworthy food in the Progressive Era align with different cultural infrastructures. Wiley and Richards typify and were part of larger networks of Progressive reform. They saw food risks, like other problems, as the products of social causes more than of individual failings; they embraced the state as an essential tool for fixing those problems; and they treated science and efficiency as the proper guides to evaluating food and designing diet. Health reform, derided by Wiley and Atwater as unscientific quackery, had more direct religious roots.[193] Those roots stretched back to Graham, through both Adventists and temperance activism, but they were refreshed by the social purity movement in their own time. Both sources made impure food an affront to God's will and food reform a matter of individual salvation. The importance of these influences is clear, too, when they fade. In the early 1900s, as Kellogg moved away from Adventist orthodoxy and social purity and toward a more scientific language of social hygiene, his specific dietary recommendations and rationale begin to sound more like those of domestic science. But Kellogg and the WCTU retained the core premise, shared by Graham, that dietary reform leads, through the individual body, to broader moral improvement, including in "the race."[194]

V. Conclusion: Legacies

None of the three food movements of the Progressive Era fully restored trust in the products of a changing food system. They did, however, achieve a new status quo, new institutions and standards for managing consumers' doubts about what to eat. These institutions and standards constitute the key legacies that the period bequeathed to later generations of food activists.

The most obvious and important institutional innovations were the Food and Drugs and Meat Inspection acts. Under these laws, the federal government assumed new responsibilities for setting standards for the content and marketing of foods. The basic identity of jam, for example, would be codified, and any added ingredients would have to be listed on the label. The USDA's Bureau of Chemistry acquired a role, if not yet real enforcement powers, in testing food additives for safety. The USDA also gained responsibility for inspecting animals before slaughter and keeping diseased meat off dining tables. And through its experiment stations, the USDA pursued the measurement of nutritional needs and food content, using that information to make dietary recommendations. In effect, consumers could now offload to government experts the problem of what to eat.[195] If a food product passed muster with the FDA and USDA, it must be safe; if it conformed to dietary guidelines, it must be good for you. The corollary is that trust in food became hostage to trust in government.

The outsourcing of trust to the FDA and USDA is part of the story, but activists in this period also aimed to empower consumers rather than relieve them of responsibilities. Domestic scientists gave women new tools for evaluating the reliability of food. They did so in part by institutionalizing home economics. Consumers, not just government experts, would get the training needed to make decisions on what to buy and how to prepare it, and they would get that training from up-to-date school instructors, not their tradition-bound mothers. Domestic scientists also endorsed the strategy of organized consumer pressure to get merchants to offer "pure" food.[196] And they cooperated with *Good Housekeeping* and other kitchen magazines in what was an early version of certification. Alongside government monitoring, private bodies would set standards, evaluate foods, and endorse the trustworthy brands. These measures—enhanced lay expertise, boycotts, certification—expanded the tactical repertoire of food activism. They were also new mechanisms for establishing trust in food.

As both scholarly and popular accounts have noted, one of the most important criteria for evaluating a food's worth during this period was "nutritionist."[197] On this point, domestic scientists and health reformers agreed that taste was an unreliable and deceptive guide to food choice. We should instead judge food on a functional basis. Does it provide the correct nutritional components? Specifically, does it contain the protein and vitamins that we need, in the correct amounts? If so, it is "good" to eat. Nutritionists could even look forward to that happy day "when the food of man shall be composed merely of the chemical elements necessary to sustain life and strength; when the kitchen and the table shall have been relegated to the garrets, and nourishment shall be scientifically prepared and measured in prescribed capsules, to be swallowed at certain intervals, [and when] the office of the palate will . . . have been abolished."[198] This functional understanding of food would prove an enduring approach to American food choice, in part because it was institutionalized in the research activities and dietary recommendations of the USDA and land grant colleges.[199]

Finally, Progressive Era food activists did more than pass along, in different forms, the ideals of "health," "natural," and "pure" for valuing food. They also helped embed those standards in economic institutions, yoking them to the power of large corporations and modern advertising. In this, they broke with Graham, for whom commercialized food production was at best suspect and most likely *un*natural. Pure food advocates, domestic scientists, and health reformers all disagreed. They were largely reconciled to a commercialized food system, albeit in different ways. For pure food advocates, government regulation would ensure that commercial food production was compatible with health and safety. Domestic scientists and health reformers went further. For home economists, large corporations with modern production facilities turning out branded products guaranteed to consumers the integrity of food. The Kelloggs did not need to outsource trust to reputable firms; they produced and marketed health food themselves. But it was not long before plenty of other companies met the call for trustworthy food, sponsoring pure food expositions and marketing their products as living up to the standards set by domestic scientists and health reformers.[200] In doing so, they both reinforced these standards and established a model for the future commercializing of other food virtues. As with federal regulation, however, there was a legacy of another kind: Faith in food became hostage to trust in corporate food producers. In the 1960s, both the governmental and business guarantors of trust would be discredited.

4

Organic Food,
1960–1990

For Robert Rodale (1930–1990), heir to his father's role as organic food's leading champion in the United States, reforming the food system could not have had higher stakes. "While today being organic is a comfort—an added plus that gives texture and meaning to life," he warned in 1971, "tomorrow being organic could be the only alternative to a technological concentration-camp style of life."[1] This is not how most contemporary consumers think of organic food. To understand how organic food could be cast as our savior from the iron cage means revisiting the movement in its heyday and in the context of "the '60s." That decade saw a tremendous upsurge in activism, including efforts to revamp the production and distribution of food. As a radical challenge to the conventional food system, the organic movement peaked in the early 1970s; as a lucrative market niche, it has been growing ever since. The case is well known to food scholars. It is both the first important protest against the post–World War II regime of industrial agriculture and processed food and a cautionary tale of how such protest can be tamed and commercialized.[2] It is less well known to social movement scholars, and this is surprising. Organic advocacy is very much a part of the otherwise well-studied 1960s cycle of protest, with close ties to the New Left and counterculture, including their attacks on corporations and technocracy. It displays the hallmarks of a "new social movement," from its post-material values to its participatory organization. And it richly illustrates the familiar dynamic of social movement cooptation: modest political concessions (above all, federal standards for and certification of "organic" food), corporate mainstreaming (symbolized by the rise of Whole Foods Market), and the seductive slide from collective rebellion to individualized lifestyle politics.

This chapter focuses on organic food advocacy in the late 1960s and 1970s, when it was still more movement than market. As a deliberate alternative to conventional agricultural methods, embraced by some home gardeners and small farmers, "organic" food in the United States predates the 1960s by two decades. It was in the late 1960s that the movement gained energy and support from young consumers. My focus will be on this period, when consumer enthusiasm and activism aligned with the advocacy work of organic farmers to produce a popular movement.

What new grievances in this period sparked action? How did organic enthusiasts frame their criticisms and goals? And how did they organize and pursue those goals? Linking these questions to long-term dynamics in the food system, I particularly emphasize the breakdown of trust in the 1960s and the short- and long-term mechanisms by which that trust was reconstructed. Among the short-term ones were some of the most transgressive features of the organic movement in its early years, including its wide-ranging critique of "unnatural" food and its countercultural co-ops. Highlighting the movement's ties to broader currents of contentious politics in this period, I also call out similarities and differences from prior eras of food protest (a theme to which I return in Chapter 5). The continuities and legacies are clearest in organic's celebration of "natural" food, its divorce of food problems from labor problems, and its eventual resort to federal regulation to rebuild trust between producers and consumers. The departures from Progressive Era food politics—departures that showcase the impact of the era's counterculture and environmentalism—include a very different orientation to science, a new way of connecting the personal and the political, and a (short-lived) call to democratize the food system.

The influence of environmentalism and the counterculture on organic advocacy once again illustrates diffusion across social movements, a mechanism discussed in Chapter 2 and well known from studies of contentious politics. Legacies from the Progressive Era can be seen as diffusion at a greater temporal distance. Social movement researchers typically focus on the "relational" diffusion (channeled through direct social ties, such as those among reform-minded women of the Progressive Era) that occurs within cycles of protest.[3] But diffusion can also take place over much longer periods of time, exceeding the life span of activists, activist communities, and formal coalitions. As the time span lengthens, other channels for diffusion take over. Formal social movement organizations, if they survive, become more important vehicles. Their mission statements, membership rules, and operating procedures all serve to carry over time particular ways of framing problems, drawing boundaries, and selecting tactics. More relevant to my cases, the agenda of a movement at one time may come to be institutionalized in non-movement organizations. For instance, Sylvester Graham's dietary advice got adopted by the Seventh-day Adventist Church, and the pure food movement's divorce between food and labor reform got ratified by the regulatory structure of government. Diffusion over long stretches of time may also be favored by the practices of collective memory,[4] as lessons from the past get embedded in and reproduced by public monuments, ritual reenactments, and popular stories. What some organic advocates cited as the unholy alliance of nutritionists and food corporations in the home economics movement offered a cautionary tale about the need for a more democratic science. More recently, the oft-told narrative of the organic pioneers Drew and Myra Goodman, whose Earthbound Farm came to symbolize the betrayal of the ideal of small-scale local agriculture, keeps alive among contemporary activists the perils of Big Organic.[5] Tracing this temporal layer of recurring social movements requires that we keep an eye out for these vehicles of long-term diffusion. Let us look first, however, at the organic movement in its transgressive prime.

I. "Big Ag," Processed Food, and Consumer Disenchantment

In the two decades after World War II, developments foreshadowed in the early twentieth century came to dominate the U.S. food system. For critics, the most important were "big agriculture," with highly mechanized, chemical-intensive farming, and industrial food processing, applying sophisticated technology to the fabrication of new food-like products.[6]

The modernization of agriculture after World War II looked toward larger operations specializing in commodity crops and making greater use of machinery to plant and harvest those crops. In these ways they brought the logic of industrial capitalism to "factories in the field."[7] Among the signs of change were bigger farms and fewer workers. The average acreage of farms more than doubled between 1945 and 1970, even while those employed in agriculture dropped from 16 percent to 4 percent of the labor force. That increase in productivity owed much to mechanization, including the shift from animal to mechanical energy. As late as 1945, mules and horses still outnumbered tractors five to one; by 1960, tractors had raced ahead.[8] But two other sources of agricultural productivity would become much more important flash points for food activism in the 1960s. One was a sharply increased use of synthetic fertilizer in place of manure, cover crops, and crop rotation, allowing more frequent plantings and higher yields. The second was a similarly dramatic increase in the use of pesticides and herbicides to reduce crop loss from insects and weeds.

The federal government could claim much of the credit for these trends. Until the late 1950s, it had sought to support farm incomes by controlling production, keeping prices up by tamping supply down. Thereafter, farm policy shifted to encourage maximum production, with the USDA compensating farms if prices for major crops fell below target levels. The effect was to favor large operations, encouraging farmers to "get big or get out."[9] The state also played a role in the development of agricultural fertilizers and pesticides through wartime research and the later development work of USDA experiment stations and public universities.[10] When big ag and chemical-intensive production came under attack, the government would be one target.

A second general trend in the postwar food system was toward products fabricated to bring convenience to consumers and added value to manufacturers. These basic goals are familiar, but they held greater sway—owing in part to the increasing participation of women in the paid labor force—and took new forms. Some, such as many frozen foods, resulted from applying new techniques to make familiar fruit, vegetables, or fish easier to store and use as needed.[11] Others involved the time-honored strategies of standardizing and mechanizing the production of foods (such as bakeshop pies) that had once been prepared by skilled hands. The greater novelty was a proliferation of commodities conjured more from the lab than from either the home or the industrial kitchen. Many of these commodities had little culinary precedent.[12] As Harvey Levenstein points out, the 1950s was "the golden age of food processing."[13] The idea was no longer simply to start with a recognizable food and figure out how to make it more quickly and cheaply. Instead, technicians worked at a more molecular level, synthesizing and combining ingredients to assemble a marketable blend of taste, texture, longevity, and convenience. Some of the components might still be traditional products of agriculture but reconstructed and enhanced with chemical flavorings and preservatives. Pringles chips (1969), for example, are almost half (dried) potatoes, compacted with other ingredients to a standard, packable shape.[14] Other products bear only a passing resemblance, in taste or composition, to familiar foods. Cheez Whiz (1953) lists "cheese culture" near the bottom of its ingredient list; less than 2 percent of Tang (1958) comes from oranges; and Cool Whip (1966) offers only trace amounts of milk.[15] Genetically engineered corn and soy were increasingly part of the processed food recipe by the 1990s.[16]

Food production controlled by large corporations and dependent on pesticides and additives set the stage for a breakdown in trust in the 1960s. Moral entrepreneurs and food scandals set the play in motion. Small farmers, squeezed by highly mechanized, large-scale competitors, helped raise the alarm. Federal subsidy programs, they charged, betrayed the family farm in favor of big ag. And while the latter might be good for "super farm technology [and] processed foods with longer shelf life," the "deficient soils" of chemical agriculture "feed deficient men." Only family farms could produce good food.[17] These complaints had been aired back in the 1930s by proponents of "Permanent Agriculture."[18] For the rise of the organic movement, however, the crisis of confidence among *consumers* rather than producers mattered most.

Consumer fears focused on food additives and pesticides. These concerns can be seen on several fronts. Mainstream newspaper coverage of the issues increased sharply in the late 1950s and into the 1960s. "How Pure Is Your Food?" asked *U.S. News and World Report* in a typical headline.[19] The magazine rounded up some dangers before assuring readers that the Food and Drug Administration (FDA) vigilantly watched over the food supply. That reassurance grew less convincing over time. Spurred in part by debates over the Food Additive Amendment of 1958, which required that new food additives be evaluated for safety, the number of *New York Times* articles addressing the issue spiked in 1959 and 1960 and remained high over the next ten years.[20] A common theme throughout this coverage was growing consumer doubt about "modern" food. "When a housewife strolls into a supermarket today she is confronted with a cornucopia of things she can shake 'n bake, brown 'n serve, whip 'n chill or heat 'n eat. But now more and more shoppers are beginning to eye the labels on products with suspicion, trying to find out whether the foods they shake, brown, heat and whip are really safe to eat."[21] Coverage of food and pesticides in the *New York Times* follows an even more dramatic arc. Through the 1950s, the newspaper published at most eleven articles a year on the topic. It averaged thirty-three per year in the 1960s, peaking at seventy-three in 1969.[22]

There were other signs of diminished trust. Anna Zeide finds the trade association for food canners worrying over the issue and devising campaigns, drawing on the best of social science expertise, to win back consumer confidence.[23] Evidently, it failed. By 1969, the Nixon White House felt obliged to call a conference of industry and consumer representatives, scientists, and regulators to address popular doubts. According to one headline, the "Food Parley Exposes a 'Trust Gap'": "Consumer advocates, for the most part, came to the conference with a generalized complaint. They feared that the public was consistently being hoodwinked by food manufacturers."[24] The summit did little to close the gap. A survey three years later found a third of respondents convinced that American food was not safe.[25]

The alternative press was more closely aligned with the young, educated consumers who would embrace organic food at the end of the 1960s. It, too, began issuing warnings early in the decade. Compared with the *New York Times*, the alternative press's analyses more often linked pesticides and additives to the amoral pursuit of gain by capitalist firms. Summing up the conclusions of his *The Poisons in Your Food* (1960), William Longgood warned readers that "we are being systematically and irresponsibly poisoned by businessmen in their quest for greater profits."[26] In this view, the rot was both culinary and social: "American food, like other American institutions, is decadent and degenerate."[27] But while mainstream and alternative newspapers differed as to underlying causes, they alerted readers to the same threats to their health. One common narrative strategy in the alternative press (much as in Progressive Era muckraking) exposed the dangers hidden in familiar and much-loved foods, from frozen desserts ("What's Lurking in My Ice Cream?"[28]) to meat and cheese. "Domestic cheeses are decreasingly food items and increasingly synthetic ones. They are artificially thickened, stabilized[,] preserved[,] flavored[,] and colored. Where color has to be added, coal-tar dyes, highly toxic and strongly suspect as a cause of cancer, may do the trick."[29] Here, too, the threats were explicitly tied to *modern* food production. "By now most of us are aware of the fact that the quality of America's food is becoming progressively worse. There are cases on record where it has already proven lethal. Yet what else could be expected from the methods which are used by modern industry to process and market food? Wholesome, natural foods are looked upon with disdain. Science has sought incessantly to improve upon nature until now there is almost nothing left that is pure and untainted." With all this meddling in nature, "It is not difficult to understand why the health of the American people is being totally undermined and why 57 per cent of the population is chronically ill."[30] After chronicling a similar roundup of additives and mass-market foods in 1971, the investigative journalist Daniel Zwerdling offered some practical recommendations: Do not eat food with artificial colors; do not eat bakery products with bleached flour; do not eat convenience foods; do not eat packaged snacks; do not eat breakfast cereals; and do not eat "imitation" foods.[31] That did not leave many options at the local supermarket.

The application of science to increasing agricultural yields and enhancing packaged food was not without precedent. But new voices and events made trends in the food system lively matters of public concern. Critical and widely circulated books played a role, and Rachel Carson deserves the credit she is usually given for exposing the impact of pesticides on food and the environment. Her *Silent Spring* (1962), this period's answer to *The Jungle*, commanded broad attention, thanks both to its devastating analysis and to the vigorous public counterattacks that ensued from the chemical industry. Carson's credentials, meticulous research, and respected publishing venues no doubt gave her indictment weight and resilience. Scruffier critics preceded Carson (*Our Daily Poison* [1955], *The Poisons in Your Food* [1960]), and many more followed her (*The Hidden Assassins* [1965], *The Chemical Feast* [1970]).[32] The mainstreaming of these critiques is suggested by the founding of the Center for Science in the Public Interest in 1971. The center made its early focus the risks of conventional foods and the need for more research on them, and its name emphasized that, in food as elsewhere, science did not necessarily serve the public good.[33] Laura Miller adds another set of voices that put food hazards on the agenda: the health foods industry. Small businesses in that industry had long hawked alternative foods as healthier than conventional ones. These products would impart enviable strength, robust health, and long lives.[34] Growing concern over additives and pesticides gave these entrepreneurs new opportunities to make their case and sell their products. Through their advertising, the profit motive helped amplify doubts about the products of mainstream food businesses.

As in the Progressive Era, periodic food scandals served to concentrate the public mind on risky—but quite normal—practices of the food industry. The year 1959 brought news of cancer-causing hormones in poultry and of a cancer-causing herbicide in cranberries. Pesticides turned up in fish in 1966; salmonella in processing facilities, three years later. And in perhaps the greatest affront to innocent consumers, baby food additives came under suspicion in 1969.[35] Confidence in the food industry may have been even more fragile thanks to a sharp spike in prices in 1966, prompting housewives to retaliate with supermarket boycotts.[36] The message that modern food corporations are not the consumer's friend could not have been more different from that of domestic scientists sixty years earlier. The contrast points to an important legacy from the Progressive Era. In that period, trust in food had been reestablished through confidence in government regulation and corporate integrity. Political movements of the 1960s would undermine that confidence. In so doing, they would reinforce doubts about food.

II. The Context of "the '60s"

"The '60s" is familiar shorthand for an upsurge in social protest that struck observers as a sharp break with the social conservatism and Cold War politics of the Eisenhower years. The cast of social movement characters includes some of the country's most storied agents of change: the Civil Rights Movement, the Free Speech Movement, the antiwar movement, the feminist movement, the environmental movement, and the counterculture. Measured by mobilization for public protest, the organic food movement was a bit player, but it was very much part of this wider cycle of protest. Of particular importance as influences on the consumer wing of the organic food movement were the counterculture, environmentalism, and consumer activism.

To start the list with the counterculture is arguably to begin as this cycle of protest is winding down. By the end of the 1960s, the era's youthful rebellion had been frustrated both by the slow pace of change and by the electoral turn to the right in 1968.[37] One response was a focus on culture as a more promising arena for protest. Social change, it seemed, could not be won through organized public protest or party politics. It could be achieved instead through the pursuit of lifestyles that were more egalitarian in personal relations, less materialistic and competitive, and more rooted in small-scale communities. Whether realistic or not, the counterculture's shift away from New Left politics had more to do with tactics than with goals. The two shared the same enemies, including big business, restrictive social roles, a morally bankrupt liberal establishment, and technology in the service of capital. The concurrent revival of environmentalism as a popular movement may appear to have little in common with the counterculture.[38] Here, after all, was an organized movement. It boasted well-established formal associations such as the Sierra Club, as well as a lively popular base; a coherent agenda for protecting the environment from corporate polluters; and a willingness to do so through legal channels. Yet the two fields of activism had in common several features that would inform organic advocacy. Both fully qualified as "postmaterial" and "new" social movements.[39] Some activists from each camp explicitly rejected materialism as one of the original sins: the priority given to economic gain threatened the environment and fostered individualism over community. On this point the two movements sometimes merged. They did so in calls to get "back to the land," and they did so in the mission statement of a leading radical publication of the day, *Mother Earth News* (launched in 1970), which placed "heavy emphasis . . . on alternative life styles, ecology, working with nature and doing more with less."[40] Environmentalism and the counterculture also targeted the same offenders.[41] Both treated capital as a threat (to nature and to human community). Both doubted the federal government could be a tool for social change, given its ties to business and its bureaucratic lethargy. And both suspected scientific institutions and researchers of doing the bidding of corporate interests. In their deep skepticism about the national government and scientific experts, environmentalists and cultural rebels repudiated Progressive orthodoxy of the early 1900s. Indeed, what were for that earlier era's activists essential tools of reform and sources of legitimacy—federal regulation and scientific expertise—had lost credibility for radicals of the late 1960s. Finally, champions of the environment and of the counterculture shared (with each other and with much of the New Left) a commitment to greater democratization across American society. That commitment was practical as well as programmatic, with radicals from both camps working together in campus ecology clubs, rural communes, and cooperative housing.[42]

At least initially, the counterculture was broadly critical of capitalism and aimed to build more democratic alternatives in everyday life. The emerging organic movement also piggybacked on the less transgressive field of consumer activism. "The consumer" had been established as a social category in the Progressive Era and as an object of political mobilization and government solicitude in the Depression. Activism on behalf of consumers was another part of the 1960s cycle of protest.[43] It took one form in the muckraking exposés of business malfeasance—unsafe products, deceptive advertising, collusion with government—by crusaders such as Ralph Nader. Nader and his allies shared the era's skepticism that government bureaucrats were able or willing to defend citizens' interests. Effective regulation had to come from below, with grassroots mobilization in consumer advocacy organizations such as public interest research groups and citizen utility boards. For those too busy for that work, there was always a subscription to *Consumer Reports*, the flagship publication of the Consumers Union. Here, independent experts, unbiased by corporate interests, presented their reviews of products to educate and empower the individual consumer. In contrast to the Progressive Era's National Consumers League, these campaigns and reviews generally did not look closely at the labor conditions behind products, and the salient public identity of beneficiaries was that of the consumer, not the producer.[44]

The growth of consumer politics in the 1960s sometimes took another form, however. Individual buyers might not only benefit from the expertise of Consumers Union testers. Their market leverage might also be mobilized and coordinated to achieve some social goal.[45] Improving working conditions could be one of those goals, as in boycotts of grapes (1965) and lettuce (1970) to force growers to meet United Farm Workers' demands.[46] In this way, progressive urban consumers might act on behalf of poorly treated minority labor. The tactic shaded into the development of a more individualistic "lifestyle politics."[47] Growing numbers of consumers came to treat their purchasing choices as means to express political (pro-labor, green, feminist) values.[48] This was a less ambitious version of a central tenet of the counterculture: social change could be advanced by changing the way each of us lives our lives. The appeal of lifestyle politics and political consumerism in the late 1960s is easy to understand. It was a moment when the possibilities for change through either institutional politics or collective protest seemed to be waning.[49] At the same time, both variants of consumer politics presented business with new opportunities to cultivate niche markets, from green goods to socially responsible investments.[50] One such niche market would prove especially lucrative: organic food.

III. The Organic Movement

At first, organic was more movement than market.[51] "Organic" came to be the term used to describe methods of renewing soil fertility and managing pests without chemical inputs, such as with rich compost and beneficial insects. The methods were pioneered by Sir Albert Howard in India and England.[52] In the United States, similar techniques gained support from agrarian reformers in the aftermath of the Dust Bowl and from J. I. Rodale in the 1940s. Rodale (1898–1971) deserves credit for coining the term; for putting wealth gained in his manufacturing business into a demonstration farm in Pennsylvania; and, most important, for popularizing organic agriculture among small farmers and gardeners through his books and his monthly magazine *Organic Gardening and Farming*.[53] It was particularly in the 1960s that organic took off as a movement. It did so, in part, in deliberate opposition to the practices and power of big agriculture, of its government sponsors, and of its scientific backers. But the movement grew even more dramatically beginning around 1969. This was when organic food rapidly gained support (and *Organic Gardening and Farming* gained readers) among young urban consumers, for whom "organic" aligned with environmental, countercultural, and consumer values. That breakthrough created a growing market for organic produce. Over time, the movement spawned successful businesses, with large growers, distributors, and retailers playing an increasingly dominant role. My account will focus more on the late 1960s and early 1970s, when organic's character as an insurgent movement is most prominent. The 1990 federal law that led (slowly) to formal standards and labeling for organic food is a fitting endpoint for this story. I also pay particular attention to consumers of organic food, both because of their role in expanding the popular base for organic food advocacy and because that is where the social movement characteristics of the case are clearest. It was through consumers that what had been a matter of agricultural techniques recommended by a relative handful of small farmers and hobbyists acquired much wider social support and a much broader political agenda. My primary sources correspond to this focus on a particular period and on a particular constituency of the movement. The alternative press flourished at this time, and it reflected urban consumers more than established farmers. During these years, editorials and reports in *Organic Gardening and Farming* also increasingly targeted consumers rather than just growers looking for horticultural advice.

A. Middle-Class Rebels

Small farmers were certainly the early risers in the U.S. organic movement. They were men and women deliberately growing produce with minimal chemical inputs. Some were following family tradition or personal experience; some were guided by *Organic Gardening and Farming*. A collection of oral histories with prominent members of the organic community features pioneers whose commitment to sustainable methods dates back to the 1950s.[54] The collection also includes newcomers from the late 1960s. The latter were not established family farmers but enthusiasts, often with urban backgrounds and university credentials, who were seeking more independent and "natural" lives. In need of tutoring, they sought instruction from personal contacts and printed guides (often published by the Rodales).[55] One center of activity was the University of California, Santa Cruz (UCSC). The campus garden's charismatic manager, Alan Chadwick, introduced volunteers to "biodynamic" alternatives to conventional agriculture. Many of his acolytes went on to operate smallholdings in Northern California and to form networks of mutual support and shared identity. The UCSC garden, one apprentice recalled, "was organic from the beginning. It was fabulous. . . . It was right in the middle of those two centers of the back-to-the-land movement and the alternative culture of the late '60s and early '70s. It was centrally placed and timely."[56] As small-scale organic production expanded, other businesses added to the momentum. Long-standing natural foods stores began to promote organic produce on health grounds, giving an early commercial boost to the movement.[57] And food co-ops, founded in the late 1960s and early 1970s by young men and women with more ideological fervor than managerial skill, soon stocked organic produce.[58]

What of the consumers who made organic a broader movement and, eventually, a substantial market? They came in two waves, both overwhelmingly middle class. Beginning in the late 1960s, the first wave consisted of young people who approached organic food as part of a larger commitment to countercultural and environmental values. Old hands welcomed them, with some reservations. Robert Rodale celebrated "the hippies, the student radicals, the new wave of far-out young people" who were gardening and eating organically. He was less comfortable with their purported communal living and nudity.[59] The owner of a natural foods store in Los Angeles also applauded the increased sales and offered a demographic label for his new customers: About a third of his business came from "the upper-class hippie group."[60] A second surge came in the late 1980s, stimulated by a new round of public alarm over pesticides, particularly revelations of toxic residues on children's food (including alar on apples). These new organic enthusiasts were no less middle class and urban than their predecessors. However, rather than cultural rebels they were conscientious consumers motivated above all by health concerns.[61]

B. The Organic Ideal versus Conventional Food

As the make-up of the organic food movement changed, so did the ideological character of its advocacy. In the 1950s and early 1960s, promoters such as J. I. Rodale framed problems in the food system primarily in terms of health—both the Earth's and the eater's. As consumers rallied to organic food in the late 1960s, indictments of the status quo and visions of change also widened. Ultimately, "organic" became shorthand for a fundamental economic, political, and cultural revamping of the food system. By 1990, this alternative vision narrowed again as federal government regulators and producers began to settle on a legal definition of "organic" that was closely focused on permissible inputs.

Building on the early advocacy work of Rodale and champions of Permanent Agriculture, critics of conventional food production in the early 1960s emphasized the need for change in agricultural techniques.[62] The organic alternative meant preserving soil fertility and managing pests with minimal chemical inputs. *Organic Gardening and Farming* gave special attention to composting, but it also promoted cover crops, crop rotation, and judicious use of manure. For pest control, farmers and gardeners were urged to shun pesticides in favor of complementary crops, beneficial insects, and plenty of manual labor. The advantages, in the first instance, were ecological. Using natural methods such as these preserved soil health and microbial diversity over time and thus constituted responsible stewardship of the land. The general notion that modern agricultural methods polluted the Earth was not new. Graham had complained that the use of manure threatened virgin soil. Early organic advocates more often framed their remedies in terms of ecological relationships among different plant and animal species; consumer enthusiasts followed suit. Without necessarily using the word, they also justified organic alternatives on grounds of sustainability—a theme missing from Graham and Kellogg.[63]

The other, relatively narrow claim by early organic advocates does echo Graham and Kellogg: organic food is healthier. J. I. Rodale rested much of his case on this point. Testifying before the House of Representatives in 1950, he assured skeptical listeners that children growing up on organic farms had greater vigor and that the spread of chemical-intensive agriculture was associated with increasing cancer rates.[64] Rodale offered no elaborate physiological theory comparable to Graham's or Kellogg's to back up these claims. He simply argued that organic methods produced food with more vitamins and minerals and fewer toxic residues, hoping to win converts with compelling anecdotes instead of hard evidence.[65] He resembled Graham and Kellogg more closely with his insistence that consuming organic food was the best medicine. Along with *Organic Gardening and Farming*, Rodale published *Prevention*, a popular magazine that directed readers toward dietary improvements and natural remedies and away from medical intervention. According to his son Robert, "It was the possibility of helping people to achieve better health that first attracted my father . . . to the organic idea."[66] It fell to Robert's generation to make a different break with Graham by renouncing asceticism. Organic food is good for you, but it also tastes better than fruit and vegetables grown in lifeless soil and shipped long distances. The inevitable *Rodale Cookbook* came in 1973, "stuffed with natural gourmet recipes."[67]

As organic food gained new enthusiasts, including many participants in other social movements of the late 1960s, advocates moved far beyond the issues of growing techniques and better health. In doing so, they applied to problems in the food system many of the ideals of the New Left and the counterculture, often quite self-consciously.[68] The indictments they leveled and the alternatives they proposed can be roughly sorted into economic, political, and cultural critiques. Each damned conventional food production for violating consumer trust, and each proposed alternative methods of producing and distributing food that would merit consumer confidence.

1. Economic Critique

The economic critique was above all an attack on big business and its pernicious effects on farms, in factories, and at retail stores. "People are realizing how much poison is sold as food by the big companies and the big market chains, and how expensive food is that includes fancy package[s] and well-known name[s]." Organic foods, by contrast, come "without poisons and expensive packages."[69] When large companies were not poisoning consumers, they were poisoning the Earth: "Big business, while searching for ever-escalating profits from agriculture, is riding roughshod over the delicate balance of nature which can't be upset if the land is going to continue to be fertile."[70] The contrast to domestic science is stark. What for Ellen Richards had been markers of reliability—food manufactured and branded by large, reputable companies—were now reasons for deep suspicion.[71]

What was a more trustworthy source of food? To begin with, it was the opposite of agribusiness: the small farm, family-owned. This ideal resembles the old Jeffersonian identification of independent farmer with political virtue. For organic advocates, alternatives to corporate agriculture had more to do with proper stewardship of the land than with good citizenship.[72] Through that ideal of stewardship, particular farming practices became more than just the means to healthier food. Whether or not corporate agriculture poisoned eaters, it was judged to erode soil, kill wildlife, and pollute groundwater. Family farmers were different. Each had a deeply rooted interest in preserving the land for future generations, and organic methods were the way to do so. After reminding readers that "company farms threaten America," *Organic Gardening and Farming*'s Jerome Goldstein went on to argue that "smallness is becoming as significant a quality of the organic method as no-pesticides and no-artificial fertilizers. . . . To protect the organic idea, we must make our national leaders aware that the organic market is a key part of the consumer movement for smallness in the marketplace."[73] A champion of organic in Austin, Texas, went further. "Family farms are based on human needs; in contrast, an agribusiness company, such as Tenneco, operates as an integrated conglomerate which perpetuates itself but gradually depletes our resources and quality of life."[74] Small-scale production and organic techniques combined to make food more trustworthy. Those assumptions informed early proposals to certify organic food. Proponents in New York made clear that organic standards represented more than market regulation. Those standards would also make "the identity of organic food growers" the key to "a code of ethics," and thus to the elimination of fraud.[75] This sort of agrarian populist attack on big business stretches back to the late nineteenth century and may have been second nature to established organic farmers.[76] For newcomers and consumers, the counterculture and New Left were more proximate influences; small could be beautiful for reasons rooted in both the 1880s and the 1960s.

What held for agribusiness and the family farm applied, as well, to other institutions in the food system. Small size and personal ties restored trust. Long before contemporary locavores "got to know" where their food came from, organic advocates urged consumers to develop more direct relations with farmers and retailers. If they could not get good food by growing it themselves (consistently the first recommendation from *Organic Gardening and Farming*), they should buy it at farm stands and farmers' markets. Organic "has come to stand for an attitude that looks upon smallness as a virtue. In an era when most city people have grown up without any personal communication with the producer of their foods, the organic route is clearly different. Suddenly, the consumer can identify the farmer, and the farmer can identify the personal needs of the consumer. No longer is the supermarket clerk or the television commercial the most vivid contact."[77] And instead of shopping at giant supermarkets, consumers should patronize the local co-op, run by men and women from the neighborhood who did not put profits before people. Closer ties to producers and retailers also gave consumers opportunities to learn more about their food. The human connection and consumer knowledge both reinforced confidence in the food.[78] Here, too, the organic alternative was far from domestic science's embrace of large companies distributing nationally branded products. "The word organic is becoming a linking symbol upon which a consumer can relate to a producer. It is a substitute for national brand advertising via television, newspapers or magazine; the word organic when truly defined cannot have a national brand name because its essence is its localization and personalization."[79] One *Organic Gardening and Farming* writer confidently predicted that, "as the Co-op plan unfolds[,] we expect the Kroger and A&P to be covered with cobwebs, and the small organic farmer to be flourishing in the countryside."[80] Others had still grander ambitions. Joining local co-ops and buying clubs, an alternative newspaper in Cincinnati argued, should be seen as nothing less than "part of a larger movement toward liberation."[81]

This economic critique, then, framed big business as remote, soulless, and concerned only with maximizing profits. These were the root causes of "poisonous" food. Those poisoned, however, and those who would benefit from reform were small producers and consumers, not labor. Much like their Progressive Era predecessors, organic advocates had a blind spot for class. They urged consumers to make purchases that benefited the small farm, the environment, and their own health but rarely the worker who harvested, processed, or served that food. And while activists made clear that consumers should be educated to shun the wrong foods, they much less often asked whether they could afford the right ones. As always, there were exceptions. Committed as they were to pesticide-free produce, organic advocates sometimes joined campaigns to also protect farm workers from pesticide exposure.[82] And when farmers in California began organizing in the early 1970s to codify what could be marketed as "organic," they had some lively discussions about including basic labor standards in that definition.[83] For their part, urban champions of organic food occasionally raised alarms about food security. That era's co-ops sometimes fell to fighting over whether food selection and pricing should be geared to winning working-class support. But members of the early California Certified Organic Farmers (CCOF) opted to omit labor conditions from organic standards, and food co-ops generally gave higher priority to virtuous farm owners than to the tastes and budgets of working-class buyers.[84]

2. Political Critique

Progressive Era campaigns for pure food sought federal intervention to guarantee consumer safety. For early organic farmers and consumers, government regulation in agriculture and food marketing only made matters worse. By 1990, most would come around to the value of a federal role in defining and certifying organic food. In the late 1960s and early 1970s, however, they hoped instead for more decentralized and democratic methods of fostering organic production.

One of the common complaints from organic farmers was that federal agricultural policies favored the very forces that spread pesticides, eroded the land, and concentrated ownership in big corporate farms. In part, this criticism echoed long-standing aversion on the part of small farmers to bureaucratic regulation, a pervasive theme in *Acres, USA,* a leading midwestern newspaper for alternative agriculture. But organic farmers also condemned agricultural subsidies that benefited large growers and conventional crops; land grant colleges and extension agents that encouraged chemical fertilizers and pesticides; and tax-funded research that catered to big agriculture. Focusing especially on land grant colleges "and their allies—the chemical and machinery firms," Robert Rodale charged that they "foul up this country by applying too many simplistic technological remedies to farm problems," using "technology to replace human hands with machines, chemicals, and special varieties of crop plants. The result has been more food produced by each farmer and on each acre, but at the same time much displacement of people to the cities . . . and often sad environmental consequences."[85] Beyond specific policies, organic advocates also resented federal officials' dismissive attitudes toward alternative agriculture. Spokesmen and scientists with the U.S. Department of Agriculture (USDA) seemed to be shills for the status quo, scoffing at organic ideals as backward, at best, and dangerous quackery, at worst: "Through the years the public has been gulled into believing that Big Brother (our 'health' authorities) guard us against hazards, that chemical pesticides . . . and the chase for the last bushel and the last dollar . . . are the only way."[86]

Small farmers, organic and conventional, had made similar charges before.[87] It was in the 1960s, however, that they were widely seconded by organic consumer advocates. The USDA, FDA, and Environmental Protection Agency (EPA) could not be relied on to safeguard the food supply. Pesticides were a particular cause for alarm. In that battle, Robert Rodale lamented, we "are getting precious little help" from our government.[88] Why did the FDA continue to "accept poisons in food, as long as they don't cause immediate death?"[89] And why was "EPA" said to stand for "Endorse Pesticides Agency"?[90] The standard answer in the alternative press was collusion. As with agricultural policy, government agencies did the bidding of food processors, chemical companies, and a medical profession with a vested interest in costly cures rather than cheap prevention. "There is more profit in a vaccination than in a meal of uncontaminated food. Doctors, commercial producers and processors of food, and the federal and local governments seem to be united in the conspiracy to keep Americans unhealthy." Real change would require "breaking the conspiracy between doctors, food producers and the government."[91]

This distrust of the federal government carried over into recommendations for political reform. Progressive Era reformers had confidence that increased government regulation could safeguard food if guided by expert knowledge and nonpartisan efficiency. Their successors in the 1960s did not reject expertise, but they wanted it turned to the service of small farms and organic techniques. More broadly, organic food advocates departed from the Progressive ideal of an enlightened administrative state by championing more decentralized and participatory agricultural decision making. The quest for local control fit well with an older strain of rural populist hostility to Washington's power. But together with an emphasis on more democratic deliberation, it also applied to food a general embrace of participatory democracy in the New Left. In response to early calls for federal certification, leading voices in the movement countered that standards should be worked out by democratic means and by regional groups that were closer to local conditions. "Certification programs are best developed by organic farmers and persons associated with the distribution and consumption of their harvests, on a *grass-roots, regional basis.*"[92] At the retail end, food co-ops won praise not just because they were small and local alternatives to giant supermarkets. They also created opportunities to "take the control of one part of [our] own lives from advertisers, the package industry, chemical manufacturers, and the profit-oriented society."[93] More, they offered a setting in which co-op members could practice grassroots democracy. As one participant recalled, here "egalitarian structures and decision-making processes facilitated their participation and cultivated their leadership skills."[94]

3. Cultural Critique

To these attacks on big business and a complicit state, organic activists added a more cultural critique of the food system. They framed conventional agriculture and processed foods as "unnatural." The term was rich in meanings, and the contrast between natural and unnatural became a general template for judging social practices and actors.[95] A second framework for denouncing the status quo focused on the uses and abuses of science and technology in modern food production. The first evil called for various returns to nature; the second, for a more populist science. Both proposals had more in common with Graham than with Progressive Era food reformers.

a. Natural versus Unnatural: The claim that conventionally produced food was unnatural referred to much more than health risks. Instead, "unnatural" and "artificial" became all-purpose terms of censure. Until the late 1960s, the censure applied primarily to how food was grown and what it contained. Under the influence of modern environmentalism and the counterculture, it came to encompass lifestyles out of harmony with nature and humanity. The antidote was "organic living," a simpler, bucolic alternative to technological society.

A starting assumption in organic's cultural critique was that natural food was, for that very reason, more trustworthy. What food qualified? One contrast involved methods of production. Organic advocates counterposed traditional methods of maintaining soil fertility (composting, careful use of manure) to synthetic fertilizer; whole foods to their refined, bleached, and processed versions; and foods composed of only a few and minimally processed ingredients (flour, sugar, butter) to those with a long list of additives developed in laboratories. Good food was unmodified from its natural state by technology. By contrast, "Science has sought incessantly to improve upon nature until now there is almost nothing left that is pure and untainted [by] . . . chemicals, preservatives, emulsifiers, carcinogenic dyes, pesticides, stabilizers, hormones, antibiotics, milling and bleaching."[96]

That basic dichotomy was not invented by the organic movement. Graham and Kellogg had made similar contrasts using a more religious language of virtuous and sinful foods. Generations of natural foods entrepreneurs continued the tradition as they hawked their wares.[97] The organic movement put a more ecological spin on "natural."[98] Some foods qualified as natural because their production aligned with an existing balance of interconnected biological processes, as when natural predators rather than pesticides protected crops from destructive insects. Violating that balance was unnatural—and unsustainable. *Organic Gardening and Farming* regularly deemed conventional agricultural techniques unnatural in this sense, inexorably depleting soil fertility and water resources.[99] Alternative press journalists agreed. Organic food represented a healthier relationship to nature, one in which men and women worked with the natural world rather than against it. That natural world had a gendered character that made it all the more trustworthy. Earlier food reformers had recommended food made by women, whether as the pious mothers or the trained experts of the home. Organic advocates were more likely to feminize nature itself. One letter to *Organic Gardening and Farming* praised the journal for supporting "lifestyles with which both our minds and Mother Earth can live."[100]

By the early 1970s, producing food in harmony with nature shaded into living in harmony with nature. *Organic Gardening and Farming*, whose original readership had been practicing farmers and gardeners, expanded its audience and began to speak of "organic living" and "natural" lifestyles. The valorization of nature here contrasted natural environments in the country with artificial urban ones, reviving much older bucolic ideals.[101] In recommending "a whole natural way of living and thinking," the journal identified such lives with "basic country values—good soil, pure water, clean air."[102] But urban consumers could also live more naturally by purchasing natural products. Equating "natural" and "wild," Robert Rodale called for a "Half Wild Way to a Better Life" for those unable to garden. Eating more wild

foods (roughage, semi-wild plants, whole grains) could bring basic country values to city dwellers.[103] Shopping at the local co-op, similarly, gave
the urban consumer some of the benefits of nature. These benefits included
not only organic food but also a small-scale setting and personal ties more
characteristic of rural living than anything to be found in a supermarket.[104]

Two other virtues distinguished organic living from the unnatural and
artificial, both of them reinforced by the wider counterculture. One was
organic's freedom from the confinements and complications of technology,
a distinction that once again valued rural over urban living. Rodale pressed
this familiar theme, and both *Organic Gardening and Farming* and the alternative press helped popularize it. Over time, Rodale's vision became increasingly dystopian. In 1965, he argued only that "the organic method is
a revolt against technology. Organic gardeners and farmers . . . look with
great suspicion on new technological developments in our field that seem to
be too great an attack on nature." Two years later, technology had become
a "cobweb" ensnaring humanity. By the early 1970s, he was warning that
"cities will become more sophisticated technological prisons," their residents watched by cameras, monitored by computers, and isolated in their
apartments.[105] Other organic advocates may not have shared this bleak vision of the future. However, they joined Rodale in making nature's virtues
encompass a technologically simpler life. Organic food was an important
part of that life. Organic living had a second merit in contrast to artificial
lifestyles. It rejected the rampant materialism of contemporary American
society. In 1970, *Organic Gardening and Farming* introduced a special section on "Organic Food Shopping and Organic Living," recommending
products that were organically grown, environmentally sound, and healthy.
But the publication added that organic living meant more than "cooperat-
ing with nature." It also meant "making do with less, and *enjoying* it."[106]
As early as 1972, attentive supporters of organic food warned of it going
mainstream, so that "eating organic food is just another bourgeois luxury."
The movement should instead encourage people to "break free from consumerism" altogether.[107] The twin rejections of technology and materialism
in favor of "nature" aligned the organic movement with a larger communal
retreat from the city, the call to get "back to the land." This complex layering
of purported benefits from going natural is suggested by one of many such
personal ads in *Mother Earth News*. "Would like to correspond with others
interested in forming a self-sustaining, rural community with emphasis
on organic farming, handcrafts, fellowship . . . and peaceful living."[108] In
this, the organic movement shared in a wider enthusiasm for natural living in the late 1960s and early 1970s, whether in religious practices, clothing, or health remedies. A lending library in Vermont made organic food
just one part of a larger offering of books that covered "natural childbirth,

breastfeeding, raising free happy children (e.g., Summerhill), and simple living" along with "organic gardening and farming."[109]

Champions of organic food, then, criticized the conventional alternative as unecological, as inauthentic, and as corrupted by technology and materialism. "Unnatural" covered all these sins. Activists framed organic as more natural in yet another way. They argued that the existing food system exemplified standardization and conformity. Organic living valued the natural by prizing individuality in the garden and society alike.[110] In part, this defense of nonconformity reflected organic activists' acute sense of being marginalized and dismissed by mainstream scientists, government officials, and industry leaders. "To be an organic gardener," Rodale lamented, "you must reject the opinions of the experts and the professors and stand up to occasional charges that you are a crackpot or faddist." Doing so is a virtue when "there are so many forces at work in our society that lead us to conformity."[111] But organic enthusiasts also pressed the analogy between standardization in the food system and in social life. They rejected both. While spokespeople for the counterculture made ticky-tacky houses and gray-suited organization men leading symbols of lifeless conformity, organic activists pointed to crop monocultures on farms and mass-produced packaged foods in supermarkets. Organic, by contrast, stood for healthy variety in garden plantings and in American culture. A report in *Organic Gardening and Farming* on a visit to a progressive school made the analogy explicit. In an article titled "The Organic Revolution Goes to College," M. C. Goldman praised a school for supporting two sorts of "natural" growth. "The idea is to let the children develop freely, with a minimum of restrictions, interference or rules. Most of the people have long hair; the townspeople call them hippies. And what's good for the scholar is good for the garden. . . . The school believes in freedom and natural harmony—and that applies to the garden as well."[112] Robert Rodale linked the ideal of natural nonconformity back to the evils of overweening technology. Reaching (like Graham) for the homely example of bread, he waxed nostalgic about the bread of America's revolutionary era. He described it as made from home-grown wheat ground at the local water mill, so different from today's plastic-wrapped factory loaf. Rodale admitted that we cannot turn back the clock. But we should find ways to free ourselves from dependence on the system that sells us that loaf. "It's Time," he headed his column, "for a New Declaration of Independence."[113]

It is with this sense of "natural" that organic advocates of the late 1960s departed most sharply from earlier food reformers. Framing organic food as health saving, no matter what the doctors tell you, closely mirrors Graham's and Kellogg's praise of natural food. So does the condemnation of conventional food as alienated by modern technology from the simple products of nature. The similarities between Grahamites and organic advocates appear, too, in the corresponding embrace of natural foods as an antidote to industrialized food.[114] But Graham offered a much narrower critique of technology. It enabled commercial interests to produce a lot of bad food, but it was not itself a form of cultural domination. The notion of organic living as more natural because it frees us from social constraints might have given further offense to Graham and Kellogg. They warned instead that eating the wrong foods subverted social order by stimulating individual passions. In the organic movement, by contrast, restrictive social norms *should* be subverted, and the conventional food system reinforced those norms at the expense of individual freedom. These different ways of linking nature, social order, and the individual appear as well in the different roles assigned to self-control. For Graham and Kellogg, proper diet strengthened self-control and in so doing reinforced standards of middle-class respectability. For some organic advocates, proper diet instead fortified individuals to liberate themselves from a confining middle-class culture.[115]

That contrast between respectability and rebellion points to a broader difference in the ways that organic food advocates connected the personal to the political (a connection every social movement must make to recruit participants). For Grahamites, as more broadly in the Second Great Awakening, the connection worked through public confession, a ritual linking personal sin and redemption to a larger project of national salvation.[116] For many Progressive women, including those who backed a pure food law, the key was to translate their familial roles and maternal natures into a public responsibility for social reform.[117] For organic advocates in the movement's heyday, following a countercultural script, the food system could be transformed by acting out one's political commitments in everyday life. That meant uncovering corporate power and technological domination hidden in the pesticide-ridden and processed food we put on the table at home and choosing to grow or buy alternatives. But it also meant breaking with traditional roles rather than either giving them dietary reinforcement (as Graham would do) or using them as a strategic resource (as in the maternalist playbook). Individuals should instead pursue social change by breaking with conventions in how they related to fellow commune members, how they bought food, and how they made decisions at the local co-op. As Warren Belasco reminds us, the call to reject traditional rules and roles percolated down even to selecting vegetables (limp and irregular could be good), preparing them (raw is better), and eating them (with fingers, from shared dishes).[118] In the expansive definition of the organic movement, these were more "natural" and became important personal strategies for social betterment.

The invidious contrast between natural and unnatural served the organic movement well as a framing device. It covered a wide range of meanings. Unmodified from some naturally occurring state, in harmony with ecological balance, an authentic way of life, a form of resistance to technology and materialism, freed from stuffy social conventions, "organic" had much to recommend it. Just as with "purity" in the Progressive Era, the very ambiguity and multiple meanings of "natural" made it a good unifying symbol. It allowed consumers with different complaints and visions, whether those worried about pesticides or those in search of personal liberation, to rally under a shared flag. It created common ground between libertarian small farmers and the countercultural consumers who energized the movement in the late 1960s. And it provided discursive tools that both enriched organic's critique of the food system and supported alliances with other rebels of the '60s. Organic activists' critique of mainstream science and their call for a populist alternative did the same.

b. Corporate versus Populist Science: Leading proponents of organic food expressed more than skepticism about the *use* of technology in farms and factories. They raised more fundamental questions about mainstream knowledge production in agricultural and nutritional sciences, the research that stood behind expert advice on how to farm and what to eat. Proponents of alternative farming methods had clashed with mainstream scientists and USDA officials before.[119] The conflict flared up again in the 1960s, fueled by New Left attacks on the unholy alliance among science, business, and the military. Late in the decade, consumers of organic food joined the fray. There were several points where beliefs in the superiority of sustainable agriculture and organic food challenged the conventional wisdom of the day. The postwar Green Revolution claimed to put scientific knowledge to the necessary task of increasing agricultural productivity. Monocultures of high-yield hybrids would boost output; synthetic fertilizers would restore soil fertility year after year; pesticides would reduce crop loss from insects; and herbicides would check weeds.[120] The idea that commercial farms could—and should—dispense with these modern tools was widely derided, perhaps most famously in Secretary of Agriculture Earl Butz's remark in 1972 that a return to organic agriculture would consign fifty million Americans to starvation.[121] In more sober language, most agricultural scientists agreed. Nutritionists also dismissed claims that organically grown food had health advantages as scientifically illiterate. The essential vitamins and minerals needed by the human body, they lectured, were present in the same quantities in conventionally grown produce. No credible studies showed benefits from eating organic, and examples of improved health or longevity among organic consumers were purely anecdotal. Conventional food manufacturers pushed the same message, concerned that health claims about organic food would cast doubt on their products.[122]

There was more at stake than competing recommendations about proper diet. Linking the issue to their critique of big business and its puppet state, organic enthusiasts charged that academic science had been fundamentally corrupted by its alliance with industry.[123] Here, too, there is a remarkable turnabout from Progressive Era reformers. For domestic scientists, modern corporations applying up-to-date science should reduce consumers' worries about food safety and adulteration. Organic advocates repudiated that model for establishing trust in food, with Robert Rodale complaining that "nutrition teachers were for a long time the captives of the food industry."[124] The skepticism took two forms. One raised doubts about modern science on philosophical grounds, as contrary to a more holistic or even spiritual understanding of the natural world. Some went as far as to redefine legitimate expertise as peasant knowledge, rooted in an almost mystical connection to the soil. These reservations about science were more prominent before World War II among some pioneers of British organic agriculture and in the work of the Austrian founder of "biodynamic" agriculture, Rudolf Steiner.[125] But they appear, as well, in the early writing of J. I. Rodale, arguing for the value of practical experience over professorial theories.[126] A later flashpoint for this clash between rival agricultural epistemologies was UCSC. There, Alan Chadwick captivated student volunteers with his biodynamic horticulture, and many of his acolytes went on to play influential roles in Northern California's organic industry. In the view of one UCSC ally, Chadwick's approach to nature stood in deliberate opposition to "reductionist scientism." Science faculty replied in kind. One emeritus professor, lobbying to have Chadwick's garden shut down, asked, "How could the university support something so antiscience [as his] approach to agriculture?"[127]

The more common argument in organic's critique of science focused less on epistemology than on the institutional context of science. Robert Rodale accepted what he called "basic" research, with its standard methods and focus on mechanisms underlying the natural world. By contrast, "applied" research to develop agricultural techniques or nutritional guidelines typically served the agenda of corporate farms and food processors. It did so for the simplest of reasons: Those corporations and manufacturers paid the research bills. Rodale's own willingness to accept the markers of legitimate science (like Kellogg's comparable faith in science) is clear from the eagerness with which he published any study backing his own claims, with the scientific credentials and university affiliations of the authors on prominent display. It was the contrary findings that showed the pervasive corruption of science by vested interests. Rodale's father had leveled this charge as early as 1950. In congressional testimony that year, he called for scientific research on the effects of chemical fertilizers and insecticides, coaching house members on standard experimental methods that should be used. A committee member responded by questioning Rodale's academic bona fides and asserting that *real* scientists agreed that organic agriculture could never achieve the productivity of current methods. "Don't let the college professors say there is no evidence," the senior Rodale retorted. "It is like going to the criminal elements and saying, 'You police crime.'" Why? Because "the college professor gets money for research. His job is based on the money given by the chemical fertilizer factories."[128] Rodale's son took up the torch, with land grant universities a favorite target. They were supposed to use public money to support farms. Instead, they catered only to agribusiness, displacing small farmers in the process.[129]

What alternatives did organic advocates offer? They certainly sought to lessen the influence of food corporations on agricultural and nutritional research. Redirecting universities and the USDA toward the needs of organic and small farms was one way to do so. "This would include developing new farm machinery (mulchers, shredders, etc.), recycling garbage (turning organic wastes, autumn leaves, etc.) into compost[,] and making these machines available to all farmers. This will be no easy task. Both government and business are committed to large-unit, mechanized, chemical farming."[130] Another proposal called on the government to increase research spending in order to offset the bias in business funding.[131] But a more ambitious vision, consistent with the movement's critique of the political status quo, was to democratize science. In this the movement went beyond Graham's evangelical attack on traditional hierarchies, including the privileged voices of doctors. There was now a need for institutional changes to make science serve the people. One version of this involved checks and balances. Universities and the federal government were likely to remain shills for corporate interests, but there could be organizations of *counter*-experts to oppose them. The *Environment Action Bulletin* and *Organic Gardening and Farming*, for example, urged the creation of "Scientific Adversary Centers" that would be "centers of technological assessment, with the sole purpose of learning and communicating to the public the *adverse* features of technological approaches. The goal is *not* destructive criticism, but rather the full development of 'the other side of the picture.'"[132] The Center for Science in the Public Interest (founded in 1971) had a similar mission and focused particularly on food issues in its early years.[133] Another proposal envisioned not organic scientists fighting corporate scientists so much as organic farmers collaborating with academic researchers to produce better science. Bob Scowcroft, founder of the Organic Farming Research Foundation (1992), recalled one version of this ideal of treating "farmers and scientists as peers." Both sides would benefit by getting "scientists out of the damn labs, and into the fields, and to see farming as a system. But at the same time get the farmers out of the fields, and into the lab and academia to understand, or get a better sense, of the science that described what they were doing."[134] The point was not to elevate peasant knowledge over academic expertise but to institutionalize a dialogue between them.[135]

My account of organic movement ideology has focused on a relatively short period, roughly from the mid-1960s to the mid-1970s. As a movement, this was organic's heyday. It was a time when a new generation of organic farmers entered the field, often inspired to build a wholesome alternative to big agriculture. They were joined by activist consumers, some merely hoping to resolve their doubts about conventional food, some also acting out ideals of an alternative society. The moment did not last. But during this period, farmers' and consumers' larger framing of problems and solutions played important roles. The invidious contrasts between unnatural and natural (in their several meanings), between big business and small farm or co-op, and between "high tech" and old-fashioned simplicity all offered standards for judging whether a food was trustworthy. They did so, importantly, at a time *before* state and federal governments developed certification programs that allowed consumers to make choices on the basis of a simple label. These contrasts also performed boundary work for movement participants, helping build collective identity. That shared identity was powerfully reinforced by organic activists' siege mentality. They knew the right way forward for food but suffered constant belittling as "fringe and kooky."[136] Their common identity also helped organic farmers, who were in some respects competitors, to work together. They visited one another's farms, traded advice and equipment, and eventually worked out common practices and standards. And it helped create ties between farmers and consumers at a time when farmers' markets were few and the modern food system connected them only through an anonymous cash nexus.[137]

Unity against whom? In contrast to the Progressive Era, distinctions between good food and bad did not map onto those between white natives and darker-skinned immigrants. Indeed, as Belasco and Aaron Bobrow-Strain show, the 1960s and 1970s saw a culinary inversion of the Progressive Era hierarchy.[138] Whereas in the earlier period "white" stood for safely pure and modern food and its WASP consumers, by the 1970s "white" signified bland and alarmingly modern industrial food—the white sugar, bleached flour, and instant rice of the supermarket. Brown sugar, flour, and rice now came out on top as virtuous foods, their consumption an act of solidarity with oppressed people of color. But while the icons of the food rebellion were brown, the rebels themselves were mostly white.[139] For the organic movement, at least, the boundaries were drawn instead against *other* whites: those of an older generation; those occupying positions of power in business, government, and academe; and those who were hopelessly square and conformist.

C. Organization and Strategy

The rebels may have been mostly white, but in other respects they were a diverse lot. Farmers ran small businesses in rural areas. Consumers had a range of motives for going organic, often lived in cities or on university campuses, and had little in the way of formal associations to coordinate their market choices. A variety of institutions and individuals filled the gap. Some catered to producers; some appealed more to consumers; and some linked the two. Together, they provided the infrastructure for a coherent movement. They also connected participants to other activist groups of the day, thus facilitating the diffusion of more general models of protest politics in the late 1960s. Those of environmentalism and the counterculture were especially important.

Even before the 1960s, organic gardening clubs (more than one hundred of them in 1955) attracted enthusiasts on a local basis for "exhibits, competition, talks," and the occasional "organic dinner."[140] Organization among commercial producers got underway in the early 1970s. The Northeast Organic Farming Association (NOFA) led the way in 1971, with branches forming in individual states. The California Certified Organic Farmers (1973), Oregon Tilth (1974), and others soon followed; by 1989, they numbered more than forty.[141] These associations served two, mutually reinforcing purposes. As trade groups, they could work out standards for what qualified for marketing as "organic," monitor members' compliance, and see that produce was labeled appropriately. Through informal meetings and farm visits, these organizations also offered mutual support for farmers defying the conventional wisdom and hoping to learn from one another.[142] Both functions made the associations important forums for building solidarity among potential competitors. And because their founding members included young men and women coming to organic from activist backgrounds of other kinds, they speeded the diffusion of themes and tactics from other movements. In NOFA, one sparkplug was Grace Gershuny, whose activist roots included living in a Montreal commune and helping run countercultural food co-ops.[143] Early members of the CCOF had similarly transgressive backgrounds. Jerry and Jean Thomas described themselves as "back to [the] landers" before discovering organic. For Amigo Bob Cantisano, the path to the CCOF passed through an urban commune and participation in the first Earth Day, in 1970. Other pioneers recounted experiences in the antiwar movement that prompted them to seek a thoroughgoing *alternative* agriculture—and thus to embrace organic.[144] The CCOF and NOFA, moreover, echoed the more general activist culture in their reliance on democratic decision making and decentralized solutions, even for market regulation.[145] The West Coast and the Northeast had a large influx of "hippie" farmers, but they were also the most influential regions for the young industry and for the movement in the early 1970s.[146]

There was a similar cross-fertilization on the consumer side. Campus organic clubs served as one organizational hub for activism. They had strong ties with other student groups, collaborating with ecology centers, for example, in recycling projects or in political campaigns involving environmental issues. "Social action aimed at tackling environmental problems on the community level," *Organic Gardening and Farming* proudly reported, "has become 'standard operating procedure' for O. G. Clubs everywhere."[147] And in some university towns, the clubs were parts of still larger local networks of alternative food production and distribution. On a visit to Ann Arbor in 1972, Jerome Goldstein found an Organic Committee, Ecology Garden, Community Garden, organic restaurant, and food co-op.[148] Natural foods shops offered another off-campus node for organic activism. As retailers, they aimed to sell consumers trustworthy produce, something promised by an organic label. But as with producer associations, their role went well beyond marketing. The stores also built demand through educational work, and their community bulletin boards and demonstration events created additional opportunities for networking.[149]

What tied organic food producers and consumers together? The most important brokers through the 1960s were the Rodale Institute and *Organic Gardening and Farming*. The latter boomed in circulation as organic food gained favor in the late 1960s, from 300,000 in 1962 to 500,000 in 1970 and 850,000 by late 1972.[150] The publication's content changed accordingly, adding to its staples of composting tips and equipment recommendations new sections on organic products, "organic living," and developments on college campuses. Rodale's magazine also helped link organic enthusiasts with environmental activism, through both editorials and more practical measures, such as issuing the pamphlet "The Organic Gardener's Guide to Complaining in the Name of the Environment." The guide's author, columnist James Olds, included advice on coalition building between organic clubs and campus ecology groups. "The link-up is essential for mobilizing enough power for change."[151]

The Rodale Institute and *Organic Gardening and Farming* also connected producers and consumers by strengthening their market ties. The top recommendation for securing good food was to grow your own. But if this was not an option, the institute and its journal offered their services as consumer guides, vetting and listing organic suppliers and supporting programs, such as farmers' markets, to enable direct buying from organic food producers.[152] At the other end of the commodity chain, the Rodale Institute encouraged farmers to get organized. It did so by sponsoring regular conferences such as the Organic Food Symposium in Allentown, Pennsylvania, in 1970, which brought together "200 major growers, distributors, shop-keepers and concerned consumers." The symposium sought to address consumers' "worry about the environment, [their] new interest in food flavor and wholesomeness," and their rejection of "the plasticized, push-button commercialism of 'modern' food production and distribution."[153] In California, the institute also jump-started collective efforts to set standards and develop labels for organic produce, efforts quickly taken over by the fledgling CCOF.[154]

The Rodales were not alone in bridging activist networks. *Mother Earth News*, for example, created common ground with its focus on do-it-yourself tools and techniques pitched to backyard gardeners as well as small commercial farmers, home tinkerers along with back-to-the-landers. The paper's enthusiastic endorsement of *Organic Gardening and Farming* also brought that magazine to a wider audience. The alternative press—local imprints of the counterculture such as Berkeley's *Barb,* Ann Arbor's *Sun,* Austin's *Rag,* and San Francisco's *Good Times*—made the same connection. The Alternative Press database shows references to *Organic Gardening and Farming* first appearing in 1969 and increasing in frequency thereafter. Small wonder that OGF became "required reading for much of the Berkeley 'hip' community."[155] And although geared more toward farmers than hippies, *Acres, USA* and *Countryside Magazine* also served as hubs for organic networking.[156]

At the cutting edge of the movement, finally, were food communes and co-ops. These alternative institutions were not initially dedicated to organic food, but they gave it a new ideological luster (and added shelf space). Rural communes proliferated in the 1960s: One estimate puts the number at ten thousand formed nationwide between 1965 and 1975.[157] Whether or not back-to-the-landers set out to grow their food by any particular method, organic agriculture's approach—working with nature rather than against it, taking care of the land, minimizing high-tech inputs—was a good fit. Back in town, there was a similar boom in co-ops, with as many as ten thousand in operation in 1969–1970.[158] They had an explicit political agenda. Ronnie Cummins, who would found the Organic Consumers Association in 1998, recalled that "in the late 1960s, those of us coming out of the civil rights movement and the antiwar movement saw [that] building a counter-culture or an alternative economy was a political strategy for radical social change. We realized that protesting in the streets and even lobbying for civil rights legislation wasn't enough, and that we needed to have fundamental changes throughout the institutions. One of those things that started as a political tactic was to build food cooperatives all over the nation."[159] There was a strong affinity between the leftist politics of many co-op founders and farmers who rejected big agriculture, self-consciously embraced ecological values, and in some cases organized as communes.[160] And ideology aside, food co-ops fostered more direct market ties between local producers and consumers. In both theory and practice, then, they gave organic the imprimatur of the most important day-to-day institutions of the counterculture. Even more than with natural foods stores, their role as local cells for leftist politics linked organic advocates to progressive activists of other stripes. In this they were part of a still larger movement that included housing co-ops, cooperative childcare, and community health clinics.[161]

Like other centers of '60s politics, food co-ops could be contentious places. Organic food was one of the points of contention. Should co-ops, as agents of the revolution, seek support from the proletariat by catering to working-class tastes and budgets? Or should they carry only healthy and green goods, even if they were more expensive? Although the outcome might seesaw with attendance at participatory meetings, green eventually won. But in organic's heyday, the debate kept issues of class and race on the agenda, making co-ops an especially important center for a more radical organic critique of the dominant food system.[162]

What sorts of social movement strategy did these organizations and individuals practice? Organic activism blended consumerist tactics with more traditional political lobbying. Each had the dual goals of building up organic as a movement and as a market, and to these ends, each sought new ways to reestablish trust in food. The consumerist strategy followed a now familiar logic: Pursue social changes by marshalling the buying power of enlightened eaters. "The best way to get farmers to use less pesticides," argued *Organic Gardening and Farming*, "is to make clear that there's a big, unfilled market for spray-free food. . . . There's a vital need for all the organic consumer pressures that can be brought to bear."[163] The strategy involved efforts on both demand and supply sides, aiming to reeducate consumers so they would buy organic and improve marketing so that organic choices would be readily available. The consumer education showcased the rich variety of organic thinking in the 1960s and early 1970s. Initially, the appeals mainly emphasized individual health. Consumers should buy organic food because it is more nutritious and less toxic. That general formula was little different from Graham's. For organic advocates, however, healthy and safe food neither demanded nor enabled self-denial. Indeed, organic promised a happy coincidence of health and pleasure because locally and organically grown fruit and vegetables tasted better.[164] Over time, the rationale for choosing organic expanded. Buying organic, customers were told, helped protect the environment. Getting organic through buying clubs and co-ops represented a "food conspiracy" to starve supermarkets. And some radicals claimed that purchasing organic was one step toward social revolution. But even with such grand ambitions, the strategy was one of conscientious consumerism, pursuing change in the food system through concerted market pressure.

That leverage could be magnified from the demand side by ensuring that the correct consumer choices were also convenient and reliable ones. Here the line blurs between organizing to mobilize a movement and to build a market. Setting up farmers' markets, helping distribute organic produce through co-ops and natural foods stores, and preparing lists of trustworthy sources all served both purposes. They could also aggregate into dense local networks of alternative economic and social institutions, as in the Bay Area Food System of the mid-1970s: "The Food System is made up of small growers, bakeries, stores and a distribution service, all run on egalitarian lines with an emphasis on regionally-produced, high-quality (usually organic), low-cost foodstuffs. The emergence of this network of decentralized, worker-owned and operated businesses in the Bay region is an exciting development to decentralists and those concerned with locally-based economic options."[165] But in practical terms, the core of the strategy remained one of building market outlets where educated consumers could buy organic food.

Boosting the supply of organic food was part of the solution, but it also created new problems of trust. As the market expanded and offered suppliers a price premium for organic produce, farmers and customers alike had to worry about fraud. What would prevent organic imposters?[166] In Vermont and New Hampshire in the early 1970s, the answer could still be personal ties because more sales were local and face-to-face.[167] More extensive markets developed faster in California. There the pioneering certification program developed by the CCOF was not only good for collective identity; it was also a deliberate strategy to reassure consumers, and one another, by policing the industry. "By setting sound, practical standards for growing crops right, then helping the grower establish a clear identity with those who buy organic food . . . , reassurance replaces doubt."[168]

The reassurance came first through voluntary action. Members of the CCOF would deputize an informal committee to visit a member's farm, inspect it for organic integrity, and approve the use of a CCOF label.[169] But as organic production and distribution expanded in volume and geographic scope, and with persistent cases of fraud, such localized and volunteer efforts gave way to more state-centered strategies. Much as with the pure food campaign, the government would again be enlisted to back consumer trust in organic purchases. Oregon led the way with a state certification program in 1973.[170] By 1990, nearly half of all states had followed suit. With growing interstate commerce in organic food and demand for it soaring in response to the publication of *Intolerable Risk: Pesticides in Our Children's Food* in 1989, federal certification finally won approval in 1990.[171] Actual definition of standards and implementation of the program would take another twelve years and prove contentious.[172] Organic farmers had plenty of doubts about government regulation. They had little faith in the USDA, and some considered federal regulation too remote. As one early organic farmer explained, "The biggest problem with the federal laws is that they are farther away from the local grower."[173] But the national program served the essential purposes of curbing fraud among producers and giving customers an easy marker of trustworthy food: the USDA organic logo. These political measures helped the market grow.

Although government certification was the most important of organic's political strategies, it was not the only focus. A second goal, again part market and part movement, was to change federal research priorities. The effort involved conventional lobbying to get politicians to throw organic at least a few crumbs from the research funding pie currently devoted to conventional agriculture. Winning that change in a farm bill might yield practical benefits, such as useful academic studies and more readily available technical advice geared to organic production. But it also had symbolic value. It established organic as a legitimate piece of U.S. agriculture and a legitimate focus for scientific analysis. After years of denigration, that two-fold recognition might count for more than the modest sums won through congressional lobbying.[174]

D. Movement to Market

These dual strategies—consumerist and political—paid off. Beginning in 1988, farm bills offered slightly increased support for research on sustainable agriculture (a diplomatic rebranding of "organic") and for conservation measures of particular interest to organic farmers.[175] More important, the National Organic Standards Board finally settled on a federal definition of organic in 1998 and began to prepare corresponding government labeling. A dramatic expansion of the organic sector followed. Sales increased ninefold between 1998 and 2015, far exceeding growth rates for conventional products. Organic's share of the market rose from 1 percent to 5 percent of total food sales over the same period.[176] Credit for that economic success is generally given to the combination of federal certification and repeated alarms over pesticide risks. The latter shows that organic advocates had educated consumers to identify organic with pesticide-free; the former made it easier for shoppers to act accordingly. But before federal or even most state certification programs took effect, organic advocates had helped rebuild trust in other ways. Farmers' markets and other direct sales leveraged personal trust. Knowing (or at least coming face-to-face with) the farmer helped consumers buy with confidence. And in a brief but important transitional period, co-ops leveraged ideological trust. Organic food, even somewhat limp, enjoyed countercultural credibility in the early 1970s precisely because of the economic and social setting in which it was purchased. A *New York Times* article introducing readers in 1972 to the burgeoning organic scene noted that shoppers were easily deceived. It was important to be able to "trust the store."[177] Co-ops let progressive consumers of the time do so.

By the 1980s, however, the balance between movement and market had clearly shifted toward the market. For consumers, buying organic food was less often taken as a revolt against big business, the corporate state, or the tyranny of modern technology. Instead, organic had become more of a conventional business (however "mission-driven"); a consumer taste (however conscientious); and, after 1990, an official USDA program.[178] Federal certification is sometimes taken to be the death knell for a more transgressive organic movement, but the trend was clear much earlier.

One small part of organic's taming involved the triumph of normal science. Early organic advocates, we saw, doubted the integrity and even the methods of mainstream agricultural and nutritional scientists. They nevertheless trumpeted academic studies when the conclusions agreed with them, and they started pushing for more research funding for organic agriculture as early as the 1960s. David Goodman and his colleagues criticize these efforts for divorcing academic research on organic farming from the larger social changes needed for a genuinely alternative agriculture.[179] But even within the arena of academic research, organic advocates' critique of the scientific enterprise had lost ground by the late 1970s. The shift is clear in microcosm at UCSC. As a new University of California campus open to experimentation, UCSC tolerated Chadwick's promotion of a holistic and experiential approach to farming in opposition to academic science. That moment soon passed. Tensions with formally trained biology faculty and the disciplinary structure of a research university helped push Chadwick out. When a new professor arrived to launch the campus's environmental studies program, he aimed "to start an academic department and develop a new major, not to coddle a wild man who planted by the moon."[180] Although UCSC remained a leading center for research and training in alternative agriculture (agroecology), it did so within a more standard framework of credentialed, peer-reviewed, academic expertise. The peers did not include practical farmers speaking with the wisdom of the soil.

Overall, however, the mainstreaming of organic was more a matter of business models and consumer tastes than scientific methods. Among organic farmers, many continued to identify their mission as changing the food system.[181] That meant stewarding the soil, saving the family farm, and building community between producers and consumers. But by the mid-1980s, organic food had become a small but growing market that offered producers a price premium and, for a time, shelter from highly capitalized big competitors. These opportunities were especially attractive to farmers squeezed by rising land values in California. In this setting, new organic

production increasingly came from farmers converting conventional operations out of economic need more than ideological commitment.[182] On the
retail side, the change is clearest with co-ops. Those that clung to participatory governance and pay-what-you-can-afford pricing often went under.
Those that survived adopted more hierarchical authority, professional management, and upscale marketing. As Michael Haedicke points out, co-op
leaders interpret many of these changes as advancing the fundamental mission to serve members, and co-ops often continue to position themselves as
virtuous alternatives to supermarkets—smaller, greener, more committed
to consumer education, more neighborly. These are real virtues but a far cry
from "conspiracies" against a capitalist food system.[183] As for the natural
foods stores that also carried organic products, they continued to do what
Miller shows they had always done: use the rhetoric of nature and health
to turn a profit. The organic boom gave them new opportunities to use that
old business model.[184]

With organic food developing into a reliable market with good returns,
the big players moved in. Some built up from modest beginnings, such as
Earthbound Farm and Whole Foods. Others were established firms buying
up or spinning off units with appropriately wholesome names, including
Smucker's Santa Cruz Organics (1989), M&M Mars' Seeds of Change (1997),
and Kellogg's Morningstar Farms Natural Touch (1999).[185] And overall, the
stores that had helped give organic its identity played a diminishing role
in retail distribution. As late as 1991, mainstream retailers accounted for
only 7 percent of organic sales; 68 percent came from "natural foods retailers," including co-ops. By 2006, the mainstream took the lead, 46 percent
to 44 percent.[186] The arrival of big business in organic markets was as much
symptom as cause of mainstreaming. Organic was worth the investment
because smaller farmers and retailers had already organized the markets
and proved their value, even before federal certification closed the deal.[187]
The shift was more than an economic one. It eroded a key institutional base
for organic as a movement for change in the food system.

Changing consumer preferences complemented shifts in the structure
of the organic food industry. Although there are no systematic survey data
on the motives behind organic purchases in the early 1970s, it is likely that
they included the rationales pushed with such enthusiasm by advocates,
including organic food as natural (in several senses), ecological, and subversive. Those inducements probably loomed larger at a time when the food was
new and required some effort to find. By the late 1980s, a poll of California
consumers found a much narrower focus on food safety. A survey of New
York co-op shoppers (presumably more politically reflective about their
consumption choices than most supermarket shoppers) in 1991 showed a
similar preoccupation.[188] The other major shift in organic consumption is

that it went upscale. Accounts of U.S. food culture from the 1960s consistently note how a marginalized countercultural preference for "authentic" and natural food gradually morphed into the cutting-edge cuisine of an educated upper middle class, with Berkeley's high-end Chez Panisse restaurant the star witness.[189] Organic was an important part of this rise in "yuppie chow."[190] And organic food, in particular, required a discerning attention to labels and standards, as well as extra income, making it a good fit with yuppies' cultural and economic capital.[191] Organic food remained virtuous food, marketed as benefiting the environment, as well as personal health. But it could also be promoted for its superior taste, to be appreciated by discerning palates. As early as 1969, ads by Berkeley's Organic Food Co-Op appealed both to "health seekers" and "discriminating gourmets."[192] The contrast with ascetic Grahamites is clear: For organic food consumers, proper diet involved no personal sacrifice. But the two sets of reformers found common ground in their status aspirations. The right foods corresponded to middle-class respectability for Grahamites and to middle-class cultural know-how for organic advocates.

The year 1990 saw a victory in passage of the federal Organic Food Production Act. As it turned out, the finish line was still twelve years away. The act established a National Organic Standards Board to develop a legal definition of organic. Although its appointees tilted toward Big Organic, the board also had some independence from the USDA, acknowledging that small farmers and consumer advocates remained deeply suspicious of that agency. Their suspicions seemed richly merited in 1997. The draft rules issued for public comment in December, among other concessions to large producers and chemical companies, allowed certified organic food to include the products of genetic engineering, irradiation, and sewage sludge (the "big three"). The ensuing outcry included more than 275,000 comments (a record at the time) and testified to the organic movement's alliances and capacity for political mobilization. Comments using standard forms from activist groups came from organized consumers (e.g., Working Assets), citizen scientists (the Center for Science in the Public Interest), and trade groups (the Organic Farmers' Marketing Association), as well as from food co-ops and *Organic Gardening and Farming*. The overwhelming focus was on the big three. But comments also complained that the USDA had subverted democracy by ignoring the board's recommendations on these issues, and they highlighted the contradiction between corporate-influenced rules and the need for consumer trust in a national organic label. According to the 35,989 letters from Working Assets members, "The USDA rejected its own advisory board's recommendations. It is succumbing to pressure from biotechnology, agribusiness and other industry giants that want to weaken the regulation of organic food production. As a consumer of organic food, I find three possible changes especially alarming and urge you to reject them: genetic engineering, irradiation and municipal waste sludge." Should the proposed rules stand, it would "jeopardize all confidence in the term organic."[193]

The focus on the big three was in part a strategic move by organic movement leaders, a way to mobilize consumer protest against the draft rules. That strategic shift had consequences. On one side, the deluge of outraged comments succeeded. In 2000, the USDA's final rule excluded the big three from its definition of organic (full implementation took two more years). From this struggle, too, emerged the Organic Consumers Association, still the leading watchdog against efforts to dilute organic standards or shift power in running the program toward Big Organic.[194] These successes also helped institutionalize a narrowing of the movement's approach compared with the early 1970s. One retreat involved a shift from organic as a holistic process of sustainable agriculture to organic as the absence of proscribed ingredients. The shift was well underway before 1997. Gershuny recalls tensions within NOFA in the early 1980s, with some members arguing for measures of soil health as a better standard.[195] Listing ingredients, however, proved more manageable for a national program; the firestorm over the big three may have locked in this approach.[196] Organic standards laid down in the National Organic Program (NOP) also ignored demands, central to the early movement, that organic be defined in part by small-scale production. Some *Organic Gardening and Farming* readers in 1972 anticipated the threat. They argued that federal organic certification would mean "bigness, centralization, specialization, etc. . . . These are the ways of corporate monoculture, not organic homesteading."[197] The issue did not vanish with the creation of the NOP. Organic advocates continued to criticize the program for ignoring, or even imposing new hardships on, small farmers. Some went on to pursue alternative certification schemes or chose to drop the formal label in favor of a market identity as "local."[198] For most consumers, however, the organic label signifies healthy eating and a green lifestyle, not an alternative to corporate monoculture. Official standards also sidelined agricultural workers. The labor conditions of organic agriculture employees had never been a priority for more than a minority of advocates. Omission of worker protections in federal organic standards largely confirmed an existing consensus in the movement.[199] It also followed from the long-term institutional separation of labor regulation from agricultural policy. In the bureaucratic language of the USDA, as it declined to include labor practices in organic standards, "other statutes cover labor and worker safety standards," and the Organic Food Production Act "does not provide the authority to include them in these regulations."[200] Finally, the contentious federal rulemaking showcased organic's narrowed defense of democracy. The earlier vision had been one of decentralized and participatory democracy, whether through farmers setting standards or co-op members running stores. That ideal was no longer an option in the NOP. Advocacy groups continued to criticize the program on narrower grounds: It gave too much weight to the big players in the industry, diluted the influence of small ones, and thus paved the way for weakening organic standards.[201] In the end, what the movement helped achieve, and the NOP institutionalized, was something of a return to the Progressive Era status quo. The federal government would again be the guarantor of trust in food for most consumers, including organic shoppers.

IV. Conclusion

Both the origin and the limits of the organic movement reflect, among other influences, legacies from the earlier campaigns for pure food and domestic science. Those campaigns bequeathed a food regime in which trust relied heavily on the credibility of government regulation, large corporations, and mainstream science. Their disrepute in the 1960s fueled doubts about the safety and healthfulness of conventional food, and those doubts brought many young consumers into the organic movement. On the other side, the movement also owes its modest policy achievements in part to institutional constraints inherited from the Progressive Era. That was the period when government management of agriculture and labor became firmly established as separate jurisdictions with distinct bureaucracies. It was also the time when USDA-sponsored research and technical assistance began its long service to the ideal of maximizing production on large farms.[202] By the 1960s, a model of "organic" agriculture that included decent pay and working conditions, small family farms, and process- rather than ingredient-based standards probably could not have won official backing.

But if institutional legacies helped ensure that federal regulation of organic food would have much in common with federal regulation of "purity," the movement in other respects was shaped more by the activist culture of its time. Those influences account for much of what was new in organic advocacy during the late 1960s and the 1970s. The movement popularized an ecological understanding of "natural" food; gave to "natural" the added meaning and merit of nonconformity; explicitly attacked corporate agriculture; insisted on a participatory approach to food certification, communes, and co-ops; and believed that the food system could be changed if we acted out our values in our individual lives.[203] These contributions to the repertoire of food movements applied to food the more general templates of the era's environmental, consumer, and countercultural politics. The influence of those models is unsurprising. Organic food activism occurred at a time and in places, such as university towns, of intense mobilization around a variety of social issues. The organizations advocating organic alternatives overlapped or allied with those of environmentalism and the counter-culture, such as campus ecological groups and urban co-ops. And many of the individuals who discovered organic farming, joined rural communes, or founded food co-ops in the late 1960s came with personal backgrounds in New Left politics.[204]

My summary of how activists framed food issues, articulated goals, developed strategies, and organized for change borrows the general categories used by social movement scholars to characterize their cases. In the context of food politics, these categories also point to mechanisms for constructing more trustworthy food. The celebration of "natural," in opposition to artificial, technological, and conformist, offered metrics for evaluating food. Consumers could use them to make their food choices. Was a given item a product of nature rather than the lab? Sold unpackaged? One of a kind in appearance or properties rather than one of many supermarket or fast-food clones? Food was also more trustworthy if embedded in more personal and authentic relationships, such as the direct ties to farmers at a roadside stand, to fellow members of the neighborhood co-op, or to familiar faces at a collectively run restaurant. And food could be validated by proxy if it was acquired in particular settings, such as co-ops, that embodied ideals of small scale, egalitarian structure, and democratic governance. These were all measures of trustworthy food that were quite different from the Progressive Era's reliance on federal regulation, modern science, and corporate branding. In some respects, organic had more in common with Graham and his critique of food products outsourced from family ties and tainted by commercial interests. But while the consumer strategy of basing trust on personal ties—know your farmer, know your food—would endure, this solution for problems of trust in other respects was short lived. The new co-ops disappeared or went mainstream, and the identification of organic with small-scale production faded for most consumers. The USDA organic label was a less personal guarantor of trust; it became the main way to earn consumer confidence. Much as organic advocates rejected Progressive Era markers of trust (approved by government regulators, manufactured by modern corporations, meeting science-based nutritional guidelines), so the organic label left its own legacies for more recent food politics. For many contemporary activists, that label exemplified the failure to construct a genuinely alternative food system. As Chapter 5 explains, their efforts to solve new problems of trust in food would be guided in part by a determination not to make the same mistakes.

5

Comparing Pasts and Present

The San Diego Roots Sustainable Food Project, launched in 2001, describes itself as "a network of citizens, farmers, chefs, gardeners, teachers, and students working to encourage the growth and consumption of regional food. From farm to fork, we focus awareness and work toward a more ecologically sound, economically viable and socially just food system in San Diego."[1] One of its major projects is Wild Willow Farm, located near the Mexican border. The farm supplies produce for a Community Supported Agriculture (CSA) program and is "where we teach people essential sustainable farming skills [and] train the next generation of sustainable farmers for our region." San Diego Roots also fosters urban agriculture through victory gardens it sponsors in local neighborhoods. And for those not ready to get their hands dirty, the organization's website offers links to help consumers find locally grown food through farmers' markets, restaurants, and CSAs. Its members envision both economic and cultural benefits: "By eating locally, not only do you get fresher, better-tasting food, but you also help support family farms . . . encourage a vibrant local economy . . . and promote community."

These practices and ideals in some ways reprise those of the early organic movement. They aim to displace conventional agribusiness in favor of small-scale, decentralized production, including on family farms. They foster more direct ties between producers and consumers, embedding commodity chains in personal relationships. San Diego Roots recommends the products of this alternative system as both healthier and tastier. And echoing the principles of many consumer activists who supported organic food in the early 1970s, the website calls for social justice but has little more to say about workers in food production or consumers with limited means. San Diego Roots also showcases some of the changes in food activism. While it shares with the organic movement a strong emphasis on environmental issues, it relies more on the contemporary language of sustainability. The organization complements its Wild Willow Farm with efforts to promote urban agriculture. And although the farm is organic, the celebration of regional production and distribution makes place, not growing methods, the primary marker of good food. Growing and consuming *local* produce is good for eaters, for the environment, and for the regional economy.

Comparing food activism of the late 1960s and the 2010s is not a matter of setting two independent cases side by side. This book has argued for treating the two as continuations of a recurring movement. In this view, we can best understand contemporary food politics by sorting out the different temporal layers of long-running tendencies of a capitalist food system and diffusion within and across time periods. This concluding chapter offers readers two more opportunities to judge the usefulness of that perspective. First, looking backward, it rounds up major similarities and differences across the book's cases of activism, connecting those similarities and differences to more general dynamics of a recurrent food movement. Second, looking forward from these case studies, it briefly brings that analysis up to date. The chapter focuses particularly on recent efforts to build local, alternative food networks (sometimes referred to as Organic 2.0). It asks how these efforts represent both familiar and distinctive responses to problems in the food system and explores how those responses reflect legacies from prior eras of food activism.

I. Themes and Variations

A. Recurrent Grievances

Judged from a distance, reformers in the 1830s, 1890s, and 1960s sounded the same notes in their critiques of conventional food. They denounced that food as unhealthy. The specific risks differed—inflammatory bread, embalmed beef, poisonous produce—but all were judged wanting in safety, nutritional value, or both. If consumers had doubts on these issues, those doubts counted as a further grievance. Many foods contained unknown or unfamiliar adulterants and additives. This raised an alarming question: How can people tell whether a food is safe to eat? Common suspicions of those who made the food reinforced anxieties. Whether they were targeting small commercial bakeries in Sylvester Graham's time, dishonest business-men in the Progressive Era, or soulless corporations in the 1960s, critics charged that producers sacrificed consumers' interests in the pursuit of profit. And for food reformers in each era, a common way to summarize these flaws was to denounce suspect food as unnatural. The critique con-trasted food that was unhealthy, lacking in transparency, and corrupted by profiteering with food closer to its natural state. Unnatural food was not merely artificial. It was the product of artifice by self-serving actors on remote farms or behind factory gates.

These themes, shared among activists across 140 years, are symptomatic of recurrent dynamics in the food system. The case studies have particu-larly highlighted commodification, delocalization, and the application of industrial methods and new technology to food production. From knead-ing bread to assembling meals, food items and food tasks that were at some point made and performed in households have moved, one by one, into the marketplace and become commodities for purchase. That shift can feed suspicions that food producers put short-term profits ahead of consumers' well-being. The relocation of food production to distant farms and factories is alienating, an activity out of sight of home, local community, even coun-try. It further distances food from customary networks and institutions of trust, whether those of face-to-face relations or government oversight. The logic of industrial production, like delocalization, also detaches food pro-duction from the personal responsibility of known individuals, the more so as ever-larger firms—meat-packers, big ag—take charge. And inventive manufacturers regularly introduce new products (margarine, Twinkies), new packaging (cans, plastic wrap), and new processes (for growing and preserving customary foods or constructing novel ones). For a time, these innovations can undermine the trust bred by long familiarity.

These dynamics are necessary parts of capitalist food production, little different from the production of clothing or cars or other goods except that, because they are things we eat, the stakes are higher with commodified food. By periodically prompting doubts about foods and food purveyors, these recurrent changes also help account for the enduring appeal of "na-ture" and personal ties (or, in the case of domestic science, the personal familiarity of a well-branded company) to validate food. Why are these doubts more widespread and vocal at some times than others? The serendip-ity of events plays some role, with scandals intermittently focusing public attention on problems that are in fact always with us. The food movements that turned doubts into demands also occurred amid wider cycles of protest, when barriers to mobilization around all manner of grievances are gener-ally lower.[2] But another side of commodified food is competition among food producers. Business rivals sometimes stoked consumers' anxieties in order to redirect their purchases, such as to "hygienic" foods, untouched by human hands, or to "natural" products, untainted by modern technology.[3]

This summary of common themes and their roots in the food system obviously splits and lumps, highlighting some differences and glossing over others. It does so deliberately, to tease out the different temporal contexts within which food activism has been shaped through its several iterations. One kind of splitting highlights some commonalities—those that have to do with the dynamics of food production—but not others. Among the "not others" is the consistent thread of "nutritionism" in American food culture. Foods are commonly evaluated not by their conformity to established culinary traditions but by their functional constituents (vitamins, carbohydrates, antioxidants, and so on). Michael Pollan is surely right that this obsession adds to our anxiety over food choices.[4] It is an approach commonly traced to Progressive Era nutritional analysis,[5] but it is clearly visible, as well, in Graham's dietary science. My summary also does some judicious lumping. It gives less attention to the distinctive challenges of each era's food regime than to similarities. Rather than contrasting urban bakers with multinational corporations or manure with pesticides, I generalize to commodification, delocalization, and technological innovation. That lumping may seem to stack the deck in favor of ambient movement cultures in accounting for specific characteristics of food protest. But the three Progressive Era cases suggest that this is the right move. In the same food regime we find quite different ways of framing problems and formulating solutions. These contrasts, along with those across the three periods, are better explained by social movement piggybacking.

B. Distinctive Responses

Grahamites were part of a larger evangelical revival that called individuals to reform society by confessing their sins and choosing the path to salvation. Fifty years later, John Harvey Kellogg joined a similar religious quest to bring morality back to a (still) unredeemed society. But pure food advocates and domestic scientists followed Progressive and maternalist scripts. They embraced science, a liberal state, and a public expression of women's responsibilities for solving social problems. Early organic activists, especially among consumers, launched a different crusade. They shared with the wider counterculture a commitment to social change through participatory democracy and personal prefigurative politics.[6] In the counterculture and in the burgeoning environmental movement they also found a more general language of opposition to corporate capitalism and technocratic control. These broader cultures of protest not only helped fuel mobilization around problems in the food system. They also steered grievances common to all these periods in very different directions.

Consider, as social movement scholars urge us to do, the particular ways in which reformers framed the threats to individual and social well-being. Grahamites raised the alarm over community morality. They linked improper foods (especially bread from city bakers) to the perils of a commercializing and urbanizing society. Eating such "stimulating" foods inflamed men's and women's baser impulses and, in the aggregate, subverted the traditional moral order. Kellogg embellished Graham's grim assessment mainly by making these evils a particularly alarming problem for America's Northern European stock, to be combated by a vigorous program of eugenic improvement. Progressives dropped the explicit language of individual sin and more clearly invoked social causes of food problems. For those advocating government action to curb adulteration and improve home economics, the main problems were self-interested businessmen and ignorant consumers. The first put inferior food on the market, and the second bought it. Early organic activists were equally severe in blaming food risks on self-interested and scoundrelly businessmen, especially when it came to pesticide use. But they pushed this critique considerably further. They offered a wide-ranging indictment of the corrupt alliance of big food corporations, complicit government officials, and captive scientists, jointly denying consumers healthy and legible food. Similarly, they joined many Grahamites and Progressive pure food advocates in censuring foods alienated from their natural state by modern technology but did not stop there. They introduced in their praise of natural food environmentalist notions of ecological balance and sustainability. And they followed countercultural models in opposing all things natural to all forms of social conformity and rampant materialism.

What was to be done? For Grahamites, proper food, like eternal salvation, was for the individual to choose. It would take self-discipline to resist the lure of stimulants and the scorn of doctors, but it was within our own power to follow the right diet and reap the rewards of good health, pious soul, and wholesome family. Kellogg largely agreed, but he made more concessions to the typical Progressive view that individuals needed help from protective laws and public education. That Progressive agenda emphasized social causes over personal responsibility and called for pure food legislation in Congress and home economics in public schools to check deceptive businesses and train future housewives. Organic farmers came to a similar conclusion in demanding certification. Government-sanctioned standards would eliminate fraud from competitors and support informed choices by consumers. But in the late 1960s and early 1970s, organic activists often called for more far-reaching changes. Good food would become available only through alternative economic and social institutions such as democratically run co-ops. These broad contrasts in social movement templates for diagnosing problems and advocating changes can also be seen in the different ways that reformers connected food problems to human "appetites." For Graham and Kellogg, our God-given taste for wholesome food had been corrupted by civilization, requiring a new spiritual discipline. For domestic scientists, in particular, our appetites were not depraved but ignorant (or perhaps misdirected by immigrant foodways) and needed reeducation to align them with the findings of nutritional science. And for countercultural organic activists, natural appetites had been subverted by the blandishments of capitalist advertising and materialism. Reviving our tastes for good food called for personal liberation from those influences.

These divergent answers to the question of what is to be done also imply different ways of connecting personal action with social change. Some of Graham's supporters did recognize the need for social institutions—properly run boardinghouses, college dining rooms, and grocery stores—to support healthy eating. But the key to transforming Americans' pathological food consumption followed an evangelical script. Community morality would be restored if we confessed our dietary sins and embraced Graham's Good Word. Progressive food reformers had other ways to translate individual action into social betterment. On the political front, the key was nonpartisan good citizenship. Restoring an "honest" marketplace required that businessmen set aside narrow self-interest and the competitive race to the bottom; a pure food law would make that possible. On the home front, the logic was more that of maternalism. Dietary health demanded of women that they better perform their natural roles as guardians of the family. Domestic science would enable them to do so with greater expertise. For early organic consumers, finally, individual choices could transform society through prefigurative politics. Rejecting corporate food and buying organic from alternative stores were lifestyle changes that would plant the seeds for a healthier and more authentic food system. All these nostrums relied in part on the great American virtue of personal responsibility. Even Progressives had faith that the individual initiative of enlightened consumers and trained housewives would help solve social problems. But the meaning of individual responsibility conformed to larger social movement cultures. For Graham, it involved triumph over individual sin. For Progressives, proper dietary choices meant substituting the guidance of science and an enlightened state for ignorant tradition and narrow self-interest. And organic activists turned "individual responsibility" into personal liberation, part of a wider subversion of technocratic control and social conformity.

More practical tactics followed. Graham and his associates relied mainly on direct persuasion to urge individuals to mend their dietary ways. This was standard evangelical operating procedure, but it is also true that the strategic alternatives of using government policy or market pressure were not practical options at the time. Beyond municipal regulation of public markets, there was little state capacity to intervene in food production or distribution. Market pressure made little sense when "the consumer" was not yet a recognized actor and could have no role within a movement that viewed the purchase of commercial food as part of the problem. Both options were open to Progressives, and they used them. Their approach to food safety applied the same tools as in dealing with other social problems. Adulteration and nutrition could be ameliorated through government intervention and concerted, conscientious consumption. By the late 1960s, the state offered food activists little hope. It was viewed more as a tool of agribusiness and food manufacturers than as an agent of change. But one Progressive Era tactic still made sense: Identify virtuous products, educate consumers to buy them, and in this way change American agriculture from within. Younger activists gave that strategy a new meaning. Those associated with *Organic Gardening and Farming*, with the alternative press, and with communes and co-ops made it part of a larger countercultural dream. They believed that fundamental change throughout society could be won, not through conventional politics, but by transforming the way in which each individual lived his or her life. In these three eras' reform strategies, activists also saw quite different roles for mainstream science. Credentialed experts such as chemists and nutritionists were essential allies for pure food activists and domestic scientists. Grahamites and organic advocates kept their distance. They did so partly because those credentialed experts were generally hostile to them. But they also did so out of a more general skepticism—whether evangelical or countercultural—of professional authority. Science *could* be an ally, but only in a more populist form, tied to biblical law in Graham's popular lectures and writing or to progressive politics by opponents of corporate agriculture and federally funded university research. Following New Left cultural analysts, organic activists took the attack on the scientific establishment one step further. Graham denounced medical experts as elitist and self-serving. For Robert Rodale and kindred critics of the food system in the late 1960s, they were part of a larger system of technocratic domination.

Many of these contrasts come together to set different standards for trustworthy food. Activists in all three eras, we have seen, endorsed natural food in opposition to the commercialized versions of their day—store-bought bread, the adulterated products of a dishonest marketplace, the plastic food of corporate America. In promoting natural food as a cure-all, Graham, Kellogg, Rodale, and any number of contemporary nutritional gurus agree.[7] But more revealing of ambient cultural influences are the different constructions of natural. For Graham and Kellogg, nature had value because it was crafted by God, and the food closest to biblical precepts had the greatest legitimacy. For advocates of a food and drug law and of domestic science, nature's bounty had more secularized virtues. Food unsullied by business artifice and conforming to the laws of nutritional science won their approval. And for organic activists, food counted as natural if it was ecologically sound and culturally subversive. Reformers in each era also invoked some version of democracy as an antidote to untrustworthy food. Graham did so in the evangelicals' populist spirit, rejecting the authority of a medical elite. Pure food advocates and domestic scientists called instead on a democratic state to protect and educate consumers. And their organic successors embraced a more participatory model: Standards should be devised, and food managed, on a decentralized democratic basis.

In all three periods, finally, reformers enlisted women to restore trust. We saw in Chapters 2 and 3 that women accounted for a third of the main Grahamite society and that they played key roles in supporting pure food legislation and in leading the domestic science movement. Chapter 4 noted that women were well represented among the founders of small organic farms and food co-ops of the late 1960s. But much as reformers praised nature in different terms, so they feminized trustworthy food in different ways. For Graham, women embodied piety, tradition, and the precommercial home; one could thus have faith in the products of their loving hands. Domestic scientists still made women a guarantor of safe and nutritious food, but only to the extent that they subscribed to modern science, not outmoded traditions. Their maternal responsibilities, moreover, extended outside the home in their capacities as expert consumers and even as employees of schools and hospitals. Organic activists enlarged the scope of maternalism still further, celebrating Mother Earth as the source of trustworthy food, to be protected and renewed.[8]

Food as God intended, food with the imprimatur of Progressive government and modern science, and food that defied oppression by state and capital offered select consumers new grounds for trust. These metrics for distinguishing good from suspect food, finally, mapped onto invidious social distinctions of different kinds. Graham's godly food was also that of the respectable and improving middle class, in contrast to both the degraded poor and the self-indulgent rich. The pure and nutritional food of the Progressive Era stood opposite the lesser fare of unassimilated and uneducated immigrants. And for its young enthusiasts, organic food drew a boundary between middle-class whites of two types: the cool and the square.

C. Inherited Influences

Many of the common themes across the three eras of food activism, I have argued, reflect recurrent dynamics in the production and distribution of food. And many features of each campaign that set it apart from the others reflect wider currents of activism and political culture in these periods. However, we should remember that these are not independent cases. Their accomplishments and failures influenced later waves of activism. Graham was certainly not the first to frame "natural" food as the key to good health, as superior to both commercial products and doctors' nostrums, and as the physiological basis for individual morality.[9] But he popularized these claims as a coherent package, and that package got passed on to Kellogg and other food reformers of the Progressive Era. Particularly with respect to Graham's dietary recommendations (avoid meat, alcohol, stimulating spices, sweets, etc.), a religious institution (the Seventh-day Adventists) and a temperance organization (the Woman's Christian Temperance Union) played key roles in transmitting his regimen into the last decades of the century. The superiority of natural food to both conventional food and orthodox medicine also got picked up by entrepreneurs, and their marketing efforts helped carry the message forward to Progressive health reformers and, later still, to champions of organic food.[10] The Progressives left legacies of their own. They added to the menu of food activism the idea of concerted consumer action to bring about change, in some cases making use of product certifications like those of *Good Housekeeping*. It was a strategy kept alive by *Good Housekeeping* but also by the National Consumers League and later the Consumers Union, becoming a taken-for-granted part of the tactical repertoire available to organic activists. The public outcry over food adulteration gave larger companies the incentive to promote their own products as "pure" and "natural." These businesses reinforced the less richly funded efforts of natural foods entrepreneurs. Progressives also went far beyond Graham in making the government a guarantor of trust in food. In doing so, they did more than make government an obvious tool for their descendants' use. They also passed along particular standards of evaluation, built into the rules and practices of the Food and Drug Administration (FDA), such as informed consumer choices tied to accurate product labeling, and of the U.S. Department of Agriculture, such as making nutritional content the chief basis for dietary recommendations. These political institutions made another bequest to the organic movement in strictly separating the regulation of food from the management of labor relations.

The Progressives, finally, left legacies in the form of fracture points. By making federal oversight and corporate integrity the foundations of consumer trust, they also made both vulnerable to a vicious circle of mistrust. When trust in the credibility of government and business declines (perhaps for reasons having little to do with food), it can raise doubts about food, as well.[11] On the other side, widespread questioning of food safety can undermine confidence in the institutions bringing it to market. For a time in the late 1960s and early 1970s, that vicious circle meant that government oversight and corporate guarantees were ruled out as options for reconstructing trust in food.

II. Lessons for Social Movements

This book's account of food activism offers lessons for social movement scholarship, as well as for food studies. The most obvious is the value of following single genres of movement over extended periods of time. Other scholars have given us valuable insights as they generalize across movements about mechanisms of contentious politics. However, keeping the focus on single genres of recurrent movements—those that confront enduring social problems such as gender inequality or labor exploitation or untrustworthy food—has its own benefits. It makes it possible to unpack the different temporal contexts within which a movement evolves, from the long run of problem-specific motors of protest and of long-term legacies, to shorter-term modeling on other movements. And although this approach leans toward the particular, it can be applied elsewhere. Within the genre of food politics, for example, we can trace similar mixtures of industry dynamics, movement legacies, and period cultures that put European opposition to genetically engineered food on a different path from its U.S. counterpart.[12] We need not stop with food. Scholars such as John Walton, Chad Goldberg, John Krinsky, and Chris Rhomberg have crafted such narratives for recurrent battles over water rights, welfare rights, and labor rights.[13]

A second lesson concerns cultural modeling. Movement scholars have done fine work on the role of "co-optable institutions" such as churches for the Civil Rights Movement or music festivals for "white power" mobilization.[14] These institutions offer indispensable resources, protection, and allies. But we should also consider how movements, in piggybacking on other movements, can borrow for their own campaigns certain ways of interpreting problems, framing solutions, choosing strategies, or organizing for battle. This is a form of diffusion in which cultural scripts are adapted to new purposes. A third lesson is to distinguish between two sorts of diffusion. The one commonly studied follows influences from one protest event or movement to another, as activists learn from one another. But diffusion also happens over much longer periods of time, skipping over the personal networks and coalitions that figure so prominently in diffusion within single cycles of protest.[15] For such long-term diffusion, we must instead look to the ways that protest discourse, strategy, or solidarities get embedded in movement organizations, political institutions, popular culture, and business behavior. Once embedded, they may become resources and constraints for much later generations of activists.

Finally, the food movements I have examined, particularly organic, are examples of consumer-based movements.[16] Although reformers in several of my cases engaged in conventional state-centered action, pressing governments for changes in food-related policies, the focus of many others was the market. The idea was that desired changes in how food was produced and consumed could be achieved if individuals selectively bought items that met certain standards (such as vegetarian, "hygienic," organic) and shunned those that did not. Many participants were not affiliated with formal movement organizations, and their "protest" more often took the form of individual consumption choices than it did collective public action. For such movements, we need to ask what holds them together: How are they "organized?"[17] Piggybacking provides one answer. Participants in the early organic movement were *also* embedded in the counterculture, the environmental movement, and the New Left. Thus, they had common scripts that supported a shared orientation toward food reform. As new bases for trust in food emerged—in effect, agreed-on directives for appropriate consumer behavior—these also helped coordinate action through the market. Some of these coordination mechanisms are movement specific. Common standards for trustworthy food are of little value for unifying consumer protest against despoilers of the environment or violators of women's rights. This gives us another reason to focus on particular genres of protest.

III. Back to the Present

Can this layering of movement causation—system dynamics, piggybacking, reform legacies—shed light on our own era of food activism? The current period is much less distinct from its predecessor. Many of the same organizations, activists, and issues that were part of organic advocacy are still at work. But the mix of the familiar and the new lends itself to a similarly layered analysis.

Consider, as a point of departure, Homegrown Organic Farms. This large marketer of fruit in California and Oregon distributes produce from more than eighty farms covering more than four thousand acres.[18] A package of its blueberries, purchased in the summer of 2018, helped this consumer know where his food came from. The label sported a QR code and instructions to "Scan me to meet your grower." Following the code led to an image of Tom and Karen Avinelis, for whom "farming just becomes a part of who you are and who your family is." The Avinelises, I learned, are committed to sustainability in family farming and to "growing healthy food." Homegrown's website offers thirty such profiles of its growers, pictured standing with their families and celebrating their roots in particular communities and parcels of land. ("'In four generations we've only moved a quarter of a mile,' Vernon [Peterson] declares, a large smile spreading across his face as he gazes out at his orchard.")

Homegrown's rhetoric echoes that heard in the early organic movement. The company idealizes the family farm. It presents organic food as better for your health. In its farmers' testimonials and its company name, Homegrown conjures a close tie between grower and consumer reminiscent of the farm stands and direct-order organic schemes of the late 1960s. In other ways, Homegrown illustrates changes since that time. Although there is still an emphasis on environmental virtues, the company's public relations points consumers toward the specific virtue of sustainability. The credibility of its fruit seems to lie not just in how but also in where it is grown. There is a new technology for winning consumers' trust by establishing via the Internet "personal" ties between them and farmers. Last, Homegrown's touting of sustainability, small farms, and personal connections comes from an established, fairly large company rather than from critical voices within the Rodale Institute. The mix of old and new themes is typical of contemporary activists responding to common problems under distinct conditions, some of them inherited from the organic movement.

Certainly, current doubts about conventional food have some familiar sources. Like activists in other periods, those today charge that the prevailing system offers us food that is unhealthy, full of artificial and obscure ingredients, and of unknown provenance. Some of these risks correspond to recurrent dynamics of the food system, even if the specific forms they take are new. There is still delocalization (imports from China); new technologies (genetic engineering); industrialized food (McDonald's); novel food (high-octane energy drinks); and food subject to commercial imperatives (the "deserts" where it is not profitable to sell healthy food).[19] Other risks reflect the concerns of our own time. The threat of climate change, for example, adds an important new dimension to organic's focus on environmental impact and sustainability. The "obesity epidemic" looms in the background of current worries about processed food and health. And 2020's global pandemic and economic shutdown give new urgency to the problem of food insecurity.

The responses have been many and tremendously varied. Some are more or less continuous with the initiatives of the organic movement.[20] Others, dating from the early 1990s, have struck observers as part of a new wave. The list usually begins with the explosion of farmers' markets and Community Supported Agriculture (CSA) programs. Farmers' markets gained favor as a way to foster organic agriculture in the 1970s, but they spread much more rapidly in the 1990s (the number increased 63 percent between 1994 and 2000 alone) and thereafter. The first CSA in the United States dates to 1985; within ten years, five hundred operated across the country.[21]

Both institutions aim to bring higher income to farmers and better produce to consumers while also shortening the distance, geographic and social, between them. Other relatively new ventures to address problems in the food system include "buy local" campaigns; food security projects to make healthy food more affordable to low-income consumers; mobilization to change the priorities of the farm bill; school garden programs, urban agriculture projects, and protests against genetically engineered foods; and Food Policy Councils to coordinate reform efforts and connect reformers with city officials.[22] The range of advocacy groups involved is equally diverse, in part because the emphasis on *local* food means local organization.[23] But even the umbrella groups operating at a national level are as varied as the food system itself. Their priorities are suggested by their names, as the following sample shows: the Center for Food Safety, Feeding America, the National Sustainable Agriculture Coalition, Obesity Action Coalition, Community Alliance with Family Farmers, Fair Trade USA, the National Organic Coalition, the Non–GMO Project, Local Harvest, and the Food Chain Workers Alliance. Adding to the rich variety of contemporary food activism, seemingly single-purpose organizations (e.g., the Pesticide Action Network) frequently join coalitions to campaign for other reform goals (e.g., the HEAL Food Alliance's efforts on behalf of more sustainable and equitable farm systems).[24] The brief overview of current activism that follows concentrates on the still-capacious category of local, alternative agriculture, both because this is probably the most prominent arena for grassroots efforts and because it is often regarded as the successor to the earlier organic movement. I also continue my focus on the consumer side of food reform movements.

A. Locavores and New Bases for Trust

With locavorism, as with organic agriculture, the initial push often came from regional farmers eager to increase direct sales and cultivate a new market niche.[25] But part of what makes a new market look more like a movement is the mobilization of consumers as ideological participants, as well as economic patrons. What kind of participants, in what kind of movement? A large literature finds that the motives of supportive consumers vary widely, and "changing the food system" is usually low on the list. Patrons of farmers' markets and CSAs are more likely to say that they want to buy healthier or better-quality produce, to support (and perhaps get to know) local farmers, or, somewhat less common, to improve the environment and build local community.[26] And what kind of movement? Scholars have raised many questions about the politics of contemporary alternative food movements. How well do activists in different campaigns combine attention to environmental

sustainability, food quality, and social justice? How far do they go in addressing inequalities of class, race, and gender? And, related to these, how successfully do they avoid catering only to affluent consumers or putting local
economic interests ahead of other considerations?[27] The usual answer to all
these questions is the same: most contemporary efforts fall short.

Cutting across the variations in motives and political valence, however,
are some common themes. Above all, there is the enthusiastic embrace of
"sustainable" and "local" food. Both terms are rich in connotations. Food
system reformers aim at sustainability in the ecological sense of production
and distribution that meet current needs while also preserving the resources
and capabilities to meet future ones. Examples include growing methods
that maintain soil fertility and meat production that does not contribute
to climate change. Community Supported Agriculture programs are seen
to promote sustainability in this sense. According to one early promoter
of these programs, a CSA "reconnects producers with consumers and em-
powers members to 'vote with their dollars' for ecologically sound, local
agriculture."[28] Over time, however, locavores have applied the term to social as well as environmental goods. A sustainable food system should also
ensure that small farmers can stay in business; that consumers (including
poor ones) have access to healthy food; and that workers in fields, factories,
and restaurants earn a living wage. Members of the Groundswell Center
"believe that our food system cannot be truly sustainable without racial
and economic justice and equitable access to healthy food, land for growing it, and dignified, fairly-compensated food system jobs."[29] "Local," too,
points to virtues of several kinds. Producing and distributing food on a
more regional basis has some instrumental value. It may contribute to environmental sustainability by reducing "food miles"; it supports local farmers
by increasing direct sales and protecting markets; it may make food purveyors more accountable because they have local reputations to protect; and it
benefits consumers' health by encouraging them to eat more fresh fruit and
vegetables. A more localized food system is also held up as a good in itself. It
embeds in the market small-scale production along with "opportunity and
fairness for small and medium-sized family farms."[30] It favors better-quality
produce—riper when picked, sold soon thereafter, perhaps representing
local heritage varieties rather than monocultures. And it fosters community
as shoppers mingle at markets, forge ties with farmers, and take pride in
local produce.[31] "The goal of the local food movement," says Local Harvest,
"is to create thriving community-based food systems that will make high
quality local food available to everyone."[32] The scholarly jury is still out on
whether small-scale local agriculture does, in fact, deliver these goods.[33]

Some of these themes have much in common with earlier responses
to commodification and delocalization. The idea that trust in food can be

restored by anchoring commodity exchange in personal ties and communal solidarity—know your farmer, patronize members of your community rather than distant and anonymous sources[34]—also appeared in the organic movement and in Graham's praise of homemade bread. And why stop with Graham? Accounts of eighteenth-century food riots also highlight the tensions between emerging national markets in food and local moral economies. Grain and bread, rioters charged, should be subject to community standards of a "just" price and to community control over local productive property. Selfish middlemen or merchants shipping food away to fetch a higher price should be subjected to popular sanction.[35] The ideal of the small producer as a counterweight to industrial production and corporate concentration can also be traced back in time: to organic's small farmers, to agrarian reformers, to Graham's local wheat growers and home bread makers, and further, at least to Jefferson's agrarian ideal.[36] Contemporary locavores' celebration of artisanal food offers a variation on the same theme. Food from skilled men and women, their hands guided by traditional craft knowledge, is preferable to food whose producers are rendered anonymous by long commodity chains and modern manufacturing.[37] For the "'locavore' craft brewer Ron Silberstein," the enemy is mass-produced malt: "Local, handcrafted malt is [the] key to bringing a sense of terroir . . . back to beer."[38]

We can also see some influences on locavorism coming from our own time's political culture. There is still the close tie, established by the organic movement, between environmentalism and food reform. But thanks in part to that tie, advocates of alternative local food systems have followed environmentalists' ideological trajectory. Early calls to patronize farmers' markets, eat seasonal local produce, and defy monocultures by cultivating distinctive regional varieties were open to criticism as elitist. These were options available to affluent consumers of "yuppie chow" and ignored issues of food access among the less privileged.[39] Environmentalists in the 1980s faced comparable rebukes for catering primarily to middle-class whites. Critical voices promoted an environmental justice agenda. Without abandoning older movement goals, they focused more systematically on the intersection of environmental problems and inequalities of class and race. They urged us to continue fighting pollution but also to publicize and organize around toxic wastes dumped in poor neighborhoods.[40] Locavores have made a similar move under the banner of food justice. They acknowledge that the problems associated with conventional food—health, quality, access—are not equally distributed. Members of the Community Alliance with Family Farmers insist that they "recognize the historic and lasting inequities in the California food and farming system. . . . Farmers of color . . . immigrant, indigenous and women farmers, should have the opportunity to create and participate in a food and agriculture system that aligns with their needs."[41] Acting on this insight, many locavore organizations are seeking broader alliances to knit together alternative networks of local food production, to reduce food insecurity, and to expand community organizing.[42] For example, adding new farmers' markets to support small growers and bring better-quality produce to consumers is still on the agenda. But there are also efforts to locate some of those markets in underserved neighborhoods and to make their goods affordable and easy to buy with Electronic Benefit Transfer (EBT) cards. Ecological sustainability is essential, but so is work toward a food system that is sustainable for its workers and poor consumers. Some branches of more recent food activism, finally, have learned from and forged links with a broader anti-globalization movement. This has meant greater attention to the roles played by global corporations and global trade in such problems as agricultural monocultures, the spread of genetically engineered crops, and a fast-food culture. It has also diffused the anti-globalization movement's language of food sovereignty, originally the battle cry of peasant movements in developing economies, into some U.S. campaigns for more localized and democratic control of food systems.[43] With a nod to the global South, the National Family Farm Coalition translates food sovereignty into "food democracy, a form of food justice, or local control."[44]

B. Piggybacking, Legacies, and the Limits of the Local Food Movement

Realizing these visions is another matter. For many critics, contemporary food activism is also shaped (or contaminated) by the prevailing politics of neoliberalism.[45] The indictments are many and plausible. Locavores often hope to bring about change through voluntary action in civil society, including by steering markets in new directions. Vote with your fork! Proponents of healthier food and opponents of genetically engineered foods commonly frame the issues in terms of consumers' right to know and to make more informed, individual choices. Compared with the early organic movement, a thoroughgoing democratization of food governance is rarely on today's agenda. The influence of neoliberalism in these areas may be overstated. As in the past, primarily voluntaristic and market-oriented strategies are paralleled by more state-centered ones. Some of them, including battles to rewrite the farm bill and to empower local Food Policy Councils, involve broad coalitions of organizations, many of which do not fit the neoliberal model. The fact that this dual-track approach can also be found in the Progressive Era also suggests that neoliberalism should not be the prime causal suspect. But food reformers do often take a distinctly neoliberal approach to the essential movement work of linking personal and political change.

Grahamites made that link through an evangelical script of individual sin and public confession. For Progressives, it had more to do with good citizenship and maternal duty. And for early organic food consumers, it took the form of prefigurative politics. Contemporary food activism continues the trajectory of organic toward embodying political goals in individualized consumer choices. Far more than in the early 1970s, this is now a general model that prevails well beyond food activism, often as a deliberate alternative to engaging with discredited political institutions.[46]

There is a third layer of influence on locavorism, involving legacies from the past. For some of these, that past is recent and the legacies are conducted through organizational continuities, policy frameworks, and the object lessons drawn from alleged failures of the organic movement. Many of the organizations and activists involved in the organic movement are still with us, now promoting local agriculture along with organic production. Among the Organic Consumers Association's current goals is "breaking the chains of corporate control" by persuading consumers to buy local products (as long as they are also organic).[47] The Rodale Institute runs a CSA, and the Cornucopia Project spun off by Rodale backs "ecologically produced local, organic and authentic" food. One of the main national organizations promoting local food systems, the National Sustainable Agriculture Coalition, includes representatives from the pioneering California Coalition of Organic Farmers, Oregon Tilth, and the Organic Farming Research Foundation. The ties are also personal. Interviews with organic pioneers in Northern California, for example, find many of them currently involved in CSAs and local food-security work.[48] At the retail end, natural foods stores and food co-ops, early sources of organic food, carried the torch into locavore campaigns.[49]

This seeding of locavorism with organic veterans may have helped keep activists focused on persistent dilemmas of building an alternative agricultural system. Tensions between movement and market, insurgency and business viability, preoccupied organic producers and distributors from the start.[50] Their successors have updated these same concerns—if Walmart sells local produce, are we winning or losing?—but have not solved them. The dilemma comes with following organic's original strategy of seeking change in the food system through the market. Locavores also update another dilemma faced by the developing organic movement: that of class and consumption. In the earlier case, the transition from countercultural organic food to a trendier counter-cuisine made good food a privilege for those with economic resources and cultural capital. Locavores built on that legacy in some ways. They continue to fight conventional food by redirecting consumer purchases, and they do so in part by making virtuous food an opportunity to display educated and discerning tastes. The specific virtues may be defined differently—local, carbon-neutral, humane, sustainable—but the link between alternative food and middle-class privilege remains.[51] Finally, today's locavores follow organic precedents in another way: What gives certain food a cachet (heritage varieties, artisanal production, local sourcing, personal ties) also makes it trustworthy. These are qualities, Laura Miller shows, that Mrs. Gooch learned to highlight in her stores' displays, each product coming with a lovingly detailed narrative of its provenance. Whole Foods bought the company, and the rhetoric.[52] Homegrown Organic Farms' QR code, leading me to the farmers and land behind the blueberries I bought, follows a similar recipe for winning my trust. These markers of good food—is it politically correct? authentic? locally sourced?—are easy to lampoon, in part because advocates are so often tone deaf when it comes to class inequality among consumers. But locavores' reliance on cultivated tastes to identify trustworthy food is not new. It is part of a lineage that goes back at least to the "discriminating gourmets" to whom Berkeley's food co-op advertised organic products in the late 1960s.[53]

Contemporary food activism is also constrained by the same framework of policy making that we saw in the early organic movement. Agroecology programs have multiplied, but the iron triangle of farm lobbying, federal funding, and university research priorities still gives conventional agriculture's agenda the upper hand.[54] Locavores have been no more successful than their organic predecessors in overcoming the institutional separation between labor and agricultural policy. And more broadly, the vision of an alternative food system, like earlier calls for organic, is out of sync with government institutions. The vision is of integrated changes in agricultural methods, market arrangements, and social policy that produce a sustainable system ecologically, economically, and socially. By contrast, policy-making institutions disperse these issues across a variety of federal agencies and congressional committees. As critics note, there is no U.S. Department of Food. The fragmentation of contemporary food activism among such issues as organic standards, obesity, environmental impact, food security, and restaurant working conditions reflects a similar fragmentation of oversight (or neglect) by local, state, and federal governments.[55] That institutional atomizing of movement energy is a legacy more from U.S. nation-state development than from prior cycles of protest, but it was ratified by the construction of the FDA by Progressive reformers and of organic standards by their counterparts in the 1980s.

Even more than with the Progressive and organic cases, finally, past activism shapes contemporary locavorism through the power of the cautionary tale.[56] Advocates for local and alternative agriculture warn against repeating the mistakes of the organic movement. The biggest mistake was to allow commercial mainstreaming.[57] Here the touchstones are Big Organic and big supermarket chains, especially Whole Foods, that apply a corporate model to organic retailing. "For many who participated in the early phase of organic farming, its subsequent history is a story of paradise lost—or, worse, sold—in which cherished ideals have simply become part of the sales pitch."[58] Julie Guthman and Michael Haedicke show that a commercial model was part of the organic movement from the start, and Haedicke adds that a movement identity persists in this sector.[59] But however faulty as history, the narrative of organic's co-optation by big capital still influences contemporary food reformers. It helps explain the appeal of personal ties and direct relationships between producer and consumer to ground trust in food, because these links are hard to duplicate by large corporations operating on a national scale.[60] It also helps explain the shift among some reformers from defining good food in terms of production techniques (pesticide- and artificial fertilizer-free "organic") to local origins.[61] Unfortunately, a preoccupation with past mistakes is no guarantee that they will not be repeated. "Local," like "organic" or "pure," has become a marketing niche for supermarkets and restaurants. An ersatz personal touch is often reproduced in ads and labels picturing happy farmers and bespoke artisans at work; fast-food chains offer in-season local products, such as lobster rolls at McDonald's in Maine.[62]

IV. Food Movements, Social Movements

I have aimed to show the advantages of analyzing recurrent social movements over the long haul. The things that make them recurrent are consequential, and those influences are easily missed by aggregating the stuff of social movements across different genres of contention. What makes such movements vary has much to do with their roots in the activism and politics distinctive to particular times. And one thing that gives them continuity is that they build on the successes and failures of their predecessors. To make this larger argument, I have deliberately set to the side ways in which food movements are also like other movements, past and present. One of these commonalities is that all social movements fall short. The limitations of my movements are not distinctive to food reform. The relative neglect of class inequalities; the perils of seeking social change through the market; the difficulties in advancing social justice goals through personalized politics; the tensions between organized collective action and decentralized participatory democracy—all are challenges that confront a wide range of movements. These dilemmas, in turn, remind us of more generally applicable lessons for contemporary social movements, more often preached than practiced. One is that consumption-based strategies alone are vulnerable to commercial co-optation, give the affluent more influence, and, for both those reasons, easily become exercises in the well-meaning display of social status. Complementing those strategies with state-centered tactics is no panacea. But involving the state calls into play a broader range of resources—and thus people—and a wider range of levers for change. A second lesson is that broadening alliances can strengthen social movements. The most familiar recommendation here is to reframe issues in more inclusive terms, such as environmental justice, human rights, or food justice.[63] Another approach, however, puts less emphasis on ideology and more on organizational vehicles such as Food Policy Councils.[64] The hope is that, while diverse participants may join such councils to advance sectional interests, they learn from one another and cultivate a wider solidarity. A third lesson is that food movements should continue to focus on issues of class inequality. These inequalities, both between rich and poor consumers and between food system workers and those who benefit from their labor, are as pronounced with organic and local food as they are in the conventional sector.[65] In the United States, they are both hidden by individualism and reconstituted as racial inequalities. Putting class front and center exposes the limits of consumption-based politics and offers a more inclusive framing of problems in the food system. In this respect, at least, the challenges for food activists are little different from those facing most other progressive U.S. social movements. But food confers some advantages. From food stamps to food safety, many aspects of the food system are already matters for state regulation. A purely market-based strategy is not an option. Food, moreover, is a point at which the personal and political clearly converge. That facilitates mobilization. Finally, food's pleasures offer one way to invite fellowship across social boundaries. These are advantages on which activists can build in crafting a more effective food movement.

Notes

CHAPTER 1

1. "Proposed Rule to Roll Back Nutrition Standards Will Jeopardize Children's Health and Nutrition," Food Research and Action Center, January 22, 2020, accessed March 14, 2020, https://frac.org/news/proposed-rule-to-roll-back-nutrition-standards-will-jeopardize-childrens-health-and-nutrition.

2. "The USDA's New Industry Friendly Hog Slaughter Inspection Is Hogwash," Food and Water Watch, September 17, 2019, accessed March 14, 2020, https://www.foodandwaterwatch.org/news/usda-new-hog-slaughter-inspection-is-hogwash; "Foodborne Illness Outbreaks," *Food Safety News*, accessed March 26, 2020, https://www.foodsafetynews.com/foodborne-illness-outbreaks.

3. "Colorado Mandatory Labeling of GMOs Initiative, Proposition 105," Ballotpedia, accessed March 15, 2020, https://ballotpedia.org/Colorado_Mandatory_Labeling_of_GMOs_Initiative,_Proposition_105_(2014).

4. "USDA's New Disclosure Rule for Genetically Engineered Food Will Leave Many Consumers in the Dark," *Consumer Reports*, December 20, 2018, accessed March 25, 2020, https://advocacy.consumerreports.org/press_release/usdas-new-disclosure-rule-for-genetically-engineered-food-will-leave-many-consumers-in-the-dark.

5. "Final GMO Labeling Rule Does Not Require Labeling of Highly Refined Ingredients from GM Crops, if No Modified Genetic Material Is Detectable," Elaine Watson, Food Navigator-USA, December 21, 2018, https://www.foodnavigator-usa.com/Article/2018/12/20/Final-GMO-labeling-rule-does-not-require-labeling-of-highly-refined-ingredients-from-GM-crops-if-no-modified-genetic-material-is-detectable.

6. Earl Blumenauer, "A Green New Deal Must Include Food and Farming," *Civil Eats*, January 30, 2019, accessed March 15, 2020, https://civileats.com/2019/01/30/a-green-new-deal-must-include-food-and-farming.

7. Beyond Meat website, accessed March 15, 2020, https://www.beyondmeat.com/products.

8. "Our Latino Communities Are Struggling with Hunger at a Much Higher Rate," Feeding America, accessed March 15, 2020, https://www.feedingamerica.org/hunger-in-america/latino-hunger-facts; "Hunger Hits African American Communities Harder," Feeding America, accessed March 15, 2020. https://www.feedingamerica.org/hunger-in-america/african-american.

9. "The Chef on a Mission to Bring Soulful, Healthy Food to All of Brooklyn," *New York Times*, August 7, 2019.

10. Nadra Nittle, "Bringing Fresh Produce to LA's Corner Stores Alone Won't Solve Food Inequality, but It's a Start," *Civil Eats*, August 19, 2019, accessed March 15, 2020, https://civileats.com/2019/08/19/bringing-fresh-produce-to-las-corner-stores-alone-wont-solve-food-inequality-but-its-a-start.

11. "President's FY 2021 Budget Would Increase Hunger and Poverty in America," Food Research and Action Center, February 10, 2020, accessed March 15, 2020, https://frac.org/news/presidents-fy-2021-budget-would-increase-hunger-and-poverty-in-america.

12. "Total Trump Food-Stamp Cuts Could Hit up to 5.3 Million Households," CBS News, December 10, 2019, accessed April 14, 2020, https://www.cbsnews.com/news/trump-administration-says-food-stamps-need-reform-advocates-say-millions-will-suffer.

13. For general discussions and typologies of food justice, see Robert Gottlieb and Anupama Joshi, *Food Justice* (Cambridge, MA: MIT Press, 2010); Eric Holt-Giménez, "Food Security, Food Justice, or Food Sovereignty? Crises, Food Movements, and Regime Change," in *Cultivating Food Justice: Race, Class, and Sustainability*, edited by Alison Hope Alkon and Julian Agyeman (Cambridge, MA: MIT Press, 2011), 309–330.

14. "Our Mission," HEAL Food Alliance, https://healfoodalliance.org/who-is-heal; Eric Holt-Giménez and Heidi Kleiner, "Food, Climate, and the Green New Deal: A Social Contract for Justice?" *Food First*, March 11, 2019, accessed March 15, 2020, https://foodfirst.org/publication/foodclimateandthegreennewdeal.

15. For overviews of contemporary food politics, including evaluations of their implicit biases, see Michael K. Goodman and Colin Sage, eds., *Food Transgressions: Making Sense of Contemporary Food Politics* (Farnham, UK: Ashgate, 2014); Alison Hope Alkon and Julie Guthman, eds., *The New Food Activism: Opposition, Cooperation, and Collective Action* (Berkeley: University of California Press, 2017); Carole Counihan and Valeria Siniscalchi, eds., *Food Activism: Agency, Democracy and Economy* (London: Bloomsbury, 2014); Eric Holt-Giménez, *Food Movements Unite: Strategies to Transform Our Food System* (Oakland, CA: Food First Books, 2011).

16. Without necessarily using the language of social movements, historical overviews include E. Melanie DuPuis, *Dangerous Digestion: The Politics of American Dietary Advice* (Berkeley: University of California Press, 2015); Charlotte Biltekoff, *Eating Right in America: The Cultural Politics of Food and Health* (Durham, NC: Duke University Press, 2013); Laura J. Miller, *Building Nature's Market: The Business and Politics of Natural Foods* (Chicago: University of Chicago Press, 2017); S. Margot Finn, *Discriminating Taste: How Class Anxiety Created the American Food Revolution* (New Brunswick, NJ: Rutgers University Press, 2017).

17. Classics include Mary Douglas, *Purity and Danger: An Analysis of Concepts of Pollution and Taboo* (London: Routledge and Kegan Paul, 1966); Stephen Mennell, *All*

Manners of Food: Eating and Taste in England and France from the Middle Ages to the Present (Urbana: University of Illinois Press, 1996); Jack Goody, *Cooking, Cuisine, and Class: A Study in Comparative Sociology* (Cambridge: Cambridge University Press, 1982).

18. For examples from different periods, see Biltekoff, *Eating Right in America*; Warren J. Belasco, *Appetite for Change: How the Counterculture Took on the Food Industry, 1966–1988*, 2d ed. (New York: Pantheon, 2007); Josée Johnston, Michelle Szabo, and Alexandra Rodney, "Good Food, Good People: Understanding the Cultural Repertoire of Ethical Eating," *Journal of Consumer Culture* 11, no. 3 (November 2011): 293–318.

19. This shift began in the 1980s with new social movement theory: see, e.g., Alberto Melucci, *Nomads of the Present: Social Movements and Individual Needs in Contemporary Society* (Philadelphia: Temple University Press, 1989). An important article that ratified the trend for American sociologists is Elizabeth A. Armstrong and Mary Bernstein, "Culture, Power, and Institutions: A Multi-institutional Politics Approach to Social Movements," *Sociological Theory* 26, no. 1 (March 2008): 74–99.

20. Compare John Krinsky, "Marxism and the Politics of Possibility: Beyond Academic Boundaries," in *Marxism and Social Movements*, edited by Colin Barker, Laurence Cox, John Krinsky, and Alf Gunvald (Leiden: Brill, 2013), 103–121, on bringing capitalism back into the study of social movements, including as a source of periodic crises to which movements of different kinds respond and as a force that structures the fault lines for social conflict. See also Beverly J. Silver and Sahan Savas Karatasli, "Historical Dynamics of Capitalism and Labor Movements," in *The Oxford Handbook of Social Movements*, edited by Donatella della Porta and Mario Diani (Oxford: Oxford University Press, 2015), 133–145. Work by Philip McMichael and Harriet Friedmann also attributes the changing character and distribution of food protest to the evolution of capitalist food production on a global scale: see Philip McMichael, "A Food Regime Genealogy," *Journal of Peasant Studies* 36, no. 1 (January 2009): 139–169; Harriet Friedmann, "From Colonialism to Green Capitalism: Social Movements and Emergence of Food Regimes," *Research in Rural Sociology and Development* 11 (2005): 227–264.

21. One example of such an approach applied to labor is Chris Rhomberg, *The Broken Table: The Detroit Newspaper Strike and the State of American Labor* (New York: Russell Sage Foundation, 2012). Kevin Gillan's discussion of temporal "vectors"—the elements that make up social movements—moving at their own paces and in their own directions is another way to appreciate the different time scales at play in any particular case of contentious politics: Kevin Gillan, "Temporality in Social Movement Theory: Vectors and Events in the Neoliberal Timescape," *Social Movement Studies* 19, no. 5–6 (2020): 516–536. As I show in this book, even the long haul of capitalist food production includes multiple time lines. Crises of trust, for example, are episodic and may be brief. The rise of consumer capitalism, contributing to new identities and social movement strategies, occurred more slowly but (in retrospect) with a clear direction.

22. Guido Möllering, "The Nature of Trust: From Georg Simmel to a Theory of Expectation, Interpretation and Suspension," *Sociology* 35, no. 2 (May 2001): 403–420; Torbjörn Bildtgård, "Trust in Food in Modern and Late-Modern Societies," *Social Science Information* 47, no. 1 (March 2008): 99–128.

23. I am especially indebted to the work of Kjaernes for this line of argument: Unni Kjaernes, "Risk and Trust in the Food Supply," in *The Handbook of Food Research*, edited by Anne Murcott, Warren Belasco, and Peter Jackson (London: Bloomsbury, 2013), 410–424; Unni Kjaernes, Mark Harvey, and Alan Warde, *Trust in Food: A Comparative and Institutional Analysis* (Basingstoke, UK: Palgrave Macmillan, 2007). See also the

essays in Christopher Ansell and David Vogel, eds., *What's the Beef? The Contested Governance of European Food Safety* (Cambridge, MA: MIT Press, 2006); Martin Thorsøe and Chris Kjeldsen, "The Constitution of Trust: Function, Configuration and Generation of Trust in Alternative Food Networks," *Sociologia Ruralis* 56, no. 2 (April 2016): 157–175; Roberta Sassatelli and Alan Scott, "Novel Food, New Markets and Trust Regimes: Responses to the Erosion of Consumers' Confidence in Austria, Italy and the UK," *European Societies* 3, no. 2 (June 2001): 213–244.

24. It is difficult to document ordinary consumers' trust in food before the era of polling. I rely mostly on the commentary of movement leaders and its apparent resonance with their followers. Anger can also quickly develop about food prices, in some cases leading to consumer boycotts or even riots. In the United States, these have tended to occur during periods of wartime stringency and have rarely involved larger critiques of the food system. See William Frieburger, "War Prosperity and Hunger: The New York Food Riots of 1917," *Labor History* 25, no. 2 (Spring 1984): 217–239; Dana Frank, "Housewives, Socialists, and the Politics of Food: The 1917 New York Cost-of-Living Protests," *Feminist Studies* 11, no. 2 (Summer 1985): 255–285; Barbara Clark Smith, "Food Rioters and the American Revolution," *William and Mary Quarterly* 51, no. 1 (January 1994): 3–38; Alan Pell Crawford, "Richmond's Bread Riot," *American History* 37, no. 2 (June 2002): 20–26. For a well-documented study of a single food—milk—see Daniel R. Block, "Protecting and Connecting: Separation, Connection, and the U.S. Dairy Economy 1840–2002," *Journal for the Study of Food and Society* 6, no. 1 (Winter 2002): 22–30.

25. For different ways of connecting the food system to anxieties about food, see Peter Jackson, *Anxious Appetites: Food and Consumer Culture* (London: Bloomsbury Academic, 2015); Frans van Waarden, "Taste, Traditions, and Transactions: The Public and Private Regulation of Food," in Ansell and Vogel, *What's the Beef?*, 35–59. The dynamics of a capitalist food system *also* involve such things as the deskilling and exploitation of labor, and that, too, has periodically sparked protest. But for the most part it has not led to *consumer* protest. Thus, in my account references to food workers are limited to noting their rarity in past food movements, either as allies or as beneficiaries of consumer action.

26. Or as sociologists say, they are socially constructed: Doug McAdam, John D. McCarthy, and Mayer N. Zald, eds., *Comparative Perspectives on Social Movements: Political Opportunities, Mobilizing Structures, and Cultural Framings* (Cambridge: Cambridge University Press, 1996).

27. Kjaernes et al., *Trust in Food*, provides comparative evidence from Western Europe for broader patterns of institutional trust and confidence in food.

28. Gabriella M. Petrick, "'Purity as Life': H. J. Heinz, Religious Sentiment, and the Beginning of the Industrial Diet," *History and Technology* 27, no. 1 (March 2011): 37–64; Miller, *Building Nature's Market*. One dairyman, in a newspaper ad in 1838, called attention to urban breweries that might use the cheap residues from distilling operations. For his own "Pure Country Milk," by contrast, he fed his cows "nothing of the swill kind": *New York Evangelist*, December 29, 1838.

29. Such advocacy groups are not themselves businesses, but their claims may be used by competitors.

30. DuPuis, *Dangerous Digestion*. On persistent worries about overstepping "natural" limits, see also Warren Belasco, "Food, Morality and Social Reform," in *Morality and Health*, edited by Allan Brandt and Paul Rozin (New York: Routledge, 1997), 185–200.

31. This general approach of exploring how cultural scripts are transposed by activists to frame problems and formulate goals has been applied to other social movements, including labor (Marc W. Steinberg, *Fighting Words: Working-Class Formation, Collective Action, and Discourse in Early Nineteenth-Century England* [Ithaca, NY: Cornell University Press, 1999]), political reform (Elisabeth S. Clemens, *The People's Lobby: Organizational Innovation and the Rise of Interest Group Politics in the United States, 1890–1925* [Chicago: University of Chicago Press, 1997]), and business mobilization (Jeffrey Haydu, *Citizen Employers: Business Communities and Labor in Cincinnati and San Francisco, 1870–1916* [Ithaca, NY: Cornell University Press, 2008]). In the following account, I emphasize *other* social movements on which food activists piggybacked as the source of protest models.

32. Doug McAdam, Sidney Tarrow, and Charles Tilly, *Dynamics of Contention* (New York: Cambridge University Press, 2001).

33. Compare Joseph R. Gusfield, "Social Movements and Social Change: Perspectives of Linearity and Fluidity," *Research in Social Movements, Conflicts and Change* 4 (1981): 317–339, on how activist communities may be nested within larger movements of cultural change.

34. Excellent studies that reflect on the role of prior outcomes in shaping later periods include John Walton, *Western Times and Water Wars: State, Culture, and Rebellion in California* (Berkeley: University of California Press, 1992) and Chris Rhomberg, *No There There: Race, Class, and Political Community in Oakland* (Berkeley: University of California Press, 2004), on protest movements; Chad Alan Goldberg, *Citizens and Paupers: Relief, Rights, and Race, from the Freedmen's Bureau to Workfare* (Chicago: University of Chicago Press, 2007), on welfare policy; and John Krinsky, "Neoliberal Times: Intersecting Temporalities and the Neoliberalization of New York City's Public-Sector Labor Relations," *Social Science History* 35, no. 3 (Fall 2011): 381–422, on municipal governance.

35. Daniel Block traces a similar dynamic in the milk industry. Moving milking away from suspect urban dairies led, down the historical line, to new worries over the anonymous products of large, distant farms. "The solutions found by one generation often led, at least partially, to the anxieties of the next": Block, "Protecting and Connecting," 23.

36. Excellent examples include Sewell on "corporate" solidarity and Traugott on the barricade in Parisian history. William H. Sewell Jr., *Work and Revolution in France: The Language of Labor from the Old Regime to 1848* (Cambridge: Cambridge University Press, 1980); Mark Traugott, *The Insurgent Barricade* (Berkeley: University of California Press, 2010).

37. Sidney Tarrow, *The Language of Contention: Revolutions in Words, 1688–2012* (New York: Cambridge University Press, 2013). For an earlier discussion of the "vocabularies" that constitute "one of the residues of movements," see Gusfield, "Social Movements and Social Change," 325.

38. Lawrence B. Glickman, *Buying Power: A History of Consumer Activism in America* (Chicago: University of Chicago Press, 2009).

39. Doug McAdam and Dieter Rucht, "The Cross-National Diffusion of Movement Ideas," *Annals of the American Academy of Political and Social Science* 528 (July 1993): 56–74; Sidney Tarrow and Doug McAdam, "Scale Shift in Transnational Contention," in *Transnational Protest and Global Activism*, edited by Donatella della Porta and Sidney Tarrow (Lanham, MD: Rowman and Littlefield, 2005), 121–147.

40. Unusually careful documentation of these transmission belts for popular discourse can be found in Walton's account of the Owens Valley water wars across several

generations and Traugott's study of barricade building over several centuries. Both include such mechanisms as popular novels and movies. Walton, *Western Times and Water Wars*; Traugott, *The Insurgent Barricade*.

41. This example more closely approximates Taylor's "abeyance structures" than other legacies discussed in this book. Verta Taylor, "Social Movement Continuity: The Women's Movement in Abeyance," *American Sociological Review* 54, no. 5 (October 1989): 761–775.

CHAPTER 2

1. *Graham Journal of Health and Longevity*, May 16, 1837, 52, May 2, 1837, 38, May 9, 1837, 48.

2. *Graham Journal of Health and Longevity*, April 4, 1837, 4.

3. Surveys include David Strang and Sarah A. Soule, "Diffusion in Organizations and Social Movements: From Hybrid Corn to Poison Pills," *Annual Review of Sociology* 24 (1998): 265–290; Nancy Whittier, "The Consequences of Social Movements for Each Other," in *The Blackwell Companion to Social Movements*, edited by David Snow, Sarah A. Soule, and Hanspeter Kriesi (Malden, MA: Blackwell, 2004), 531–551; Sarah A. Soule, "Diffusion Processes within and across Movements," in Snow et al., *The Blackwell Companion to Social Movements*, 294–310; Rebecca Kolins Givan, Kenneth M. Roberts, and Sarah A. Soule, eds., *The Diffusion of Social Movements: Actors, Mechanisms, and Political Effects* (Cambridge: Cambridge University Press, 2010); Donatella della Porta and Alice Mattoni, eds., *Spreading Protest: Social Movements in Times of Crisis* (Colchester, UK: ECPR, 2014).

4. Doug McAdam, Sidney Tarrow, and Charles Tilly, *Dynamics of Contention* (New York: Cambridge University Press, 2001); Charles Tilly and Sidney Tarrow, *Contentious Politics* (Boulder, CO: Paradigm, 2007).

5. U.S. Census Bureau, *Historical Statistics of the United States, Colonial Times to 1970* (Washington, DC: U.S. Department of Commerce, Bureau of the Census, 1975), series D 167–81, K 240–50, X 420–23.

6. John F. Kasson, *Rudeness and Civility: Manners in Nineteenth-Century Urban America* (New York: Hill and Wang, 1990), 21; Bruce Laurie, *Working People of Philadelphia, 1800–1850* (Philadelphia: Temple University Press, 1980), 9.

7. Surveys include Clarence H. Danhof, *Change in Agriculture: The Northern United States, 1820–1870* (Cambridge, MA: Harvard University Press, 1969); R. Douglas Hurt, *American Agriculture: A Brief History* (West Lafayette, IN: Purdue University Press, 2002).

8. Sarah F. McMahon, "A Comfortable Subsistence: The Changing Composition of Diet in Rural New England, 1620–1840," *William and Mary Quarterly* 42, no. 1 (January 1985): 25–65.

9. Much food *processing* (e.g., canning, pickling) was not yet widely commodified.

10. Cindy R. Lobel, "Consuming Classes: Changing Food Consumption Patterns in New York City, 1790–1860," Ph.D. diss. (City University of New York, 2003).

11. Courtney Fullilove, "The Price of Bread: The New York City Flour Riot and the Paradox of Capitalist Food Systems," *Radical History Review*, no. 118 (Winter 2014): 15–41.

12. Daniel R. Block, "Protecting and Connecting: Separation, Connection, and the U.S. Dairy Economy 1840–2002," *Journal for the Study of Food and Society* 6, no. 1

(Winter): 22–30; Michael Egan, "Organizing Protest in the Changing City: Swill Milk and Social Activism in New York City, 1842–1864," *New York History* 86, no. 3 (Summer 2005): 205–225.

13. *Graham Journal of Health and Longevity*, September 15, 1838, 289.

14. William A. Alcott, ed., *The Moral Reformer and Teacher on the Human Constitution* (Boston: Light and Horton, 1835–1836), vol. 1, 208.

15. "Public Letter from New York City Physicians," *New York Evangelist*, August 18, 1838, 9.

16. "Advertisement," *New York Evangelist*, December 29, 1838.

17. *Graham Journal of Health and Longevity*, September 15, 1838, 289.

18. Roger Horowitz, "The Politics of Meat Shopping in Antebellum New York City," in *Meat, Modernity, and the Rise of the Slaughterhouse*, edited by Paula Young Lee (Durham: University of New Hampshire Press, 2008), 167–177; Roger Horowitz, *Putting Meat on the American Table: Taste, Technology, Transformation* (Baltimore: Johns Hopkins University Press, 2006).

19. Gergely Baics, "Feeding Gotham: A Social History of Urban Provisioning, 1780–1860," Ph.D. diss. (Northwestern University, Evanston, IL, 2009); Horowitz, "The Politics of Meat Shopping in Antebellum New York City"; Helen Tangires, *Public Markets and Civic Culture in Nineteenth-Century America* (Baltimore: Johns Hopkins University Press, 2003).

20. Hurt, *American Agriculture*; Fullilove, "The Price of Bread."

21. *Poughkeepsie Casket*, September 8, 1838, 85.

22. In the United States as a whole, homemade bread still accounted for more than 90 percent of consumption as late as 1890. Aaron Bobrow-Strain, *White Bread: A Social History of the Store-Bought Loaf* (Boston: Beacon, 2012), 20. But in the larger northeastern cities where Grahamites flourished, commercial bakeries were already more numerous in the 1830s (and in Boston, owners were organizing counterprotests against Graham). As with other moral panics, their threat was symbolic as well as real, and observers seized on the most alarming anecdotes of baking conditions and methods. On moral panics, see Erich Goode and Nachman Ben-Yehuda, *Moral Panics: The Social Construction of Deviance* (Cambridge, MA: Blackwell, 1994).

23. *Masonic Mirror*, October 22, 1825, 2.

24. *Zion's Herald*, August 3, 1836, 123.

25. Sean Wilentz, *Chants Democratic: New York City and the Rise of the American Working Class, 1788–1850* (New York: Oxford University Press, 1984), 139–140, 232; Alcott, *The Moral Reformer and Teacher on the Human Constitution*, vol. 1, 173.

26. The most important exception is the long history of "food riots." For the United States, see Barbara Clark Smith, "Food Rioters and the American Revolution," *William and Mary Quarterly* 51, no. 1 (January 1994): 3–38.

27. Charles Sellers, *The Market Revolution: Jacksonian America, 1815–1846* (New York: Oxford University Press, 1991); Melvyn Stokes and Stephen Conway, eds., *The Market Revolution in America: Social, Political, and Religious Expressions, 1800–1880* (Charlottesville: University Press of Virginia, 1996).

28. The following brief survey draws on Wilentz, *Chants Democratic*; Laurie, *Working People of Philadelphia*.

29. This was a stratum quite different from the technical and managerial wage labor of the late twentieth century—more entrepreneurial, less credentialed, more dispersed among small businesses. For the early nineteenth-century U.S. middle class, the best

source is Stuart M. Blumin, *The Emergence of the Middle Class: Social Experience in the American City, 1760–1900* (Cambridge: Cambridge University Press, 1989). See also Burton J. Bledstein and Robert D. Johnston, eds., *The Middling Sorts: Explorations in the History of the American Middle Class* (New York: Routledge, 2001); Melanie Archer and Judith R. Blau, "Class Formation in Nineteenth-Century America: The Case of the Middle Class," *Annual Review of Sociology* 19 (1993): 17–41.

30. Sven Beckert, "Propertied of a Different Kind: Bourgeoisie and Lower Middle Class in the Nineteenth-Century United States," in Bledstein and Johnston, *The Middling Sorts*, 285–95.

31. Karen Halttunen, *Confidence Men and Painted Women: A Study of Middle-Class Culture in America, 1830–1870* (New Haven, CT: Yale University Press, 1982); Kasson, *Rudeness and Civility*; Rodney Hessinger, *Seduced, Abandoned, and Reborn: Visions of Youth in Middle-Class America, 1780–1850* (Philadelphia: University of Pennsylvania Press, 2005).

32. Wilentz, *Chants Democratic*; Steven J. Ross, *Workers on the Edge: Work, Leisure, and Politics in Industrializing Cincinnati, 1788–1890* (New York: Columbia University Press, 1985); William F. Hartford, *Money, Morals, and Politics: Massachusetts in the Age of the Boston Associates* (Boston: Northeastern University Press, 2001).

33. Marvin Meyers, *The Jacksonian Persuasion: Politics and Belief* (Stanford, CA: Stanford University Press, 1960).

34. Linda Young, *Middle-Class Culture in the Nineteenth Century: America, Australia, and Britain* (Houndmills, UK: Palgrave, 2003); Blumin, *The Emergence of the Middle Class*; Paul Boyer, *Urban Masses and Moral Order in America, 1820–1920* (Cambridge, MA: Harvard University Press, 1978).

35. Stephen P. Rice, *Minding the Machine: Languages of Class in Early Industrial America* (Berkeley: University of California Press, 2004); Blumin, *The Emergence of the Middle Class*.

36. Blumin, *The Emergence of the Middle Class*.

37. Richard L. Bushman, *The Refinement of America: Persons, Houses, Cities* (New York: Vintage, 1992); Mary P. Ryan, *Cradle of the Middle Class: The Family in Oneida County, New York, 1790–1865* (New York: Cambridge University Press, 1981).

38. Kathleen D. McCarthy, *American Creed: Philanthropy and the Rise of Civil Society, 1700–1865* (Chicago: University of Chicago Press, 2003); Timothy R. Mahoney, *Provincial Lives: Middle-Class Experience in the Antebellum Middle West* (Cambridge: Cambridge University Press, 1999).

39. Blumin, *The Emergence of the Middle Class*.

40. Mark A. Noll, *America's God: From Jonathan Edwards to Abraham Lincoln* (New York: Oxford University Press, 2002).

41. Nathan O. Hatch, *The Democratization of American Christianity* (New Haven, CT: Yale University Press, 1989); Ronald G. Walters, *American Reformers, 1815–1860*, rev. ed. (New York: Hill and Wang, 1997); Frances FitzGerald, *The Evangelicals: The Struggle to Shape America* (New York: Simon and Schuster, 2017).

42. Ryan, *Cradle of the Middle Class*; Paul E. Johnson, *A Shopkeeper's Millennium: Society and Revivals in Rochester, New York, 1815–1837* (New York: Hill and Wang, 1978); John S. Gilkeson Jr., *Middle-Class Providence, 1820–1940* (Princeton, NJ: Princeton University Press, 1986).

43. Anthony F. C. Wallace, *Rockdale: The Growth of an American Village in the Early Industrial Revolution* (New York: W. W. Norton, 1972); Paul Faler, "Cultural Aspects of

the Industrial Revolution: Lynn, Massachusetts Shoemakers and Industrial Morality, 1826–1860," *Labor History* 15, no. 3 (Summer, 1974): 367–394; Boyer, *Urban Masses and Moral Order in America*.

44. The following overview draws especially on Johnson, *A Shopkeeper's Millennium*; Hatch, *The Democratization of American Christianity*; Walters, *American Reformers*; Michael P. Young, *Bearing Witness against Sin: The Evangelical Birth of the American Social Movement* (Chicago: University of Chicago Press, 2006).

45. Doug McAdam, *Political Process and the Development of Black Insurgency, 1930–1970* (Chicago: University of Chicago Press, 1982).

46. Ryan, *Cradle of the Middle Class*; Sellers, *The Market Revolution*; Young, *Bearing Witness against Sin*; Scott C. Martin, *Devil of the Domestic Sphere: Temperance, Gender, and Middle-Class Ideology, 1800–1860* (DeKalb, IL: Northern Illinois University Press, 2008).

47. Joseph R. Gusfield, *Symbolic Crusade: Status Politics and the American Temperance Movement* (Urbana: University of Illinois Press, 1963); Paul E. Johnson, "Drinking, Temperance and the Construction of Identity in Nineteenth-Century America," *Social Science Information* 25, no. 2 (June 1986): 521–530; Holly Berkley Fletcher, *Gender and the American Temperance Movement of the Nineteenth Century* (New York: Routledge, 2008).

48. Johnson, *A Shopkeeper's Millennium*, 8.

49. Ibid. Johnson's study of Rochester finds that it was particularly those employers who had abandoned traditional ties and obligations to their workforce who were most likely to participate in temperance advocacy.

50. The best book on the Grahamites is Stephen Nissenbaum, *Sex, Diet, and Debility in Jacksonian America: Sylvester Graham and Health Reform* (Westport, CT: Greenwood, 1980). The following account also draws on James C. Whorton, *Crusaders for Fitness: The History of American Health Reformers* (Princeton, NJ: Princeton University Press, 1982); Jayme A. Sokolow, *Eros and Modernization: Sylvester Graham, Health Reform, and the Origins of Victorian Sexuality in America* (Rutherford, NJ: Fairleigh Dickinson University Press, 1983); Edith Walters Cole, "Sylvester Graham, Lecturer on the Science of Human Life: The Rhetoric of a Dietary Reformer," Ph.D. diss. (Indiana University, Bloomington, 1975).

51. *Graham Journal of Health and Longevity*, May 2, 1837, 38.

52. Sylvester Graham, *Lectures on the Science of Human Life* (Boston: Marsh, Capen, Lyon and Webb, 1839), 1:539.

53. Ibid., 2:419.

54. Alcott, *The Moral Reformer and Teacher on the Human Constitution*, vol. 1, 173.

55. Graham, *Lectures on the Science of Human Life*, 2:18–19; Sylvester Graham, *The Aesculapian Tablets of the Nineteenth Century* (Providence, RI: Weeden and Cory, 1834), vi.

56. Graham, *Lectures on the Science of Human Life*, 1:20.

57. Ibid., 1:24.

58. Arthur Foote, ed., *A Defence of the Graham System of Living, or, Remarks on Diet and Regimen: Dedicated to the Rising Generation* (New York: W. Applegate, 1835), 29.

59. Graham, *Lectures on the Science of Human Life*, 1:420–421.

60. Graham, *The Aesculapian Tablets of the Nineteenth Century*, vii; Graham, *Lectures on the Science of Human Life*, 2:403–404, 537.

61. Graham, *The Aesculapian Tablets of the Nineteenth Century*, 14, original punctuation.

62. *Graham Journal of Health and Longevity*, January 8, 1839, 108.

63. Sylvester Graham, *A Lecture to Young Men on Chastity* (Boston: Light and Stearns, Crocker and Brewster, 1838), 40.

64. Graham, *Lectures on the Science of Human Life*, 2:339–340, 352–353.

65. Ibid., 2:353–354.

66. Foote, *A Defence of the Graham System of Living*, 13.

67. Quoted in William B. Walker, "The Health Reform Movement in the United States, 1830–1870," Ph.D. diss. (Johns Hopkins University, Baltimore, 1955), 122–123.

68. Graham, *Lectures on the Science of Human Life*, 2:18.

69. Ibid., 2:421.

70. Ibid., 2:449.

71. Ibid., 2:455.

72. *Graham Journal of Health and Longevity*, May 16, 1837, 52.

73. Graham, *Lectures on the Science of Human Life*, 2:648.

74. Alcott, *The Moral Reformer and Teacher on the Human Constitution*, vol. 1, 65–66; Foote, *A Defence of the Graham System of Living*; Graham, *Lectures on the Science of Human Life*, 1:28–29.

75. Graham, *The Aesculapian Tablets of the Nineteenth Century*, 33.

76. Foote, *A Defence of the Graham System of Living*, 4.

77. Graham, *Lectures on the Science of Human Life*, 2: 537–538.

78. Mary Mann, a Grahamite cookbook author, may have been more realistic about feeding people than was Graham. While agreeing that "we are not to gratify our ignoble appetites, but to build up purely and devoutly those temples of the Holy Spirit which our bodies were designed to be," and threatening a dyspeptic hell for dietary sinners, she also offered diners hope for salvation, and here on earth. By carefully substituting inoffensive ingredients for unhealthy ones, cooks can ensure that "Christian lovers of pastry need not think their gastronomic pleasures at an end." Quoted in Sidonia C. Taupin, "Christianity in the Kitchen, or a Moral Guide for Gourmets," *American Quarterly* 15, no. 1 (Spring 1963): 86–87.

79. Graham, *Lectures on the Science of Human Life*, 1:505.

80. Graham, *The Aesculapian Tablets of the Nineteenth Century*, vii.

81. Graham, *Lectures on the Science of Human Life*, 2:33.

82. William A. Alcott, *Forty Years in the Wilderness of Pills and Powders; or, The Cogitations and Confessions of an Aged Physician* (Boston: J. P. Jewett, 1859), 378.

83. Graham, *The Aesculapian Tablets of the Nineteenth Century*, iv.

84. *Graham Journal of Health and Longevity*, March 30, 1839, 116.

85. Graham, *The Aesculapian Tablets of the Nineteenth Century*, 18.

86. Ibid., 27.

87. Ibid., 45.

88. American Physiological Society, *Constitution of the American Physiological Society.* (Boston: Marsh, 1837), 3–4.

89. *A Lecture to Young Men* went through fifteen editions over ten years; the book version of Graham's popular *Lectures on the Science of Human Life* was a flop. Sokolow, *Eros and Modernization*, 167.

90. Sokolow, *Eros and Modernization*, 71.

91. *Providence Patriot*, November 22, 1834, 2.

92. William A. Alcott, ed., *The Library of Health and Teacher on the Human Constitution* (Boston: George W. Light, 1837–1842), vol. 3, 72; Sokolow, *Eros and Modernization*, 147, 150–151; Nissenbaum, *Sex, Diet, and Debility in Jacksonian America*.

93. *Graham Journal of Health and Longevity*, June 22, 1839, 202.

94. Ibid., January 19, 1839, 40.

95. Walker, "The Health Reform Movement in the United States," 139–140.

96. *Graham Journal of Health and Longevity*, April 18, 1837, 24.

97. Ibid., May 9, 1837, 48; Sokolow, *Eros and Modernization*, 48; Cole, "Sylvester Graham," 225, 235.

98. Andrew F. Smith, *Eating History: 30 Turning Points in the Making of American Cuisine* (New York: Columbia University Press, 2009), 33–34; Taupin, "Christianity in the Kitchen," 86.

99. Nissenbaum, *Sex, Diet, and Debility in Jacksonian America*, 143–144.

100. Nicolas Larchet, "Food Reform Movements," in *The Oxford Encyclopedia of Food and Drink in America*, edited by Andrew F. Smith (New York: Oxford University Press, 2012), 796–805.

101. On earlier food riots, see Thomas S. Wermuth, "'The Women! in This Place Have Risen in a Mob': Women Rioters and the American Revolution in the Hudson River Valley," *Hudson River Valley Review* 20, no. 1 (Summer 2003): 65–71; Smith, "Food Rioters and the American Revolution." On locavores, see Laura B. DeLind and Anne E. Ferguson, "Is This a Women's Movement? The Relationship of Gender to Community-Supported Agriculture in Michigan," *Human Organization* 58, no. 2 (Summer 1999): 190–200; Cynthia Abbott Cone and Andrea Myhre, "Community-Supported Agriculture: A Sustainable Alternative to Industrial Agriculture?" *Human Organization* 59, no. 2 (Summer 2000): 187–197.

102. The theme dominates Marxist accounts such as Sellers, *The Market Revolution*, and more cultural interpretations such as Halttunen, *Confidence Men and Painted Women*.

103. Nissenbaum, *Sex, Diet, and Debility in Jacksonian America*, 127.

104. Halttunen, *Confidence Men and Painted Women*.

105. Graham, *The Aesculapian Tablets of the Nineteenth Century*, xi.

106. Martin Cornelius Van Buren, "The Indispensable God of Health: A Study of Republican Hygiene and the Ideology of William Alcott," Ph.D. diss. (University of California, Los Angeles, 1977), 216.

107. Quoted in Ann Douglas, *The Feminization of American Culture* (New York: Knopf, 1977), 52. See also Nancy F. Cott, *The Bonds of Womanhood: "Woman's Sphere" in New England, 1780–1835* (New Haven, CT: Yale University Press, 1977).

108. *Graham Journal of Health and Longevity*, August 3, 1839, 250.

109. Gusfield, *Symbolic Crusade*, 50; Johnson, "Drinking, Temperance and the Construction of Identity in Nineteenth-Century America."

110. Graham, *Lectures on the Science of Human Life*, 2:460.

111. *Graham Journal of Health and Longevity*, November 23, 1839, 392.

112. Alcott, *The Library of Health and Teacher on the Human Constitution*, vol. 2, 162–163.

113. On the growing popularity of parlors and pianos as badges of middle-class respectability, see Bushman, *The Refinement of America*; Kasson, *Rudeness and Civility*. Alcott, less exclusively focused on diet than Graham, made practical and healthful clothing another marker of social distinction from the tyranny of fashion. He reported, with approval, a Utica Maternal Association resolution indicting dress that was "injurious to health" and going on to complain that "fashion and custom became to us what caste is in India . . . [and have a] pernicious influence on the community." Alcott, *The Moral Reformer and Teacher on the Human Constitution*, vol. 1, 65–66.

114. Van Buren, "The Indispensable God of Health," 161–163.

115. Alcott, *The Library of Health and Teacher on the Human Constitution*, 1:134.

116. Walters, *American Reformers*, 103; Thomas H. LeDuc, "Grahamites and Garrisonites," *New York History* 20, no. 2 (April 1939): 189–191.

117. Graham, *The Aesculapian Tablets of the Nineteenth Century*, 19.

118. Ibid., 45.

119. Ibid., 16.

120. Ibid., 87; Walters, *American Reformers*, 148.

121. Walters, *American Reformers*; Young, *Bearing Witness against Sin*.

122. *Graham Journal of Health and Longevity*, January 19, 1839, 25. Dietary evangelists' challenge to mainstream medical authority would also appear in a range of alternative health movements of the time, including water cures, homeopathy, and botanics: Walker, "The Health Reform Movement in the United States, 1830–1870," 19; Sokolow, *Eros and Modernization*, 110.

123. Young, *Bearing Witness against Sin*.

124. In the temperance crusade, the move toward more coercive approaches to limiting alcohol consumption mostly came after the 1830s. The closest Grahamites seem to have come to involving the state was a (failed) effort in 1839 to have the Massachusetts legislature authorize an infirmary where care for the sick could be provided according to Graham's principles: *Graham Journal of Health and Longevity*, March 30, 1839, 116.

125. Lawrence B. Glickman, "'Buy for the Sake of the Slave': Abolitionism and the Origins of American Consumer Activism," *American Quarterly* 56, no. 4 (December 2004): 889–912; Carol Faulkner, "The Root of the Evil: Free Produce and Radical Antislavery, 1820–1860," *Journal of the Early Republic* 27, no. 3 (Fall 2007): 377–405.

126. For one survey, see Steven Shapin, "'You Are What You Eat': Historical Changes in Ideas about Food and Identity," *Historical Research* 87, no. 237 (August 2014): 377–392.

127. Walters, *American Reformers*, 148.

CHAPTER 3

1. National Pure Food and Drug Congress, *Journal of Proceedings of the National Pure Food and Drug Congress Held in Columbian University Hall, Washington, D.C., March 2, 3, 4, and 5, 1898* (Washington, DC: n.p., 1898), 4.

2. *New England Kitchen*, November 1894, 186. The full title of the publication was *New England Kitchen Magazine: A Monthly Journal of Domestic Science*.

3. *American Kitchen*, March 1900, 206.

4. The changes included such things as a trend toward more peaceful protest and modular tactics. See Charles Tilly, *Contentious Performances* (New York: Cambridge University Press, 2008); Charles Tilly, *Popular Contention in Great Britain 1758–1834* (Cambridge, MA: Harvard University Press, 1995). Other examples of this aggregating approach include work on patterns of diffusion (Dan Wang and Sarah Soule, "Social Movement Organizational Collaboration: Networks of Learning and the Diffusion of Protest Tactics, 1960–1995," *American Journal of Sociology* 117, no. 6 [December 2012]: 1674–1722); the routinization of protest (Doug McAdam, Robert J. Sampson, Simon Weffer, and Heather MacIndoe, "'There Will Be Fighting in the Streets': The Distorting Lens of Social Movement Theory," *Mobilization* 10, no. 1 [February 2005]: 1–18); and the general drift toward a "movement society" (Sarah A. Soule and Jennifer Earl,

"A Movement Society Evaluated: Collective Protest in the United States, 1960–1986," *Mobilization* 10, no. 3 [October 2005]: 345–364).

5. Alberto Melucci, *Challenging Codes: Collective Action in the Information Age* (Cambridge: Cambridge University Press, 1996); Manuel Castells, *The Power of Identity* (Malden, MA: Blackwell, 1997).

6. Roger Horowitz, *Putting Meat on the American Table: Taste, Technology, Transformation* (Baltimore: Johns Hopkins University Press, 2006); William Cronon, *Nature's Metropolis: Chicago and the Great West* (New York: W. W. Norton, 1991).

7. Aaron Bobrow-Strain, *White Bread: A Social History of the Store-Bought Loaf* (Boston: Beacon, 2012), 20, 55.

8. Katherine Leonard Turner, *How the Other Half Ate: A History of Working-Class Meals at the Turn of the Century* (Berkeley: University of California Press, 2014); Robert Dirks, *Food in the Gilded Age: What Ordinary Americans Ate* (Lanham, MD: Rowman and Littlefield, 2016).

9. Mark William Wilde, "Industrialization of Food Processing in the United States, 1860–1960," Ph.D. diss. (University of Delaware, Newark, 1988), 245. For another survey, see Bruce Kraig, *A Rich and Fertile Land: A History of Food in America* (London: Reaktion, 2017).

10. Wilde, "Industrialization of Food Processing"; Turner, *How the Other Half Ate*; Anna Zeide, *Canned: The Rise and Fall of Consumer Confidence in the American Food Industry* (Berkeley: University of California Press, 2018).

11. Lorine Swainston Goodwin, *The Pure Food, Drink, and Drug Crusaders, 1879–1914* (Jefferson, NC: McFarland, 1999), 43.

12. Waverly Root and Richard de Rochemont, *Eating in America: A History* (New York: Ecco, 1981); Ann Vileisis, *Kitchen Literacy: How We Lost Knowledge of Where Food Comes from and Why We Need to Get It Back* (Washington, DC: Island Press/Shearwater, 2008); Gabriella M. Petrick, "'Purity as Life': H. J. Heinz, Religious Sentiment, and the Beginning of the Industrial Diet," *History and Technology* 27, no. 1 (March 2011): 37–64.

13. These products were especially easy to recognize because of another trend underway in this period. From crop monocultures in agriculture to mass production in food processing, there was a growing uniformity in what Americans ate. See Paul Freedman, *American Cuisine: And How It Got This Way* (New York: Liveright, 2019). This homogenization of food was not a target for Progressive Era food reformers, however.

14. Jean-Louis Flandrin and Massimo Montanari, *Food: A Culinary History from Antiquity to the Present* (New York: Columbia University Press, 1999); Margaret Visser, *The Rituals of Dinner: The Origins, Evolution, Eccentricities, and Meaning of Table Manners* (New York: Grove Weidenfeld, 1991); James Harvey Young, *Pure Food: Securing the Federal Food and Drugs Act of 1906* (Princeton, NJ: Princeton University Press, 1989).

15. Suzanne White Junod, "Food Standards in the United States: The Case of the Peanut Butter and Jelly Sandwich," in *Food, Science, Policy, and Regulation in the Twentieth Century: International and Comparative Perspectives*, edited by David F. Smith and Jim Phillips (London: Routledge, 2000), 167–188; Gabriella M. Petrick, "The Arbiters of Taste: Producers, Consumers and the Industrialization of Taste in America, 1900–1960," Ph.D. diss. (University of Delaware, Newark, 2006); Adam D. Shprintzen, "Looks like Meat, Smells like Meat, Tastes like Meat: Battle Creek, Protose and the Making of Modern American Vegetarianism," *Food, Culture and Society* 15, no. 1 (March 2012): 113–128.

16. *Good Housekeeping*, February 1907, 189.

17. *New England Kitchen*, December 1894, 241.

18. Katherine Leonard Turner, "Buying, Not Cooking," *Food, Culture and Society* 9, no. 1 (Spring 2006): 13–39.

19. General Federation of Women's Clubs, *Proceedings of the Biennial Meetings*, 8th Biennial Meeting, 1906, 170.

20. Harvey Levenstein, *Revolution at the Table: The Transformation of the American Diet* (Berkeley: University of California Press, 2003); Tracey Deutsch, *Building a Housewife's Paradise: Gender, Politics, and American Grocery Stores in the Twentieth Century* (Chapel Hill: University of North Carolina Press, 2010).

21. Vileisis, *Kitchen Literacy*.

22. *New England Kitchen*, December 1894, 243.

23. Susan Strasser, *Never Done: A History of American Housework* (New York: Pantheon, 1982); Susan Strasser, *Satisfaction Guaranteed: The Making of the American Mass Market* (New York: Pantheon Books, 1989); Ellen Gruber Garvey, *The Adman in the Parlor: Magazines and the Gendering of Consumer Culture, 1880s to 1910s* (New York: Oxford University Press, 1996); Maureen A. Flanagan, *America Reformed: Progressives and Progressivisms, 1890s–1920s* (New York: Oxford University Press, 2007); Lawrence B. Glickman, *Buying Power: A History of Consumer Activism in America* (Chicago: University of Chicago Press).

24. Deutsch, *Building a Housewife's Paradise*; Turner, *How the Other Half Ate*.

25. Strasser, *Never Done*; Vileisis, *Kitchen Literacy*.

26. General Federation of Women's Clubs, *Proceedings of the Biennial Meetings*, 8th Biennial Meeting, 1906, 171.

27. For comparative perspectives on this era of food regulation, see Ilyse D. Barkan, "Industry Invites Regulation: The Passage of the Pure Food and Drug Act of 1906," *American Journal of Public Health* 75, no. 1 (January 1985): 18–26; Madeleine Ferrières, *Sacred Cow, Mad Cow: A History of Food Fears* (New York: Columbia University Press, 2006); Uwe Spiekermann, "Redefining Food: The Standardization of Products and Production in Europe and the United States, 1880–1914," *History and Technology* 27, no. 1 (March 2011): 11–36; Unni Kjaernes, "Risk and Trust in the Food Supply," in *The Handbook of Food Research*, edited by Anne Murcott, Warren Belasco, and Peter Jackson (London: Bloomsbury, 2013), 410–424.

28. *Good Health*, January 1883.

29. *Good Housekeeping*, January 4, 1890, 105.

30. Quoted in Young, *Pure Food*, 75.

31. *Good Housekeeping*, April 1913, 540.

32. Goodwin, *The Pure Food, Drink, and Drug Crusaders*, 43, quoting from New York's *Evening Post*.

33. Strasser, *Never Done*, 243; Vileisis, *Kitchen Literacy*.

34. For women in the workforce, added worry came from having to rely on suspect milk for their infants: Flanagan, *America Reformed*, 47.

35. Ellen H. Richards, *Food Materials and Their Adulterations* (Boston: Home Science, 1898), 8–10.

36. *New England Kitchen*, December 1894, 243.

37. Nancy Tomes, *The Gospel of Germs: Men, Women, and the Microbe in American Life* (Cambridge, MA: Harvard University Press, 1998).

38. *Good Health*, March 1882; Petrick, "The Arbiters of Taste," 64.

39. Young, *Pure Food*, 132.

40. *Good Health*, May 1899, 298. *Good Health*, as an advocate of vegetarianism, had extra incentive to publicize the horrors of slaughterhouses.

41. Levenstein, *Revolution at the Table*, 32; Young, *Pure Food*, 76; Tomes, *The Gospel of Germs*, 168–170; Wilde, "Industrialization of Food Processing," chap. 4.

42. *National Provisioner*, February 1, 1902, 19.

43. Classic and more recent surveys include Samuel P. Hays, "The Politics of Reform in Municipal Government in the Progressive Era," *Pacific Northwest Quarterly* 55, no. 4 (October 1964): 157–169; Melvyn Dubofsky, *Industrialism and the American Worker, 1865–1920* (Arlington Heights, IL: AHM, 1975); John D. Buenker, John C. Burnham, and Robert M. Crunden, *Progressivism* (Cambridge, MA: Schenkman, 1976); Alan Dawley, *Struggles for Justice: Social Responsibility and the Liberal State* (Cambridge, MA: Harvard University Press, 1991); Flanagan, *America Reformed*.

44. Ronald Steel, *Walter Lippmann and the American Century* (New York: Vintage, 1981), 49, quoting Van Wyck Brooks. Overviews and major interpretations of Progressive reform include Richard Hofstadter, *The Age of Reform* (New York: Vintage, 1955); Gabriel Kolko, *The Triumph of Conservatism: A Reinterpretation of American History, 1900–1916* (Chicago: Quadrangle, 1967); Robert H. Wiebe, *The Search for Order, 1877–1920* (New York: Hill and Wang, 1967); Dawley, *Struggles for Justice*; Michael McGerr, *A Fierce Discontent: The Rise and Fall of the Progressive Movement in America, 1870–1920* (New York: Free Press, 2003); Flanagan, *America Reformed*.

45. Hofstadter, *The Age of Reform*; Kolko, *The Triumph of Conservatism*; James Weinstein, *The Corporate Ideal in the Liberal State: 1900–1918* (Boston: Beacon, 1968); Wiebe, *The Search for Order*; Linda Gordon, "Putting Children First: Women, Maternalism, and Welfare in the Early Twentieth Century," in *United States History as Women's History*, edited by Linda Kerber, Alice Kessler-Harris, and Kathryn Kish Sklar (Chapel Hill: University of North Carolina Press, 1995), 63–86.

46. Flanagan, *America Reformed*; Glen Gendzel, "What the Progressives Had in Common," *Journal of the Gilded Age and Progressive Era* 10, no. 3 (July 2011): 331–339; Daniel T. Rodgers, "Capitalism and Politics in the Progressive Era and in Ours," *Journal of the Gilded Age and Progressive Era* 13, no. 3 (July 2014): 379–386.

47. Daniel T. Rodgers, *Atlantic Crossings: Social Politics in a Progressive Age* (Cambridge, MA: Harvard University Press, 1998).

48. Frederick Winslow Taylor, *The Principles of Scientific Management* (New York: Harper and Row, 1911); Mauro F. Guillén, *Models of Management: Work, Authority, and Organization in a Comparative Perspective* (Chicago: University of Chicago Press, 1994).

49. John G. Sproat, *"The Best Men": Liberal Reformers in the Gilded Age* (New York: Oxford University Press, 1968); Martin J. Schiesl, *The Politics of Efficiency: Municipal Administration and Reform in America, 1800–1920* (Berkeley: University of California Press, 1977).

50. Samuel Haber, *Efficiency and Uplift: Scientific Management in the Progressive Era, 1890–1920* (Chicago: University of Chicago Press, 1964); Robert A. Burnham, "The Boss Becomes a Manager: Executive Authority and City Charter Reform, 1880–1929," in *Making Sense of the City: Local Government, Civic Culture, and Community Life in Urban America*, edited by Robert B. Fairbanks and Patricia Mooney-Melvin (Columbus: Ohio State University Press, 2001), 75–94.

51. Kenneth Finegold, *Experts and Politicians: Reform Challenges to Machine Politics in New York, Cleveland, and Chicago* (Princeton, NJ: Princeton University Press, 1995);

Yehouda Shenhav, *Manufacturing Rationality: The Engineering Foundations of the Managerial Revolution* (New York: Oxford University Press, 1999).

52. Suzanne Lebsock, "Women and American Politics, 1880–1920," in *Women, Politics, and Change*, edited by Louise Tilly and Patricia Gurin (New York: Russell Sage Foundation, 1990), 35–62; Philip J. Ethington, "Recasting Urban Political History: Gender, the Public, the Household, and Political Participation in Boston and San Francisco During the Progressive Era," *Social Science History* 16, no. 2 (Summer 1992): 301–333; Elisabeth Israels Perry, "Men Are from the Gilded Age, Women Are from the Progressive Era," *Journal of the Gilded Age and Progressive Era* 1, no. 1 (January 2002): 25–48.

53. General Federation of Women's Clubs, *Proceedings of the Biennial Meetings*, 7th Biennial Meeting, 1904, 94.

54. Shelton Stromquist, *Reinventing "The People": The Progressive Movement, the Class Problem, and the Origins of Modern Liberalism* (Urbana: University of Illinois Press, 2006).

55. Reinhard Bendix, *Work and Authority in Industry: Ideologies of Management in the Course of Industrialization* (Berkeley: University of California Press, 1974); Shenhav, *Manufacturing Rationality*.

56. Kathryn Kish Sklar, "Two Political Cultures in the Progressive Era: The National Consumers' League and the American Association for Labor Legislation," in *United States History as Women's History*, edited by Linda Kerber, Alice Kessler-Harris, and Kathryn Kish Sklar (Chapel Hill: University of North Carolina Press, 1995), 36–62; Bonj Szczygiel, "'City Beautiful' Revisited: An Analysis of Nineteenth-Century Civic Improvement Efforts," *Journal of Urban History* 29, no. 2 (December 2003): 107–132.

57. *Club Woman*, April 1898, 6.

58. Overviews include David J. Pivar, *Purity Crusade: Sexual Morality and Social Control, 1868–1900* (Westport, CT: Greenwood, 1973); David J. Pivar, *Purity and Hygiene: Women, Prostitution, and the "American Plan," 1900–1930* (Westport, CT: Greenwood, 2002); Nicola Beisel, *Imperiled Innocents: Anthony Comstock and Family Reproduction in Victorian America* (Princeton, NJ: Princeton University Press, 1997); Ruth Clifford Engs, *Clean Living Movements: American Cycles of Health Reform* (Westport, CT: Praeger, 2001).

59. Pivar, *Purity Crusade*.

60. Surveys include Ruth Bordin, *Woman and Temperance: The Quest for Power and Liberty, 1873–1900* (Philadelphia: Temple University Press, 1981); Lebsock, "Women and American Politics"; Holly Berkley Fletcher, *Gender and the American Temperance Movement of the Nineteenth Century* (New York: Routledge, 2008).

61. Alison M. Parker, *Purifying America: Women, Cultural Reform, and Pro-censorship Activism, 1873–1933* (Urbana, IL: University of Illinois Press, 1997); Beisel, *Imperiled Innocents*.

62. Hofstadter, *The Age of Reform*; Beisel, *Imperiled Innocents*.

63. In *Woman and Temperance*, Bordin highlights WCTU documents that point to social causes of intemperance. But she allows that this view was more associated with Willard than representative of the WCTU as a whole, and, accordingly, recedes after 1897.

64. Pivar, *Purity Crusade*, 266.

65. Paul Boyer, *Urban Masses and Moral Order in America, 1820–1920* (Cambridge, MA: Harvard University Press, 1978); Pivar, *Purity Crusade*; Sharon Anne Cook, "'Do not . . . Do Anything That You Cannot Unblushingly Tell Your Mother': Gender and Social Purity in Canada," *Social History* 30, no. 60 (November 1997): 215–238.

66. Gergely Baics, "Feeding Gotham: A Social History of Urban Provisioning, 1780–1860," Ph.D. diss. (Northwestern University, Evanston, IL, 2009); Michael Egan, "Organizing Protest in the Changing City: Swill Milk and Social Activism in New York City, 1842–1864," *New York History* 86, no. 3 (Summer 2005): 205–225.

67. The best surveys are Young, *Pure Food*; Goodwin, *The Pure Food, Drink, and Drug Crusaders*; Mitchell Okun, *Fair Play in the Marketplace: The First Battle for Pure Food and Drugs* (Dekalb: Northern Illinois University Press, 1986).

68. The following sketch draws from Maurice Natenburg, *The Legacy of Doctor Wiley* (Chicago: Regent House, 1957) and Harvey Washington Wiley, *Harvey W. Wiley: An Autobiography* (Indianapolis: Bobbs-Merrill, 1930).

69. Wiley, *Harvey W. Wiley*, 199–200.

70. National Pure Food and Drug Congress, *Journal of Proceedings*, 4.

71. Ibid., 8–9.

72. Ibid., 32.

73. General Federation of Women's Clubs, *Proceedings of the Biennial Meetings*, 8th Biennial Meeting, 1906, 355.

74. National Pure Food and Drug Congress, *Journal of Proceedings*, 66.

75. Ibid., 4.

76. *Good Housekeeping*, October 1902, 240–242.

77. National Pure Food and Drug Congress, *Journal of Proceedings*, 16.

78. Ibid., 42. Wiley, too, "revealed a fundamental preference for the natural over the artificial": Young, *Pure Food*, 104. Graham was hardly the first to celebrate nature as opposed to the sophistications of urban civilization. For Progressive Era food reformers, however, he was the most important and commonly cited predecessor applying that standard to food.

79. Goodwin, *The Pure Food, Drink, and Drug Crusaders*.

80. Young, *Pure Food*, 159.

81. U.S. Senate, *Memorial from the National Pure Food and Drug Congress*, do. no. 233, 55th Cong., 2d sess. (Washington, DC: U.S. Government Printing Office, 1898), 1.

82. *Table Talk*, November 1913, 641.

83. National Consumers League Records, reel 3, Organization Files, minutes of 1905 annual meeting, 2–3.

84. National Pure Food and Drug Congress, *Report of Proceedings of the Second Annual Convention of the National Pure Food and Drug Congress Held in Columbia University Hall, Washington, D. C., January 18, 19, 20 and 21, 1899* (Hightstown, NJ: Barr, 1899), 10.

85. Quoted in *New York Times*, June 13, 1906.

86. *American City*, June 1912, 805.

87. Quoted in Young, *Pure Food*, 80.

88. Donna J. Wood, "The Strategic Use of Public Policy: Business Support for the 1906 Food and Drug Act," *Business History Review* 59, no. 3 (Autumn 1985), 403; Young, *Pure Food*.

89. R. James Kane, "Populism, Progressivism, and Pure Food," *Agricultural History* 38, no. 3 (July 1964): 161–166.

90. Alan I. Marcus, "Setting the Standard: Fertilizers, State Chemists, and Early National Commercial Regulation, 1880–1887," *Agricultural History* 61, no. 1 (Winter 1987): 47–73; Jonathan Dine Wirtschafter, "The Genesis and Impact of the Medical Lobby: 1898–1906," *Journal of the History of Medicine and Allied Sciences* 13, no. 1 (January

1958): 15–49; Oscar Edward Anderson, *The Health of a Nation: Harvey W. Wiley and the Fight for Pure Food* (Chicago: University of Chicago Press, 1958); Jessica J. Mudry, *Measured Meals: Nutrition in America* (Albany: State University of New York Press, 2009).

91. Quoted by Anderson, *The Health of a Nation*, 181.

92. Quoted by Young, *Pure Food*, 184.

93. Turner, *How the Other Half Ate*.

94. Marcus, "Setting the Standard"; Sarah T. Phillips, Dale Potts, Adrienne Petty, Mark Schultz, Sam Stalcup, and Anne Effland, *Reflections on One Hundred and Fifty Years of the United States Department of Agriculture* (Hanover, PA: Agricultural History Society, 2013).

95. Theda Skocpol, *Protecting Soldiers and Mothers: The Political Origins of Social Policy in the United States* (Cambridge, MA: Harvard University Press, 1992).

96. Anderson, *The Health of a Nation*.

97. Jeffrey Haydu, "Frame Brokerage in the Pure Food Movement, 1879–1906," *Social Movement Studies* 11, no. 1 (January 2012): 1–17. This pattern of common rallying cries that mean different things to diverse constituents can be found even within single organizations. The WTCU's federal structure and local autonomy allowed its branches to pursue their own versions of "home protection": Bordin, *Woman and Temperance*.

98. The standard accounts are Anderson, *The Health of a Nation*, and Young, *Pure Food*.

99. Ferrières, *Sacred Cow, Mad Cow*; David F. Smith and Jim Phillips, eds., *Food, Science, Policy, and Regulation in the Twentieth Century: International and Comparative Perspectives* (London: Routledge, 2000). On the movement of Progressive ideas among Western countries, see Rodgers, *Atlantic Crossings*.

100. *American Kitchen*, November 1900, 88.

101. *Proceedings of the Annual Conference*, 1899, 4. I use "domestic science" and "home economics" interchangeably, for variety.

102. Useful secondary sources include Laura Shapiro, *Perfection Salad: Women and Cooking at the Turn of the Century* (Berkeley: University of California Press, 1986); Carolyn M. Goldstein, "Mediating Consumption: Home Economics and American Consumers, 1900–1940," Ph.D. diss. (University of Delaware, Newark, 1994); Joel A. Tarr and Mark Tebeau, "Managing Danger in the Home Environment, 1900–1940," *Journal of Social History* 29, no. 4 (Summer 1996): 797–816; Megan J. Elias, *Stir It Up: Home Economics in American Culture* (Philadelphia: University of Pennsylvania Press, 2008).

103. Quoted in Caroline L. Hunt, *The Life of Ellen H. Richards* (Boston: Whitcomb and Barrows, 1912), 57. I rely on Hunt's biography in this paragraph.

104. Wilbur O. Atwater, "The Chemistry of Food and Nutrition," *The Century* 34, no. 1 (May 1887): 59–74; K. J. Carpenter, "The Life and Times of W. O. Atwater (1844–1907)," *Journal of Nutrition* 124 (1994): 1707S–1714S; Mudry, *Measured Meals*.

105. *Good Housekeeping*, March 1900, 122.

106. *American Kitchen*, January 1903, 169.

107. *Good Housekeeping*, May 14, 1887, 13–14, November 23, 1889, 51–53.

108. *New England Kitchen*, October 1894, 43; General Federation of Women's Clubs, *The Club Woman*, May 1904, 13. Early in her career, Richards argued that such an approach was preferable to government intervention. "'Perhaps the day will come when an association of housekeepers will be formed in each large town or city, with one of their number as a chemist. Some similar arrangement would be far more effective in checking adulteration than a dozen acts passed by Congress'": quoted in Hunt, *The Life of Ellen H. Richards*, 185. By the 1900s, domestic scientists treated consumer expertise and federal regulation as complementary.

109. *Good Housekeeping*, February 1895, 47.

110. *Good Housekeeping*, April 1912, 555–556.

111. *Club Woman*, October 1897; *Proceedings of the Annual Conference*, 1902, 88.

112. National Consumers League, *Annual Reports* (New York: National Consumers League, 1907–1909), 53, 55.

113. *New York Times*, September 18, 1910.

114. *American Kitchen*, March 1900, 206.

115. Ibid., August 1900, 162.

116. Ibid., August 1898, 155.

117. Ibid., September 1901, 204.

118. Strasser, *Never Done*.

119. *Proceedings of the Annual Conference*, 1900, 29–34.

120. Ibid., 1901, 108.

121. *New England Kitchen*, September 1894, 299; *American Kitchen*, August 1900, 199–203.

122. *American Kitchen*, August 1900, 199.

123. *Good Housekeeping*, October 1894, 146.

124. Ibid., August 1913, 253. Progressive Era household engineers such as Lillian Gilbreth and Christine Frederick took the next step, applying such tools of scientific management as time and motion study to the physical tasks of running a household: Strasser, *Never Done*.

125. *Proceedings of the Annual Conference*, 1899, 1908. Names with ambiguous gender were coded as male.

126. Shapiro, *Perfection Salad*; Goldstein, "Mediating Consumption"; Sarah Stage and Virginia B. Vincenti, eds., *Rethinking Home Economics: Women and the History of a Profession* (Ithaca, NY: Cornell University Press, 1997).

127. *Table Talk*, April 1917, 27.

128. *New England Kitchen*, May 1894, 80–81.

129. Turner notes that in the eyes of middle-class reformers, poor and working-class women would always fall short of home economists' standards. They lacked the resources to keep kitchen equipment fully separate from other living spaces and the time to prepare their husbands' lunches rather than having them buy from carts and pubs near work: Turner, *How the Other Half Ate*, 139.

130. Levenstein, *Revolution at the Table*; Hamilton Cravens, "Establishing the Science of Nutrition at the USDA: Ellen Swallow Richards and Her Allies," in *The United States Department of Agriculture in Historical Perspective*, edited by Alan I. Marcus and Richard Lowitt (Washington, DC: Agricultural History Society, 1991), 122–133.

131. The Food and Drugs Act applied only to interstate commerce, but many states had comparable laws governing intrastate commerce.

132. The food exhibits also changed in sponsorship. Earlier ones were commonly organized by the Department of Agriculture and state food authorities in cooperation with women's groups. Over time, commercial interests began to play a growing role. *New England Kitchen*, October 1894, 42–43; National Consumers League Records, reel 4, Organization Files, 1911 annual report, 46; Shapiro, *Perfection Salad*; Goodwin, *The Pure Food, Drink, and Drug Crusaders*.

133. *San Francisco Chronicle*, May 10, 1909.

134. By 1907, Mudry calculates, experiment stations had "performed more than 100 studies and published more than 56 'dietaries' for eaters of various demographic characteristics": Mudry, *Measured Meals*, 182, n. 21.

135. Goldstein, "Mediating Consumption"; U.S. Senate, Committee on Agriculture and Forestry, *Bureau of Domestic Science* (Washington, DC: U.S. Government Printing Office, 1908).

136. *Club Woman*, March 1904, 27.

137. *Federation Bulletin*, October 1905, 11.

138. *Good Housekeeping*, October 1905, 361.

139. General Federation of Women's Clubs, *Proceedings of the Biennial Meetings*, 8th Biennial Meeting, 1906, 354.

140. Goodwin, *The Pure Food, Drink, and Drug Crusaders*; Anderson, *The Health of a Nation*; *Federation Bulletin*, May 1905, 270; National Consumers League Records, reel 16, Office File, Chartered Leagues, Massachusetts, Executive Committee minutes, February 1, 1905, May 3, 1905.

141. Donatella della Porta and Lorenzo Mosca, "In Movimento: 'Contamination' in Action and the Italian Global Justice Movement," *Global Networks* 7, no. 1 (January 2007): 1–27; Sidney Tarrow and Doug McAdam, "Scale Shift in Transnational Contention," in *Transnational Protest and Global Activism*, edited by Donatella della Porta and Sidney Tarrow (Lanham, MD: Rowman and Littlefield, 2005), 121–147.

142. Engs, *Clean Living Movements*, puts this health movement in the larger context of Progressive Era social purity. Gerald Carson offers a more popular account, focusing on Kellogg in *Cornflake Crusade* (New York: Arno Press, 1976), and Ronald L. Numbers highlights the religious roots of Kellogg's health nostrums in *Prophetess of Health: Ellen G. White and the Origins of Seventh-Day Adventist Health Reform* (Knoxville: University of Tennessee Press, 1992).

143. Biographical overviews include Richard W. Schwarz, *John Harvey Kellogg, M.D.* (Nashville: Southern Publishing Association, 1970); Numbers, *Prophetess of Health*; Howard Markel, *The Kelloggs: The Battling Brothers of Battle Creek* (New York: Pantheon, 2017).

144. For a fictional account of life and therapy at the San, see T. Coraghessan Boyle, *The Road to Wellville* (New York: Viking, 1993).

145. On the commercial side of Kellogg's, in which John Harvey's younger brother Will played an outsize role, see Markel, *The Kelloggs*.

146. *Good Health*, March 1882, 94.

147. Henry Perky, quoted in National Pure Food and Drug Congress, *Journal of Proceedings*, 42.

148. *Good Health*, April 1893, 119.

149. *American Kitchen*, December 1901, 91.

150. Harriet Higbee, quoted in *Club Woman*, February 1898, 152.

151. *Good Health*, November 1885, 341.

152. *Health Reformer*, February 1873, 38–39.

153. *Club Woman*, October 1898, 181.

154. Ibid., October 1899, 181.

155. John Harvey Kellogg and Ella E. Kellogg, *Social Purity: An Address and a Talk to Girls: An Address on the Social Purity Pledge* (Battle Creek, MI: Good Health, 1889), 8.

156. John Harvey Kellogg, *Plain Facts for Young and Old* (Burlington, IA: I. F. Segner, 1882), 391.

157. Daniel Sack, *Whitebread Protestants: Food and Religion in American Culture* (New York: St. Martin's, 2000); Stacy J. Williams, "Personal Prefigurative Politics: Cooking Up an Ideal Society in the Woman's Temperance and Woman's Suffrage Movements,

1870–1920," *Sociological Quarterly* 58, no. 1 (November 2017): 72–90; *Good Health*, January 1899, 28–29.

158. *What to Eat*, February 1907, 45.

159. *Good Health*, May 1886, 153.

160. Ibid., 371–372.

161. Ibid., March 1899, 130.

162. *Proceedings of the Annual Conference*, 1908, 22.

163. *Good Health*, January 1892, 9.

164. Leading eugenicists included Irving Fisher, Charles Eliot, and Russell Chittenden.

165. *Good Health*, November 1913, 549–580, January 1914, 2–4; Schwarz, *John Harvey Kellogg*, 222–223; *Table Talk*, February 1913, 63.

166. Horace Fletcher, *The A.B.-Z. of Our Own Nutrition* (New York: Frederick A. Stokes, 1903), 73–74.

167. On Kellogg's eugenics, see Markel, *The Kelloggs*, chap. 13.

168. *Good Health*, January 1887, 14–15.

169. Carson, *Cornflake Crusade*, 183.

170. See Stacy Williams's study of temperance cookbooks: Stacy Jeanne Williams, "Recipes for Resistance: Feminist Political Discourse About Cooking, 1870–1985," Ph.D. diss. (University of California, San Diego, 2017). See also Bordin, *Woman and Temperance*.

171. Pivar, *Purity Crusade*, 228, 281–283. John Harvey and Ella also contributed their own lectures on the virtues of chastity and the evils of masturbation.

172. In *Prophetess of Health*, Numbers traces this history, adding specific biographical connections. These include an additional historical path, from Graham to the water cure advocate James Caleb Jackson, whose upstate New York spa impressed Ellen White with its hydropathy, its vegetarian fare, and its breakfast "granula"—the model for Kellogg's granola.

173. Bordin, *Woman and Temperance*, 109; Williams, "Personal Prefigurative Politics."

174. *Good Health*, January 1899, 56.

175. Ibid., July 1900, 441.

176. Sack, *Whitebread Protestants*.

177. *Good Health*, July 1900, 442; Dirks, *Food in the Gilded Age*, 134; Schwarz, *John Harvey Kellogg*, 76 (on National Cash Register).

178. Schwarz, *John Harvey Kellogg*, 76.

179. Ibid., 82–84.

180. *Good Health*, April 1911, 321.

181. Schwarz, *John Harvey Kellogg*, 100.

182. *Good Health*, December 1899, 737.

183. Ibid., July 1900, 430–431.

184. Markel, *The Kelloggs*. John Harvey Kellogg did have lines he would not cross. Commercializing God's health food as breakfast cereal was acceptable. Adding sugar to corn flakes to boost sales, as Will Kellogg did, was not: Schwarz, *John Harvey Kellogg*, 211.

185. National Pure Food and Drug Congress, *Report of Proceedings*, 5.

186. *Proceedings of the Annual Conference*, 1907, 161.

187. Quoted in Young, *Pure Food*, 216.

188. *New England Kitchen*, December 1894, 241.

189. *Good Housekeeping*, October 1905, 361.

190. *Table Talk*, November 1913, 640.

191. Wilbur O. Atwater, "Food and Diet," in *Yearbook of the United States Department of Agriculture, 1894*, United States Department of Agriculture (Washington, DC: U.S. Government Printing Office, 1895), 368.

192. *New England Kitchen*, April 1894, 10.

193. *Good Housekeeping*, November 1914, 627–628; Deborah I. Levine, "Managing American Bodies: Diet, Nutrition, and Obesity in America, 1840–1920," Ph.D. diss. (Harvard University, Cambridge, MA, 2008), 121–122.

194. On the WCTU's less explicit embrace of eugenics notions, see Riiko Bedford, "Heredity as Ideology: Ideas of the Woman's Christian Temperance Union of the United States and Ontario on Heredity and Social Reform, 1880–1910," *Canadian Bulletin of Medical History* 32, no. 1 (Spring 2015): 77–100.

195. Vileisis, *Kitchen Literacy*.

196. In this they mirrored (and perhaps learned from) the more politicized market strategy of the National Consumers League: Kathryn Kish Sklar, "The Consumers' White Label Campaign of the National Consumers' League 1898–1919," in *Getting and Spending: European and American Consumer Societies in the Twentieth Century*, edited by Susan Strasser, Charles McGovern, and Matthias Judt (New York: Cambridge University Press, 1998), 17–35.

197. For scholarly accounts, see Levenstein, *Revolution at the Table*; Mudry, *Measured Meals*. For a popular account, see Michael Pollan, *In Defense of Food: An Eater's Manifesto* (New York: Penguin, 2008).

198. *Good Housekeeping*, April 1895, 139.

199. Land grant colleges were state universities founded with money from the sale of federal land granted for this purpose under the Morrill Acts of 1862 and 1890.

200. Michael Lesy and Lisa Stoffer, *Repast: Dining Out at the Dawn of the New American Century, 1900–1910* (New York: W. W. Norton, 2013).

CHAPTER 4

1. *Organic Gardening and Farming*, September 1971, 33.

2. Valuable surveys include David Nowacek, "The Organic Foods System from 1969–1996: A Defense of Associative Order and Democratic Control Over a Market," M.A. diss. (University of Wisconsin, Madison, 1997); Julie Guthman, *Agrarian Dreams: The Paradox of Organic Farming in California* (Berkeley: University of California Press, 2004); Warren J. Belasco, *Appetite for Change: How the Counterculture Took on the Food Industry, 1966–1988*, 2d ed. (New York: Pantheon, 2007); Brian K. Obach, *Organic Struggle: The Movement for Sustainable Agriculture in the United States* (Cambridge, MA: MIT Press, 2015); Lisa F. Clark, *The Changing Politics of Organic Food in North America* (Cheltenham, UK: Edward Elger, 2015).

3. Doug McAdam and Dieter Rucht, "The Cross-National Diffusion of Movement Ideas," *Annals of the American Academy of Political and Social Science* 528 (July 1993): 56–74; Sarah A. Soule, "Diffusion Processes within and across Movements," in *The Blackwell Companion to Social Movements*, edited by David Snow, Sarah A. Soule, and Hanspeter Kriesi (Malden, MA: Blackwell, 2004), 294–310.

4. For a general introduction to scholarship on collective memory, see Jeffrey K. Olick and Joyce Robbins, "Social Memory Studies: From 'Collective Memory' to the Historical

Sociology of Mnemonic Practices," *Annual Review of Sociology* 24 (1998): 105–140; Wulf Kansteiner, "Finding Meaning in Memory: A Methodological Critique of Collective Memory Studies," *History and Theory* 41, no. 2 (May 2002): 179–197. Examples from the social movement literature include Hiro Saito, "Reiterated Commemoration: Hiroshima as National Trauma," *Sociological Theory* 24, no. 4 (December 2006): 353–376; Robert S. Jansen, "Resurrection and Appropriation: Reputational Trajectories, Memory Work, and the Political Use of Historical Figures," *American Journal of Sociology* 112, no. 4 (January 2007): 953–1007; Bill Rolston, "'Trying to Reach the Future through the Past': Murals and Memory in Northern Ireland," *Crime, Media, and Culture* 6, no. 3 (December 2010): 285–307.

5. Michael Pollan uses the term to describe agribusiness that meets federal organic standards but is in other respects little different from conventional agriculture. Michael Pollan, *The Omnivore's Dilemma: A Natural History of Four Meals* (New York: Penguin, 2006).

6. On the emerging logic of conventional agriculture in the twentieth century, see Deborah Fitzgerald, *Every Farm a Factory: The Industrial Ideal in American Agriculture* (New Haven, CT: Yale University Press, 2003). Its application after World War II is surveyed in Margaret FitzSimmons, "The New Industrial Agriculture: The Regional Integration of Specialty Crop Production," *Economic Geography* 62, no. 4 (October 1986): 334–353; David Goodman and Michael Redclift, *Refashioning Nature: Food, Ecology, and Culture* (London: Routledge, 1991); R. Douglas Hurt, *American Agriculture: A Brief History* (West Lafayette, IN: Purdue University Press, 2002). On the rise of high-tech food processing, see Mark William Wilde, "Industrialization of Food Processing in the United States, 1860–1960" (Ph.D. diss., University of Delaware, Newark, 1988); Melanie Warner, *Pandora's Lunchbox: How Processed Food Took Over the American Meal* (New York: Scribner, 2013). See also case studies such as Aaron Bobrow-Strain, *White Bread: A Social History of the Store-Bought Loaf* (Boston: Beacon, 2012).

7. The phrase is from Carey McWilliams, *Factories in the Field: The Story of Migratory Farm Labor in California* (Boston: Little, Brown, 1939).

8. Carolyn Dimitri, Anne Effland, and Neilson Conklin, *The 20th Century Transformation of U.S. Agriculture and Farm Policy*, Economic Information Bulletin no. 3 (Washington, DC: USDA Economic Research Service, 2005). After 1960, the census stopped counting work animals.

9. The quote is commonly attributed to Earl Butz, Secretary of Agriculture under President Richard Nixon. I have been unable to locate an original source for that attribution, and Nathan A. Rosenberg and Bryce Wilson Stucki ("The Butz Stops Here: Why the Food Movement Needs to Rethink Agricultural History," *Journal of Food Law and Policy* 13, no. 1 [Spring 2017]: 12–25) find his predecessor Ezra Taft Benson saying the same thing. For the general shift in agricultural policy toward maximizing output, see Mrill Ingram and Helen Ingram, "Creating Credible Edibles: The Organic Agriculture Movement and the Emergence of U.S. Federal Organic Standards," in *Routing the Opposition: Social Movements, Public Policy, and Democracy*, edited by David S. Meyer, Valerie Jenness, and Helen Ingram (Minneapolis: University of Minnesota Press, 2005), 121–148; Goodman and Redclift, *Refashioning Nature.*

10. Ingram and Ingram, "Creating Credible Edibles."

11. Shane Hamilton, "The Economies and Conveniences of Modern-Day Living: Frozen Foods and Mass Marketing, 1945–1965," *Business History Review* 77, no. 1 (Spring 2003): 33–60; Paul Josephson, "The Ocean's Hot Dog: The Development of the Fish Stick," *Technology and Culture* 49, no. 1 (January 2008): 41–61.

12. Wilde, "Industrialization of Food Processing in the United States"; Gabriella M. Petrick, "The Arbiters of Taste: Producers, Consumers and the Industrialization of Taste in America, 1900–1960" (Ph.D. diss., University of Delaware, Newark, 2006).

13. Harvey Levenstein, *Paradox of Plenty: A Social History of Eating in Modern America* (Berkeley: University of California Press, 2003), 101.

14. Marion Nestle, "Latest Court Ruling: Pringles Are Potato Chips (Sort Of)," *Food Politics*, May 26, 2009, accessed April 21, 2020, https://www.foodpolitics.com/2009/05 /latest-court-ruling-pringles-are-potato-chips-sort-of.

15. Andrew F. Smith, *Fast Food and Junk Food: An Encyclopedia of What We Love to Eat* (Santa Barbara, CA: Greenwood, 2012); Sarah Jampel, "Is Cool Whip Food?" *Food52*, April 8, 2016, accessed April 21, 2020, https://food52.com/blog/16524-is-cool-whip-food -looking-back-on-50-years.

16. Sheldon Krimsky and Roger P. Wrubel, *Agricultural Biotechnology and the Environment: Science, Policy, and Social Issues* (Urbana: University of Illinois Press, 1996); Daniel Charles, *Lords of the Harvest: Biotech, Big Money, and the Future of Food* (Cambridge, MA: Perseus, 2001). Other genetically engineered foods have since come on the market.

17. Charles Walker Jr., "Good Food/Family Farms," *Acres, USA*, June 1972, 4–5.

18. Randal S. Beeman and James A. Pritchard, *A Green and Permanent Land: Ecology and Agriculture in the Twentieth Century* (Lawrence: University Press of Kansas, 2001).

19. "How Pure Is Your Food?" *U.S. News and World Report*, December 7, 1959, 86–90.

20. A search for "food and additive*" found thirty articles in 1959 and fifty-six in 1960.

21. "Food Safety a Worry in Era of Additives," *New York Times*, November 9, 1969.

22. Calculated from search results for "food and pesticide*."

23. Anna Zeide, *Canned: The Rise and Fall of Consumer Confidence in the American Food Industry* (Berkeley: University of California Press, 2018).

24. *New York Times*, December 9, 1969.

25. Jerome Goldstein, ed., *The New Food Chain: An Organic Link Between Farm and City* (Emmaus, PA: Rodale, 1973), ix.

26. *Sedition*, October 15, 1971, 2.

27. *San Jose Red Eye*, November 27–December 3, 1969, 7.

28. Alternative Features Service, December 1, 1972, 7.

29. *Good Times*, February 12, 1971, 12.

30. *Los Angeles Free Press*, September 19, 1969, 37.

31. *Ramparts*, June 1971, 54.

32. The examples are from Kauffman's longer list: Jonathan Kauffman, *Hippie Food: How Back-to-the-Landers, Longhairs, and Revolutionaries Changed the Way We Eat* (New York: William Morrow, 2018), 113.

33. Andrew F. Smith, *Eating History: 30 Turning Points in the Making of American Cuisine* (New York: Columbia University Press, 2009).

34. Laura J. Miller, *Building Nature's Market: The Business and Politics of Natural Foods* (Chicago: University of Chicago Press, 2017).

35. *New York Times*, December 11, 1959, November 10, 1959, November 22, 1959, February 9, 1966, July 3, 1969, July 16, 1969.

36. Ibid., March 5, 1967; *Organic Gardening and Farming*, January 1967, 29.

37. David Murray, "The American Counterculture," *Journal of American Studies* 42, no. 1 (April 2008): 155; Peter Braunstein and Michael William Doyle, eds., *Imagine*

Nation: The American Counterculture of the 1960s and '70s (New York: Routledge, 2002); Jeremi Suri, "The Rise and Fall of an International Counterculture, 1960–1975," *American Historical Review* 114, no. 1 (February 2009): 61–68; Doug Rossinow, "The New Left in the Counterculture: Hypotheses and Evidence," *Radical History Review* 67 (Winter 1997): 79–120.

38. Angela G. Mertig, Riley E. Dunlap, and Denton E. Morrison, "The Environmental Movement in the United States," in *Handbook of Environmental Sociology*, edited by Riley E. Dunlap and William Michelson (Westport, CT: Greenwood, 2000), 448–481; Andrew G. Kirk, *Counterculture Green: The Whole Earth Catalog and American Environmentalism* (Lawrence: University Press of Kansas, 2007); Adam Rome, "'Give Earth a Chance': The Environmental Movement and the Sixties," *Journal of American History* 90, no. 2 (September 2003): 525–554; Keith M. Woodhouse, "The Politics of Ecology: Environmentalism and Liberalism in the 1960s," *Journal for the Study of Radicalism* 2, no. 2 (Fall 2008): 53–84; Christopher C. Sellers, *Crabgrass Crucible: Suburban Nature and the Rise of Environmentalism in Twentieth-Century America* (Chapel Hill: University of North Carolina Press, 2012).

39. Ronald Inglehart, *The Silent Revolution: Changing Values and Political Styles among Western Publics* (Princeton, NJ: Princeton University Press, 1977); Alberto Melucci, *Challenging Codes: Collective Action in the Information Age* (Cambridge: Cambridge University Press, 1996).

40. *Mother Earth News*, January 1970, 5.

41. Rome, "Give Earth a Chance."

42. Rossinow, "The New Left in the Counterculture"; Ryan H. Edgington, "'Be Receptive to the Good Earth': Health, Nature, and Labor in Countercultural Back-to-the-Land Settlements," *Agricultural History* 82, no. 3 (Summer 2008): 279–308.

43. Robert N. Mayer, *The Consumer Movement: Guardians of the Marketplace* (Boston: Twayne, 1989); Lawrence B. Glickman, *Buying Power: A History of Consumer Activism in America* (Chicago: University of Chicago Press, 2009).

44. Matthew Hilton, "Social Activism in an Age of Consumption: The Organized Consumer Movement," *Social History* 32, no. 2 (May 2007): 121–143; Glickman, *Buying Power*.

45. Michele Micheletti, *Political Virtue and Shopping: Individuals, Consumerism, and Collective Action* (New York: Palgrave Macmillan, 2003); Jeffrey Haydu and David Kadanoff, "Casing Political Consumerism," *Mobilization* 15, no. 2 (June 2010): 159–177; Dhavan V. Shah, Lewis A. Friedland, Chris Wells, Young Mie Kim, and Hernando Rojas, "Communication, Consumers, and Citizens: Revisiting the Politics of Consumption," *Annals of the American Academy of Political and Social Science* 644, no. 1 (November 2012): 6–19.

46. Marshall Ganz, *Why David Sometimes Wins: Leadership, Organization, and Strategy in the California Farm Worker Movement* (New York: Oxford University Press, 2009).

47. Manuel Castells, *The Power of Identity* (Malden, MA: Blackwell, 1997); W. Lance Bennett, "Branded Political Communication: Lifestyle Politics, Logo Campaigns, and the Rise of Global Citizenship," in *Politics, Products, and Markets: Exploring Political Consumerism Past and Present*, edited by Michele Micheletti, Adreas Føllesdal, and Dietlind Stolle (New Brunswick, NJ: Transaction, 2004), 101–125.

48. National Consumers League women in the 1890s and abolitionists in the 1850s had also expressed political values by purchasing sweatshop-free undergarments and slave-free sugar. Lifestyle politics puts more emphasis on the public performance of

those values than on the concerted strategy of improving working conditions or ending slavery.

49. Rossinow, "The New Left in the Counterculture"; Braunstein and Doyle, *Imagine Nation*.

50. Thomas Frank, *The Conquest of Cool: Business Culture, Counterculture, and the Rise of Hip Consumerism* (Chicago: University of Chicago Press, 1997).

51. Both Guthman, *Agrarian Dreams*, and Michael A. Haedicke, *Organizing Organic: Conflict and Compromise in an Emerging Market* (Stanford, CA: Stanford University Press, 2016), show that elements of market and movement, and tensions between them, were clear from the start. The balance between those elements clearly shifted over time.

52. Matthew Reed, *Rebels for the Soil: The Rise of the Global Organic Food and Farming Movement* (London: Earthscan, 2010); Beeman and Pritchard, *A Green and Permanent Land*.

53. Indicating its early focus, the magazine was named *Organic Gardening* from its launch in 1943 until 1954. On the early history of organic agriculture, see Philip Conford, *The Origins of the Organic Movement* (Edinburgh: Floris, 2001); Suzanne Peters, "The Land in Trust" (Ph.D. diss., McGill University, Montreal, 1979); Obach, *Organic Struggle*.

54. The oral histories are in Regional History Project, University of California, Santa Cruz, "Cultivating a Movement: Organic and Sustainable Farming," https://library.ucsc.edu/reg-hist/cultiv/home.

55. Peters, "The Land in Trust"; Edgington, "Be Receptive to the Good Earth"; Jeffrey Jacob, *New Pioneers: The Back-to-the-Land Movement and the Search for a Sustainable Future* (University Park: Pennsylvania State University Press, 1997); interviews with Stephen Kaffka, Jim Nelson, Zea Sonnabend, and Jerry and Jean Thomas, in Regional History Project, University of California, Santa Cruz, "Cultivating a Movement."

56. Interview with Stephen Kaffka, in Regional History Project, University of California, Santa Cruz, "Cultivating a Movement." On Chadwick, see Nowacek, "The Organic Foods System from 1969–1996"; Obach, *Organic Struggle*; *Berkeley Barb*, July 23–29, 1976. Another inspiration was Scott Nearing and his socialist self-sufficiency in Vermont: *Great Speckled Bird*, April 16, 1973. For the northeastern counterparts in early organic agriculture, see Grace Gershuny, *Organic Revolutionary: A Memoir of the Movement for Real Food, Planetary Healing, and Human Liberation* (Middletown, DE: Joes Brook, 2016); Kauffman, *Hippie Food*.

57. Miller, *Building Nature's Market*; Guthman, *Agrarian Dreams*; *Mother Earth News*, May 1970.

58. Craig Cox, *Storefront Revolution: Food Co-ops and the Counterculture* (New Brunswick, NJ: Rutgers University Press, 1994); Craig B. Upright, *Grocery Activism: The Radical History of Food Cooperatives in Minnesota* (Minneapolis: University of Minnesota Press, 2020); *San Jose Free University*, Winter–Spring 1972.

59. *Organic Gardening and Farming*, September 1969, 22.

60. Ibid., November 1970, 39.

61. Desmond A. Jolly, "Differences between Buyers and Nonbuyers of Organic Produce and Willingness to Pay Organic Price Premiums," *Journal of Agribusiness* 9, no. 1 (Spring 1991): 97–111; Guthman, *Agrarian Dreams*.

62. Conford, *The Origins of the Organic Movement*; Peters, "The Land in Trust"; Beeman and Pritchard, *A Green and Permanent Land*.

63. *Organic Gardening and Farming*, April 1964, 24–26; Peters, "The Land in Trust." Reading source material from the early organic movement is an exercise in retrospective humility. Much of what we associate with contemporary food reform is already there. The summary analysis in Cornucopia Project, *Empty Breadbasket? The Coming Challenge to America's Food Supply and What We Can Do About It* (Emmaus, PA: Rodale, 1981), is especially prescient. It rounds up now familiar perils (monocultures, CAFOs, food miles, obesity, climate change) and offers now familiar recommendations (such as renewable energy, direct marketing, buying local, regionalized food systems, and farmers' markets).

64. U.S. House of Representatives, *Hearings before the House Select Committee to Investigate the Use of Chemicals in Food Products* (Washington, DC: U.S. Government Printing Office, 1950), 862–867.

65. Rodale's rhetorical style is already on full display in *Pay Dirt: Farming and Gardening with Composts* (New York: Rodale, 1945).

66. *Organic Gardening and Farming*, March 1964, 25.

67. Ibid., October 1973, 82.

68. Interviews with Scott Roseman and Zea Sonnabend, in Regional History Project, University of California, Santa Cruz, "Cultivating a Movement"; Gershuny, *Organic Revolutionary*.

69. *San Jose Free University*, Winter–Spring 1972, 2.

70. *Ann Arbor Sun*, April 11–25, 1975, 19.

71. On organic's opposition to big business, see Kauffman, *Hippie Food*; Clark, *The Changing Politics of Organic Food in North America*.

72. Wendell Berry gets credit for this shift from a civic to an agrarian notion of good citizenship. See Kimberly K. Smith, *Wendell Berry and the Agrarian Tradition: A Common Grace* (Lawrence: University Press of Kansas, 2003).

73. *Organic Gardening and Farming*, May 1972, 98.

74. *The Rag*, October 22, 1973, 6.

75. *Organic Gardening and Farming*, May 1973, 6.

76. Beeman and Pritchard, *A Green and Permanent Land*; Guthman, *Agrarian Dreams*. Gershuny, *Organic Revolutionary*, notes that the populist impulse was stronger among midwestern than among northeastern organic farmers.

77. Environment Action Bulletin and Organic Gardening and Farming, *The Organic Guide to Colleges and Universities* (Emmaus, PA: Rodale Press, 1973), 54–55.

78. Examples include articles in *Organic Gardening and Farming* by Floyd Allen (March 1971), Jerome Olds (May 1971), and Robert Rodale (June 1971).

79. Goldstein, *The New Food Chain*, 2.

80. Environment Action Bulletin and Organic Gardening and Farming, *The Organic Guide to Colleges and Universities*, 27.

81. *The Peacemaker*, February 6, 1971, 1.

82. *Organic Gardening and Farming*, November 1963, 17–19.

83. Robert Gottlieb and Anupama Joshi, *Food Justice* (Cambridge, MA: MIT Press, 2010), 185; interview with Amigo Bob Cantisano, in Regional History Project, University of California, Santa Cruz, "Cultivating a Movement."

84. It is possible that the proposal failed in part because the member of the fledgling CCOF who paid the highest dues was also a target of organizing efforts by the United Farm Workers. See Guthman, *Agrarian Dreams*, 119. Cox, *Storefront Revolution*; Upright, *Grocery Activism*; *Good Times*, February 12, 1971.

85. Environment Action Bulletin and Organic Gardening and Farming, *The Organic Guide to Colleges and Universities*, 48.

86. *Acres, USA*, January 1975, 23–24.

87. The precursors include advocates of "Permanent Agriculture" in the 1930s (Beeman and Pritchard, *A Green and Permanent Land*) and J. I. Rodale in the 1940s (Rodale, *Pay Dirt*).

88. *Organic Gardening and Farming*, April 1963, 28–29.

89. *Good Times*, February 12, 1971, 12.

90. *Acres, USA*, September 1974, 2.

91. *Good Times*, February 12, 1971, 12.

92. *Organic Gardening and Farming*, April 1973, 89, original emphasis.

93. *The Peacemaker*, February 6, 1971, 1–2.

94. Cox, *Storefront Revolution*, 43.

95. This theme is emphasized in Belasco's excellent history of the "countercuisine," *Appetite for Change*.

96. *Los Angeles Free Press*, September 19, 1969, 37.

97. Miller, *Building Nature's Market*.

98. Peters, "The Land in Trust." Agrarian reformers in the 1930s promoted their own ecological perspective in their critique of conventional agriculture. See Beeman and Pritchard, *A Green and Permanent Land*. But it was the organic movement, alongside modern environmentalism, that popularized an ecological framing of "natural" among consumers.

99. See, e.g., *Organic Gardening and Farming*, July 1966, 19–21.

100. Ibid., March 1970, 8. One important alternative newspaper giving extensive coverage to organic food was *Mother Earth News*.

101. Edgington, "Be Receptive to the Good Earth"; Peters, "The Land in Trust"; Beeman and Pritchard, *A Green and Permanent Land*.

102. *Organic Gardening and Farming*, November 1968, 20.

103. Ibid., December 1974, 38–39.

104. Edgington, "Be Receptive to the Good Earth."

105. *Organic Gardening and Farming*, December 1965, 18; May 1967, 27; September 1975, 45.

106. Ibid., November 1974, 77, original emphasis. The ideal of "organic living" in the early 1970s is still a transgressive one in its critique of conformity, technology, and consumerism. Much as organic food evolved towards "yuppie chow" (Julie Guthman, "From the Ground Up: California Organics and the Making of 'Yuppie Chow,'" in *Alternative Food Geographies: Representation and Practice*, edited by Damian Maye, Lewis Holloway, and Moya Kneafsey [Oxford: Elsevier, 2007], 241–254), so organic living became, by the next generation of the Rodales, Maria Rodale's "organic style." See Maria McGrath, *Food for Dissent: Natural Foods and the Consumer Counterculture since the 1960s* (Amherst: University of Massachusetts Press, 2019).

107. *Chicago Seed*, January 15, 1972, 10.

108. *Mother Earth News*, November 1971, 101.

109. *Equality*, April–June 1966, 6–7.

110. Belasco, *Appetite for Change*, is particularly valuable on this point. See also Maria McGrath, "Recipes for a New World: Utopianism and Alternative Eating in Vegetarian Natural-Foods Cookbooks, 1970–84," in *Eating in Eden: Food and American Utopias*, edited by Etta M. Madden and Martha L. Finch (Lincoln: University of Nebraska Press, 2006), 162–183.

111. *Organic Gardening and Farming*, April 1962, 23.

112. Ibid., January 1970, 60.

113. Ibid., September 1976, 48.

114. Kellogg is different here, with his confidence that modern science and industrial ingenuity could make healthful grains and meat alternatives convenient parts of the popular diet.

115. Joseph Gusfield offers a nuanced account of the meanings of nature in the Second Great Awakening and the counterculture. He is particularly attentive to the central importance of individual control in the clash between nature and commercial urban life. Gusfield shows that self-mastery is seen as necessary to resist corruption by the marketplace, whether that corruption takes the form of sexual license (in the 1830s) or shallow consumerism (in the 1960s). Joseph R. Gusfield, "Nature's Body and the Metaphors of Food," in *Cultivating Differences: Symbolic Boundaries and the Making of Inequality*, edited by Michèle Lamont and Marcel Fournier (Chicago: University of Chicago Press, 1992), 75–103. The benefits of resistance are different, however. In one case, it is a matter of preserving middle-class status expectations, in the other, breaking free of them.

116. Michael P. Young, *Bearing Witness against Sin: The Evangelical Birth of the American Social Movement* (Chicago: University of Chicago Press, 2006).

117. Linda Gordon, "Putting Children First: Women, Maternalism, and Welfare in the Early Twentieth Century," in *United States History as Women's History*, edited by Linda Kerber, Alice Kessler-Harris, and Kathryn Kish Sklar (Chapel Hill: University of North Carolina Press, 1995), 63–86; Elisabeth S. Clemens, *The People's Lobby: Organizational Innovation and the Rise of Interest Group Politics in the United States, 1890–1925* (Chicago: University of Chicago Press, 1997).

118. Belasco, *Appetite for Change*.

119. Beeman and Pritchard, *A Green and Permanent Land*.

120. Peter Pringle, *Food, Inc.: Mendel to Monsanto—The Promises and Perils of the Biotech Harvest* (New York: Simon and Schuster, 2003); Reed, *Rebels for the Soil*.

121. *New York Times*, April 16, 1972.

122. Miller, *Building Nature's Market*, shows that this battle had been fought many times before, pitting natural foods entrepreneurs against mainstream scientists, doctors, and food manufacturers.

123. This line of argument mirrors broader critiques (during this same period) of science as a handmaiden to capital. See David Noble, *America by Design: Science, Technology, and the Rise of Corporate Capitalism* (New York: Alfred A. Knopf, 1977).

124. Environment Action Bulletin and Organic Gardening and Farming, *The Organic Guide to Colleges and Universities*, 2.

125. Conford, *The Origins of the Organic Movement*, follows this theme of traditional or peasant knowledge versus a more detached and atomistic modern science, focusing on European organic thought. See also Peters, "The Land in Trust."

126. Rodale, *Pay Dirt*.

127. Paul A. Lee, *There Is a Garden in the Mind: A Memoir of Alan Chadwick and the Organic Movement in California* (Berkeley, CA: North Atlantic, 2013), xi, 51. Volunteers in Chadwick's garden recalled similar tensions. See Regional History Project, University of California, Santa Cruz, "Cultivating a Movement."

128. U.S. House of Representatives, *Hearings Before the House Select Committee to Investigate the Use of Chemicals in Food Products*, 867.

129. Environment Action Bulletin and Organic Gardening and Farming, *The Organic Guide to Colleges and Universities*, 48. Similar criticisms run through *Acres, USA*. On the long-running battles between organic and conventional agriculture over research funding, see Ingram and Ingram, "Creating Credible Edibles."

130. *East Village Other*, February 4, 1970, 20; Environment Action Bulletin and Organic Gardening and Farming, *The Organic Guide to Colleges and Universities*, 51–53.

131. *Organic Gardening and Farming*, July 1973, 60–61, March 1976, 158.

132. Environment Action Bulletin and Organic Gardening and Farming, *The Organic Guide to Colleges and Universities*, 69.

133. Smith, *Eating History*.

134. Interview with Bob Scowcraft, in Regional History Project, University of California, Santa Cruz, "Cultivating a Movement."

135. David Goodman and his colleagues suggest that organic activists conceded too much in their quest for legitimacy. By focusing narrowly on relevant scientific research, they lost sight of the broader context of institutionalized power in the food system. David Goodman, E. Melanie DuPuis, and Michael K. Goodman, *Alternative Food Networks: Knowledge, Place and Politics* (New York: Routledge, 2012).

136. Interview with Larry Jacobs, in Regional History Project, University of California, Santa Cruz, "Cultivating a Movement." See also the interview with Ken Kimes and Sandra Ward, in ibid.; Obach, *Organic Struggle*.

137. On relations among farmers and between farmers and consumers, see especially the oral histories in Regional History Project, University of California, Santa Cruz, "Cultivating a Movement." I discuss the institutional arrangements for these ties below.

138. Belasco, *Appetite for Change*; Bobrow-Strain, *White Bread*.

139. The charge that organic neglected issues of food and race appears early on, as in *Chicago Seed*, January 15, 1972, and was a sore point for *Organic Gardening and Farming* (see, e.g., the issue dated February 1972, 8).

140. *Organic Gardening and Farming*, August 1960, 11; Obach, *Organic Struggle*, 38.

141. Obach, *Organic Struggle*, 57.

142. Haedicke, *Organizing Organic*, notes that priorities differed from one organization to another. The CCOF moved more quickly into certification than did NOFA because it had earlier market opportunities. See also Nowacek, "The Organic Foods System from 1969–1996"; Guthman, *Agrarian Dreams*.

143. Gershuny, *Organic Revolutionary*.

144. Regional History Project, University of California, Santa Cruz, "Cultivating a Movement"; Guthman, *Agrarian Dreams*, 112.

145. *Organic Gardening and Farming*, April 1973, 89. See also Nowacek, "The Organic Foods System from 1969–1996."

146. Haedicke, *Organizing Organic*.

147. *Organic Gardening and Farming*, April 1972, 140.

148. Ibid., 132–138.

149. Miller, *Building Nature's Market*; *Organic Gardening and Farming*, November 1970, 39–42.

150. *Organic Gardening and Farming*, June 1962, 17; March 1970, 40; September 1972, 42.

151. Ibid., August 1970, 61.

152. Direct buying included precursors to community-supported agriculture programs, as well as shopping at roadside stands. See ibid., March 1971, 43–44, May 1971, 91.

153. Ibid., August 1970, 38.

154. Interviews with Janet Brians and Cantisano, in Regional History Project, University of California, Santa Cruz, "Cultivating a Movement."

155. Letter to the editor, *Organic Gardening and Farming*, August 1971, 21.

156. Garth Youngberg, "Alternative Agriculturalists: Ideology, Politics, and Prospects," in *The New Politics of Food*, edited by Don F. Hadwiger and William P. Browne (Lexington, MA: Lexington Books, 1978), 227–246.

157. Kauffman, *Hippie Food*, 185.

158. Maria McGrath, "'That's Capitalism, Not a Co-op': Countercultural Idealism and Business Realism in 1970s U.S. Food Co-ops," *Business and Economic History On-Line* 2 (2004): 2. See also Robert Sommer, "More Than Cheap Cheese: The Food Co-op Movement in the United States," *Research in Social Movements, Conflicts and Change* 7 (1984): 71–94; Haedicke, *Organizing Organic*; Upright, *Grocery Activism*.

159. Quoted in Obach, *Organic Struggle*, 41.

160. Cox, *Storefront Revolution*.

161. Ibid.; McGrath, *Food for Dissent*. Belasco makes a similar case for "hip" businesses of the early 1970s, such as Celestial Seasonings and the Moosewood Restaurant, cooperatively owned and making countercultural iconography part of their market appeal: Belasco, *Appetite for Change*.

162. Stephanie Hartman, "The Political Palate: Reading Commune Cookbooks," *Gastronomica* 3, no. 2 (Spring 2003): 29–40; Upright, *Grocery Activism*. By the late 1990s, professionalized organizations operating on a national scale played a far more important role. Farmers and processors joined the Organic Foods Production Association of North America (established in 1984; renamed the Organic Trade Association in 1990), taking a particularly close interest in federal standards. Consumers had the Organic Consumers Association (1998), vigilant if not always successful in protecting national standards from dilution. See, e.g., Haedicke, *Organizing Organic*; Clark, *The Changing Politics of Organic Food in North America*. But these associations are more a part of the story of organic's shift from movement to market, helping institutionalize a narrower approach to constructing an alternative food system. They will make a brief appearance in Chapter 5 as vehicles carrying the influence of the organic movement into contemporary food politics.

163. *Organic Gardening and Farming*, March 1970, 43.

164. See, e.g., ibid., July 1961, 15.

165. *Berkeley Barb*, November 26–December 2, 1976, 6. On similar networks in Ann Arbor, see L. Kauffman, *South San Francisco: A History* (San Francisco: Self-published, 1976), 15; Kauffman, *Hippie Food*, 15.

166. *Organic Gardening and Farming*, March, May, and June 1971.

167. Gershuny, *Organic Revolutionary*, 60.

168. *Organic Gardening and Farming*, June 1971, 69.

169. For these early practices, see recollections in Regional History Project, University of California, Santa Cruz, "Cultivating a Movement"; Guthman, *Agrarian Dreams*.

170. Clark, *The Changing Politics of Organic Food in North America*, 87.

171. National Resources Defense Council, *Intolerable Risk: Pesticides in Our Children's Food* (New York: The Council, 1989).

172. Nowacek, "The Organic Foods System from 1969–1996"; Ingram and Ingram, "Creating Credible Edibles"; Garth Youngberg and Suzanne P. DeMuth, "Organic Agriculture in the United States: A 30-Year Retrospective," *Renewable Agriculture and Food Systems* 28, no. 4 (December 2013): 294–328; Haedicke, *Organizing Organic*.

173. Interview with Barney Bricmont, in Regional History Project, University of California, Santa Cruz, "Cultivating a Movement." Two accounts that are especially good on growers' ambivalence are Haedicke, *Organizing Organic*, and Obach, *Organic Struggle*.

174. *Organic Gardening and Farming*, July 1973, 60–61; Youngberg, "Alternative Agriculturalists," 239–241.

175. Ingram and Ingram, "Creating Credible Edibles."

176. Haedicke, *Organizing Organic*, 83; Obach, *Organic Struggle*, 138.

177. *New York Times*, April 9, 1972.

178. Even in 1990, the national organic program was more a promise than a reality. It arrived only in 2000. The general story of organic's assimilation is well told in Belasco, *Appetite for Change*, which emphasizes the consumer market, and Guthman, *Agrarian Dreams*. A more popular version is the discussion of Big Organic in Pollan, *The Omnivore's Dilemma*. These and similar accounts make it easy to keep my retelling short.

179. Goodman et al., *Alternative Food Networks*, 134.

180. Lee, *There Is a Garden in the Mind*, 137. See also the recollections of Chadwick at UCSC by Orin Martin and Amigo Bob Cantisano, in Regional History Project, University of California, Santa Cruz, "Cultivating a Movement."

181. Timothy Vos, "Visions of the Middle Landscape: Organic Farming and the Politics of Nature," *Agriculture and Human Values* 17, no. 3 (September 2000): 245–256; Laura Sayre, "The Politics of Organic Farming: Populists, Evangelicals and the Agriculture of the Middle," *Gastronomica* 11, no. 2 (May 2011): 38–47; Haedicke, *Organizing Organic*.

182. Guthman, *Agrarian Dreams*.

183. Michael A. Haedicke, "'Keeping Our Mission, Changing Our System': Translation and Organizational Change in Natural Foods Co-ops," *Sociological Quarterly* 53, no. 1 (2012): 44–67. Here I do not so much disagree with Haedicke as see the glass as half empty. See also John Case and Rosemary C. R. Taylor, eds., *Co-ops, Communes and Collectives: Experiments in Social Change in the 1960s and 1970s* (New York: Pantheon, 1979); McGrath, "That's Capitalism, Not a Co-op"; Anne Meis Knupfer, *Food Co-ops in America: Communities, Consumption, and Economic Democracy* (Ithaca, NY: Cornell University Press, 2013).

184. Miller, *Building Nature's Market*.

185. Philip H. Howard, "Consolidation in the North American Organic Food Processing Sector, 1997 to 2007," *International Journal of Sociology of Agriculture and Food* 16, no. 1 (April 2009): 13–30.

186. Haedicke, *Organizing Organic*, 86.

187. Obach, *Organic Struggle*, 82.

188. Jolly, "Differences between Buyers and Nonbuyers of Organic Produce and Willingness to Pay Organic Price Premiums"; Barbara Goldman and Katherine L. Clancy, "A Survey of Organic Produce Purchases and Related Attitudes of Food Cooperative Shoppers," *American Journal of Alternative Agriculture* 6, no. 2 (June 1991): 89–96.

189. David Kamp, *The United States of Arugula: The Sun-Dried, Cold-Pressed, Dark-Roasted, Extra Virgin Story of the American Food Revolution* (New York: Broadway, 2006); Warren J. Belasco, *Appetite for Change*; Kauffman, *Hippie Food*; McGrath, *Food for Dissent*.

190. Guthman, "From the Ground Up."

191. Josée Johnston and Shyon Baumann, *Foodies: Democracy and Distinction in the Gourmet Foodscape* (New York: Routledge, 2010).

192. See, e.g., *Berkeley Barb*, January 24–30, 1969.

193. The quotes and numbers are from the fragmentary web archive "National Organic Program Proposed Rule," U.S. Department of Agriculture, Agricultural Marketing Service, accessed July 31, 2018, https://web.archive.org/web/19990219172106/http://www.ams.usda.gov/nop/view.htm. See also the analysis of the comments in Stephen Zavestoski, Stuart Shulman, and David Schlosberg, "Democracy and the Environment on the Internet: Electronic Citizen Participation in Regulatory Rulemaking," *Science, Technology, and Human Values* 31, no. 4 (July 2006): 383–408. On the tortuous history of the National Organic Program, see Ingram and Ingram, "Creating Credible Edibles"; Obach, *Organic Struggle*; Haedicke, *Organizing Organic*.

194. Obach, *Organic Struggle*; Clark, *The Changing Politics of Organic Food in North America*; Haedicke, *Organizing Organic*.

195. Gershuny, *Organic Revolutionary*, 63–65.

196. Since 2000, much of the focus of advocacy groups such as the Organic Consumers Association and the Rodale Institute has been on resisting efforts to loosen restrictions on allowable ingredients. On the general shift from process to product, see Clark, *The Changing Politics of Organic Food in North America*.

197. *Organic Gardening and Farming*, July 1972, 10–11.

198. Obach, *Organic Struggle*; Haedicke, *Organizing Organic*. The initiative to develop a "Regenerative Organic Certification" program is one recent effort to restore something of organic's early vision, with the salutary addition of standards for farm labor pay and collective bargaining rights. See the Regenerative Organic Certification website at https://regenorganic.org/.

199. Christy Getz, Sandy Brown, and Aimee Shreck, "Class Politics and Agricultural Exceptionalism in California's Organic Agriculture Movement," *Politics and Society* 36, no. 4 (December 2008): 478–507.

200. U.S. Department of Agriculture, Agricultural Marketing Service, "National Organic Program: Final Rule," *Federal Register*, vol. 65, no. 246, December 21, 2000, 80556. See also Joshua Sbicca, *Food Justice Now! Deepening the Roots of Social Struggle* (Minneapolis: University of Minnesota Press, 2018).

201. Daniel Jaffee and Philip H. Howard, "Corporate Cooptation of Organic and Fair Trade Standards," *Agriculture and Human Values* 27, no. 4 (December 2010): 387–399. Haedicke, *Organizing Organic*, notes that, on this point, organic advocates' alliance with environmental and consumer groups did not serve them well. The environmental and consumer groups had less interest in producers' democratic self-governance.

202. Fitzgerald, *Every Farm a Factory*.

203. Among farmers, in particular, these features of organic advocacy had independent and earlier sources. For example, the embrace of local and participatory governance can also be traced to grassroots agrarian movements and to a long-standing suspicion of central government regulation. See Patrick H. Mooney and Theodore J. Majka, *Farmers' and Farm Workers' Movements: Social Protest in American Agriculture* (New York: Twayne, 1995); Smith, *Wendell Berry and the Agrarian Tradition*.

204. This pattern of applying a more general movement template to food issues appears in other food activism of the time—notably, in opposition to genetically engineered food. In this case, the template involved the New Left critique of mainstream science and corporate control over life itself. Rachel A. Schurman and William A. Munro, *Fighting for the Future of Food: Activists versus Agribusiness in the Struggle over Biotechnology* (Minneapolis: University of Minnesota Press, 2010).

CHAPTER 5

1. San Diego Roots Sustainable Food Project, accessed May 3, 2020, http://www
.sandiegoroots.org/history.html. All of the quotes in the paragraph are from this website.

2. Sidney Tarrow, *Power in Movement: Social Movements and Contentious Politics*
(Cambridge: Cambridge University Press, 1998); Debra C. Minkoff, "The Sequencing
of Social Movements," *American Sociological Review* 62, no. 5 (October 1997): 779–799.

3. Nancy F. Koehn, "Henry Heinz and Brand Creation in the Late Nineteenth Century: Making Markets for Processed Food," *Business History Review* 73, no. 3 (Autumn
1999): 349–393; Laura Miller, *Building Nature's Market: The Business and Politics of
Natural Foods* (Chicago: University of Chicago Press, 2017).

4. Michael Pollan, *In Defense of Food: An Eater's Manifesto* (New York: Penguin,
2008).

5. Harvey Levenstein, *Paradox of Plenty: A Social History of Eating in Modern
America* (Berkeley: University of California Press, 2003); Jessica J. Mudry, *Measured
Meals: Nutrition in America* (Albany: State University of New York Press, 2009).

6. "Prefigurative politics" refers to social movements modeling a more just society
in their own collective practices, such as by making decisions on a participatory basis.
Stacy Williams adds that individuals may do the same in their personal behavior and
consumption choices. Stacy J. Williams, "Personal Prefigurative Politics: Cooking Up
an Ideal Society in the Woman's Temperance and Woman's Suffrage Movements, 1870–
1920," *Sociological Quarterly* 58, no. 1 (November 2017): 72–90.

7. Maria McGrath, *Food for Dissent: Natural Foods and the Consumer Counterculture
since the 1960s* (Amherst: University of Massachusetts Press, 2019).

8. See Chapter 4. Women continue to be overrepresented among locavore "activists."
See Laura B. DeLind and Anne E. Ferguson, "Is This a Women's Movement? The Relationship of Gender to Community-Supported Agriculture in Michigan"; Cynthia A. Cone
and Andrea Myhre, "Community-Supported Agriculture: A Sustainable Alternative to
Industrial Agriculture?" *Human Organization* 58, no. 2 (Summer 1999): 190–200. Calls
from reformers such as Michael Pollan for the revival of home cooking to save our waist-
lines and our palates from processed food also seem to assign special responsibility to
women (especially when combined with narratives that trace the decline of home cooking
to the rise of feminism). See Michael Pollan, "Out of the Kitchen, Onto the Couch," *New
York Times*, July 29, 2009. But trustworthy food today is not feminine in the same way
it was for Graham or Richards. For one thing, women's cooking is sometimes redefined
as fostering a sustainable earth as well as a healthy family. Women are seen not as mere
housewives, Peggy Orenstein observes, but as "femivores": Peggy Orenstein, "The Femivore's Dilemma," *New York Times*, March 11, 2010. Further, "good food" reflects not their
piety but a new appreciation for quality and taste. Proper diet issues from more cultivated
palates rather than from nutritional education. On locavorism, gender, and elite tastes, see
Josée Johnston, Michelle Szabo, and Alexandra Rodney, "Good Food, Good People: Understanding the Cultural Repertoire of Ethical Eating," *Journal of Consumer Culture* 11,
no. 3 (November 2011): 293–318; Kate Cairns, Josée Johnston, and Shyon Bauman, "Caring about Food: Doing Gender in the Foodie Kitchen," *Gender and Society* 24, no. 5 (October 2010): 591–615; S. Margot Finn, *Discriminating Taste: How Class Anxiety Created the
American Food Revolution* (New Brunswick, NJ: Rutgers University Press, 2017).

9. Joseph R. Gusfield, "Nature's Body and the Metaphors of Food," in *Cultivating Differences: Symbolic Boundaries and the Making of Inequality*, edited by Michèle Lamont

and Marcel Fournier (Chicago: University of Chicago Press, 1992), 75–103; E. Melanie DuPuis, "Angels and Vegetables: A Brief History of Food Advice in America," *Gastronomica* 7, no. 2 (Summer 2007): 34–44.

10. Miller, *Building Nature's Market*.

11. Unni Kjaernes, "Risk and Trust in the Food Supply," in *The Handbook of Food Research*, edited by Anne Murcott, Warren Belasco, and Peter Jackson (London: Bloomsbury, 2013), 410–424.

12. Rachel A. Schurman and William A. Munro, *Fighting for the Future of Food Activists versus Agribusiness in the Struggle over Biotechnology* (Minneapolis: University of Minnesota Press, 2010).

13. John Walton, *Western Times and Water Wars: State, Culture, and Rebellion in California* (Berkeley: University of California Press, 1992); Chad Alan Goldberg, *Citizens and Paupers: Relief, Rights, and Race, from the Freedmen's Bureau to Workfare* (Chicago: University of Chicago Press, 2007); John Krinsky, "Neoliberal Times: Intersecting Temporalities and the Neoliberalization of New York City's Public-Sector Labor Relations," *Social Science History* 35, no. 3 (Fall 2011): 381–422; Chris Rhomberg, *The Broken Table: The Detroit Newspaper Strike and the State of American Labor* (New York: Russell Sage Foundation, 2012).

14. Aldon D. Morris, *The Origins of the Civil Rights Movement: Black Communities Organizing for Change* (New York: Free Press, 1984); Robert Futrell and Pete Simi, "Free Spaces, Collective Identity, and the Persistence of U.S. White Power Activism," *Social Problems* 51, no. 1 (February 2004): 16–42.

15. Pamela E. Oliver and Daniel J. Myers, "Networks, Diffusion, and Cycles of Collective Action," in *Social Movements and Networks: Relational Approaches to Collective Action*, edited by Mario Diani and Doug McAdam (New York: Oxford University Press, 2003), 173–203; Donatella della Porta and Lorenzo Mosca, "In Movimento: 'Contamination' in Action and the Italian Global Justice Movement" *Global Networks* 7, no. 1 (January 2007): 1–27; Gemma Edwards, "Infectious Innovations? The Diffusion of Tactical Innovation in Social Movement Networks, the Case of Suffragette Militancy," *Social Movement Studies* 13, no. 1 (2014): 48–69.

16. On "political consumerism" or "conscientious consumption" movements, see Michele Micheletti, *Political Virtue and Shopping: Individuals, Consumerism, and Collective Action* (New York: Palgrave Macmillan, 2003); W. Lance Bennett, "Branded Political Communication: Lifestyle Politics, Logo Campaigns, and the Rise of Global Citizenship," in *Politics, Products, and Markets: Exploring Political Consumerism Past and Present*, edited by Michele Micheletti, Andreas Føllesdal, and Dietlind Stolle (New Brunswick, NJ: Transaction, 2004), 101–125; Boris Holzer, "Political Consumerism between Individual Choice and Collective Action: Social Movements, Role Mobilization and Signalling," *International Journal of Consumer Studies* 30, no. 5 (September 2006): 405–415; Lawrence B. Glickman, *Buying Power: A History of Consumer Activism in America* (Chicago: University of Chicago Press, 2009); Dhavan V. Shah, Douglas M. McLeod, Lewis Friedland, and Michelle R. Nelson, "The Politics of Consumption/The Consumption of Politics," *Annals of the American Academy of Political and Social Science* 611, no. 1 (May 2007): 6–15; Philip Balsiger, "Making Political Consumers: The Tactical Action Repertoire of a Campaign for Clean Clothes," *Social Movement Studies* 9, no. 3 (August 2010): 311–329; Jeffrey Haydu and David Kadanoff, "Casing Political Consumerism," *Mobilization* 15, no. 2 (June 2010): 159–177; Dhavan V. Shah, Lewis A. Friedland, Chris Wells, Young Mie Kim, and Hernando Rojas, "Communication, Consumers,

and Citizens: Revisiting the Politics of Consumption," *Annals of the American Academy of Political and Social Science* 644, no. 1 (November 2012): 6–19; Caroline Heldman, *Protest Politics in the Marketplace: Consumer Activism in the Corporate Age* (Ithaca, NY: Cornell University Press, 2017).

17. Ross Haenfler, "Collective Identity in the Straight Edge Movement: How Diffuse Movements Foster Commitment, Encourage Individualized Participation, and Promote Cultural Change," *Sociological Quarterly* 45, no. 4 (Autumn 2004): 785–805; Elizabeth Cherry, "Veganism as a Cultural Movement: A Relational Approach," *Social Movement Studies* 5, no. 2 (September 2006): 155–170; Holzer, "Political Consumerism between Individual Choice and Collective Action."

18. Homegrown Organic Farms, http://www.hgofarms.com; Imogen Rose-Smith, "Institutional, Impact Investing Find Common Ground in Agriculture," *Institutional Investor*, accessed February 1, 2021, https://www.institutionalinvestor.com/article /b14z9v43y8b6zd/institutional-impact-investing-find-common-ground-in-agriculture.

19. Overviews include Michael Pollan, *The Omnivore's Dilemma: A Natural History of Four Meals* (New York: Penguin, 2006); Marion Nestle, *Eat Drink Vote: An Illustrated Guide to Food Politics* (New York: Rodale, 2013); Robert Gottlieb and Anupama Joshi, *Food Justice* (Cambridge, MA: MIT Press, 2010).

20. G. W. Feenstra, "Local Food Systems and Sustainable Communities," *American Journal of Alternative Agriculture* 12, no. 1 (March 1997): 28–36. The Cornucopia Project, launched by Robert Rodale in the late 1970s, was one important bridge between the organic and locavore movements. Its early publications anticipated many locavore priorities, and its affiliates have been consistent advocates for alternative agriculture.

21. Patricia Allen, *Together at the Table: Sustainability and Sustenance in the American Agrifood System* (University Park: Pennsylvania State University Press, 2004).

22. Roundups of these problems in the food system, together with many other examples, are in Allen, *Together at the Table*; Patricia Allen, Margaret FitzSimmons, Michael Goodman, and Keith Warner, "Shifting Plates in the Agrifood Landscape: The Tectonics of Alternative Agrifood Initiatives in California," *Journal of Rural Studies* 19, no. 1 (January 2003): 61–75; Jennifer Meta Robinson and James R. Farmer, *Selling Local: Why Local Food Movements Matter* (Bloomington: Indiana University Press, 2017). "Buy local" campaigns became common from about 1999: see C. Clare Hinrichs and Patricia Allen, "Selective Patronage and Social Justice: Local Food Consumer Campaigns in Historical Context," *Journal of Agricultural and Environmental Ethics* 21, no. 4 (August 2008): 329–352. "Food security" is a new term for an old problem addressed by earlier groups, including the Black Panthers in their breakfast program. See Raj Patel, "Survival Pending Revolution: What the Black Panthers Can Teach the U.S. Food Movement," in Holt-Giménez, *Food Movements Unite!* 115–135. The Hartford Food System (1978) seems to have been the first to combine the goals of food security with local agricultural sustainability. See Elizabeth Henderson, "Rebuilding Local Food Systems from the Grassroots Up," in *Hungry for Profit: The Agribusiness Threat to Farmers, Food, and the Environment*, edited by Fred Magdoff, John Bellamy Foster, and Frederick H. Buttel (New York: Monthly Review, 2000), 175–188. On the farm bill, see Daniel Imhoff, *Food Fight! The Citizen's Guide to the Next Food and Farm Bill* (Healdsburg, CA: Watershed Media, 2012). On protest against genetically engineered foods, see Schurman and Munro, *Fighting for the Future of Food*; Frederick H. Buttel, "The Environmental and Post-environmental Politics of Genetically Modified Crops and Foods," *Environmental Politics* 14, no. 3 (June 2005): 309–323. The first Food Policy

Council was in Knoxville and dates from 1977. The primary goal of these councils is to bring together stakeholders within and outside government to pool expertise and resources in dealing with issues such as food security, nutrition, and local agriculture. For accounts of their diffusion, see Kate Clancy, Janet Hammer, and Debra Lippoldt, "Food Policy Councils," in *Remaking the North American Food System: Strategies for Sustainability*, edited by C. Clare Hinrichs and Thomas A. Lyson (Lincoln: University of Nebraska Press, 2007), 121–143; Patrick H. Mooney, Keiko Tanaka, and Gabriele Ciciurkaite, "Food Policy Council Movement in North America: A Convergence of Alternative Local Agrifood Interests?" *Research in Rural Sociology and Development* 21 (2014): 229–255; Alethea Harper, Annie Shattuck, Eric Holt-Giménez, Alison Alkon, and Frances Lambrick, *Food Policy Councils: Lessons Learned*, Institute for Food and Development Policy, 2009, accessed May 3, 2020, http://foodfirst.org/publication/food-policy-councils-lessons-learned.

23. One systematic overview of these groups is Allen, *Together at the Table*.

24. "HEAL Member Organizations," HEAL Food Alliance, accessed May 17, 2020, https://healfoodalliance.org/who-is-heal/ourmembers.

25. Marcia R. Ostrom, "Toward a Community Supported Agriculture: A Case Study of Resistance and Change in the Modern Food System," Ph.D. diss. (University of Wisconsin, Madison, 1997); David Goodman and Michael Goodman, "Localism, Livelihoods, and the 'Post-Organic': Changing Perspectives on Alternative Food Networks in the United States," in *Alternative Food Geographies: Representation and Practice*, edited by Damien Maye, Lewis Holloway, and Moya Kneafsey (Oxford: Elsevier, 2007), 23–38.

26. These generalizations are based on a number of case studies, none of them using strictly representative samples. Cone and Myhre, "Community-Supported Agriculture"; Cynthia A. Cone and A. Kakaliouras, "Community Supported Agriculture: Building Moral Community or an Alternative Consumer Choice," *Culture and Agriculture* 15, no. 51–52 (March 1995): 28–31; Kenneth Brandon Lang Loughridge, "Community Supported Agriculture (CSA) in the Mid-Atlantic United States: A Sociological Analysis," Ph.D. diss. (University of Wisconsin, Madison, 2002); Jack R. Kloppenburg, Jr., Sharon Lezberg, Kathryn De Master, George W. Stevenson, and John Hendrickson, "Tasting Food, Tasting Sustainability: Defining the Attributes of an Alternative Food System with Competent, Ordinary People," *Human Organization* 59, no. 2 (Summer 2000): 177–186; Theresa Selfa and Joan Qazi, "Place, Taste, or Face-to-Face: Understanding Producer-Consumer Networks in 'Local' Food Systems in Washington State," *Agriculture and Human Values* 22, no. 4 (December 2005): 451–464; Patricia Allen and Clare Hinrichs, "Buying into 'Buy Local': Engagements of United States Local Food Initiatives," in *Alternative Food Geographies: Representation and Practice*, edited by Damian Maye, Lewis Holloway, and Moya Kneafsey (Oxford: Elsevier, 2007), 255–272; Zachary Schrank and Katrina Running, "Individualist and Collectivist Consumer Motivations in Local Organic Food Markets," *Journal of Consumer Culture* 18, no. 1 (February 2018): 184–201; Nathan McClintock and Michael Simpson, "Stacking Functions: Identifying Motivational Frames Guiding Urban Agriculture Organizations and Businesses in the United States and Canada," *Agriculture and Human Values* 35, no. 1 (March 2018): 19–39.

27. Julie Guthman and E. Melanie DuPuis, "Embodying Neoliberalism: Economy, Culture, and the Politics of Fat," *Environment and Planning. D, Society and Space* 24, no. 3 (June 2006): 427–448; Goodman and Goodman, "Localism, Livelihoods, and the 'Post-Organic'"; Jeff Pratt, "Food Values: The Local and the Authentic," *Critique of*

Anthropology 27, no. 3 (September 2007): 285–300; Mark Winne, *Closing the Food Gap: Resetting the Table in the Land of Plenty* (Boston: Beacon, 2008); Gottlieb and Joshi, *Food Justice*; Alison Hope Alkon and Julian Agyeman, eds., *Cultivating Food Justice: Race, Class, and Sustainability* (Cambridge, MA: MIT Press, 2011); Holt-Giménez, *Food Movements Unite*; Noha Shawki, "The 2008 Food Crisis as a Critical Event for the Food Sovereignty and Food Justice Movements," *International Journal of Sociology of Agriculture and Food* 19, no. 3 (October 2012): 423–444; Z. W. Brent, C. M. Schiavoni, and A. Fraejas, "Contextualising Food Sovereignty: The Politics of Convergence among Movements in the USA," *Third World Quarterly* 36, no. 3 (2015): 618–635; Alison Hope Alkon and Julie Guthman, eds., *The New Food Activism: Opposition, Cooperation, and Collective Action* (Berkeley: University of California Press, 2017). Emily Huddart Kennedy and her colleagues, drawing on interviews with Canadian locavores, find them more progressive (notably in advocating democratic governance as an antidote to corporate food control) in their critiques than in their remedies. Emily Huddart Kennedy, John R. Parkins, and Josée Johnston, "Food Activists, Consumer Strategies, and the Democratic Imagination: Insights from Eat-Local Movements," *Journal of Consumer Culture* 18, no. 1 (February 2018): 149–168.

28. Robyn Van En Center, Wilson College, accessed May 18, 2020, https://www.wilson.edu/robyn-van-en-center.

29. Groundswell Center for Local Food and Farming, accessed May 18, 2020, https://groundswellcenter.org/core-values.

30. The quote is from the National Sustainable Agriculture Coalition, accessed May 18, 2020, https://sustainableagriculture.net/our-work.

31. Goodman, "The Quality 'Turn' and Alternative Food Practices"; Allen, *Together at the Table*; Selfa and Qazi, "Place, Taste, or Face-to-Face"; Thomas A. Lyson, "Civic Agriculture and the North American Food System," in Hinrichs and Lyson, *Remaking the North American Food System*, 19–32. Chad Lavin draws a sharper contrast between organic and local "authenticity" in Chad Lavin, *Eating Anxiety: The Perils of Food Politics* (Minneapolis, MN: University of Minnesota Press, 2013). The first is distinguished from problematic food by chemicals, the second by distance. This contrast underestimates early organic activists' explicit support for local farming and localized sourcing as parts of a better food system.

32. "About Us," LocalHarvest, accessed May 18, 2020, https://www.localharvest.org/about.jsp.

33. One hopeful early account is Neva Hassanein, *Changing the Way America Farms: Knowledge and Community in the Sustainable Agriculture Movement* (Lincoln: University of Nebraska Press, 1999). Various cautionary notes can be found in Allen, *Together at the Table*; C. Clare Hinrichs, "The Practice and Politics of Food System Localization," *Journal of Rural Studies* 19, no. 1 (January 2003): 33–45; Michael Winter, "Embeddedness, the New Food Economy and Defensive Localism," *Journal of Rural Studies* 19, no. 1 (January 2003): 23–32; David Goodman, E. Melanie DuPuis, and Michael K. Goodman, *Alternative Food Networks: Knowledge, Place and Politics* (New York: Routledge, 2012).

34. C. Clare Hinrichs, "Embeddedness and Local Food Systems: Notes on Two Types of Direct Agricultural Market," *Journal of Rural Studies* 16, no. 3 (July 2000): 295–303; DeLind and Ferguson, "Is This a Women's Movement?"; Martin Thorsøe and Chris Kjeldsen, "The Constitution of Trust: Function, Configuration and Generation of Trust in Alternative Food Networks," *Sociologia Ruralis* 56, no. 2 (April 2016): 157–175.

35. E. P. Thompson, "The Moral Economy of the English Crowd in the Eighteenth Century," *Past and Present* 50, no. 1 (February 1971): 76–136; J. Stevenson, "Food Riots in England, 1792–1818," in *Popular Protest and Public Order: Six Studies in British History 1790–1920*, edited by R. Quinault and J. Stevenson (New York: St. Martin's, 1974), 33–74; Anthony James Coles, "The Moral Economy of the Crowd: Some Twentieth-Century Food Riots," *Journal of British Studies* 18, no. 1 (Autumn 1978): 157–176; Barbara Clark Smith, "Food Rioters and the American Revolution," *William and Mary Quarterly* 51, no. 1 (January 1994): 3–38. Classic food riots often included a call for local authorities to take responsibility for price controls. Contemporary locavores are more likely to rely on reconfigured markets.

36. Kimberly K. Smith, *Wendell Berry and the Agrarian Tradition: A Common Grace* (Lawrence: University Press of Kansas, 2003); Allen, *Together at the Table*.

37. On the appeal (and marketing) of artisanal food, see Josée Johnston and Shyon Baumann, *Foodies: Democracy and Distinction in the Gourmet Foodscape* (New York: Routledge, 2010); Siddhartha Shome, "The Social Vision of the Alternative Food Movement," in *The Oxford Handbook of Food, Politics, and Society*, edited by Ronald J. Herring (Oxford: Oxford University Press, 2015), 523–542. This idealization of food craftsmen, handicraft methods, and local traditions is especially prominent in the Slow Food movement. See Anne Meneley, "Extra Virgin Olive Oil and Slow Food," *Anthropologica* 46, no. 2 (2004): 165–176; Adrian Peace, "Barossa Slow: The Representation and Rhetoric of Slow Food's Regional Cooking," *Gastronomica* 6, no. 1 (February 2006): 51–59.

38. "Locavore Brewing: The Secret Is in the Malt," *San Francisco Business Times*, n.d., accessed May 18, 2020, https://www.bizjournals.com/sanfrancisco/feature/city-of -alameda/2018/locavore-brewing-the-secret-is-in-the-malt.html.

39. Julie Guthman, "From the Ground Up: California Organics and the Making of 'Yuppie Chow,'" in *Alternative Food Geographies: Representation and Practice*, edited by Damian Maye, Lewis Holloway, and Moya Kneafsey (Oxford: Elsevier, 2007), 241–254.

40. David Naguib Pellow and Robert J. Brulle, eds., *Power, Justice, and the Environment: A Critical Appraisal of the Environmental Justice Movement* (Cambridge, MA: MIT Press, 2005); Angela G. Mertig, Riley E. Dunlap, and Denton E. Morrison, "The Environmental Movement in the United States," in *Handbook of Environmental Sociology*, edited by Riley E. Dunlap and William Michelson (Westport, CT: Greenwood, 2000), 448–481.

41. Community Alliance with Family Farmers, accessed May 18, 2020, https://www .caff.org/about.

42. Allen, *Together at the Table*; Winne, *Closing the Food Gap*; E. Melanie DuPuis, Jill Lindsey Harrison, and David Goodman, "Just Food?" in *Cultivating Food Justice: Race, Class, and Sustainability*, edited by Alison Hope Alkon and Julian Agyeman (Cambridge, MA: MIT Press, 2011), 283–307; Eric Holt-Giménez and Yi Wang, "Reform or Transformation? The Pivotal Role of Food Justice in the U.S. Food Movement," *Race/Ethnicity* 5, no. 1 (Autumn 2011): 83–102.

43. Brenda Biddle, "Food Sovereignty and Protest," in *The International Encyclopedia of Revolution and Protest*, vol. 3, edited by Immanuel Ness (Chichester, UK: Wiley-Blackwell, 2009), 1210–1212; Holt-Giménez, *Food Movements Unite*; Shawki, "The 2008 Food Crisis as a Critical Event for the Food Sovereignty and Food Justice Movements"; Brent et al., "Contextualising Food Sovereignty."

44. "What Is Food Sovereignty?" National Family Farm Coalition (NFFC), accessed May 18, 2020, https://nffc.net/what-we-do/food-sovereignty. The NFFC is also "proud

to be a member of La Via Campesina, the international peasant movement leading the fight for food sovereignty."

45. Kelly Donati, "The Pleasure of Diversity in Slow Food's Ethics of Taste," *Food, Culture and Society* 8, no. 2 (Fall 2005): 227–242; Hinrichs and Allen, "Selective Patronage and Social Justice"; Holt-Giménez and Wang, "Reform or Transformation?"; Alison Hope Alkon, "Food Justice," in *Routledge International Handbook of Food Studies*, edited by Ken Albala (London: Taylor and Francis, 2013), 295–305. Activism in the name of food sovereignty and allied to the anti-globalization movement is in part a struggle *against* neoliberalism. So, too, is any concerted effort to reduce free-market control of food prices and supplies.

46. Micheletti, *Political Virtue and Shopping*; Dietlind Stolle, Marc Hooghe, and Michele Micheletti, "Politics in the Supermarket: Political Consumption as a Form of Political Participation," *International Political Science Review* 26, no. 3 (July 2005): 245–269; Dhavan V. Shah, Douglas M. McLeod, Eunkyung Kim, Sun Young Lee, Melissa R. Gotlieb, Shirley S. Ho, and Hilde Breivik, "Political Consumerism: How Communication and Consumption Orientations Drive 'Lifestyle Politics,'" *Annals of the American Academy of Political and Social Science* 611, no. 1 (May 2007): 217–235; Shah et al., "Communication, Consumers, and Citizens."

47. This quote and the following examples are all drawn from the organizations' websites, accessed in November 2018.

48. Regional History Project, University of California, Santa Cruz, "Cultivating a Movement: Organic and Sustainable Farming," https://library.ucsc.edu/reg-hist/cultiv/home.

49. Miller, *Building Nature's Market*. For other examples, see Ostrom, "Toward a Community Supported Agriculture." Similar continuities can be found between the organic movement and contemporary activism around genetically modified foods: Frederick H. Buttel, "The Global Politics of GEOs: The Achilles' Heel of the Globalization Regime?" in *Engineering Trouble: Biotechnology and Its Discontents*, edited by Rachel A. Schurman and Dennis Doyle Takahashi Kelso (Berkeley: University of California Press, 2003), 152–173.

50. Michael A. Haedicke, *Organizing Organic: Conflict and Compromise in an Emerging Market* (Stanford, CA: Stanford University Press, 2016).

51. On these more recent connections among class, foodie-ism, and politically correct eating in the United States and elsewhere, see Johnston et al., "Good Food, Good People"; Peace, "Barossa Slow"; Jessica Paddock, "Positioning Food Cultures: 'Alternative' Food as Distinctive Consumer Practice," *Sociology* 50, no. 6 (December 2016): 1039–1055.

52. Miller, *Building Nature's Market*. On the "supermarket pastoral," see Pollan, *The Omnivore's Dilemma*.

53. Without pinpointing organic food as the source, some popular accounts also trace elite culinary fashions back to the "hippie food" of the late 1960s. David Kamp, *The United States of Arugula: The Sun-Dried, Cold-Pressed, Dark-Roasted, Extra Virgin Story of the American Food Revolution* (New York: Broadway, 2006); Jonathan Kauffman, *Hippie Food: How Back-to-the-Landers, Longhairs, and Revolutionaries Changed the Way We Eat* (New York: William Morrow, 2018).

54. Mrill Ingram and Helen Ingram, "Creating Credible Edibles: The Organic Agriculture Movement and the Emergence of U.S. Federal Organic Standards," in *Routing the Opposition: Social Movements, Public Policy, and Democracy*, edited by David S. Meyer,

Valerie Jenness, and Helen Ingram (Minneapolis: University of Minnesota Press, 2005), 121–148; Amory Starr, "Local Food: A Social Movement?" *Cultural Studies—Critical Methodologies* 10, no. 6 (December 2010): 479–490; Goodman et al., *Alternative Food Networks*.

55. Allen, *Together at the Table*; Mooney et al., "Food Policy Council Movement in North America."

56. Whittier's "anti-spillover" from one generation of feminist movement to another also highlights the potential power of the negative example. Nancy Whittier, *Feminist Generations: The Persistence of the Radical Women's Movement* (Philadelphia: Temple University Press, 1995).

57. Goodman and Goodman, "Localism, Livelihoods, and the 'Post-Organic.'"

58. Steven Shapin, "Paradise Sold: What Are You Buying When You Buy Organic?" *New Yorker*, vol. 82, no. 13, May 15, 2006, 84–88; Josée Johnston, "The Citizen-Consumer Hybrid: Ideological Tensions and the Case of Whole Foods Market," *Theory and Society* 37, no. 3 (June 2008): 229–270.

59. Julie Guthman, *Agrarian Dreams: The Paradox of Organic Farming in California* (Berkeley: University of California Press, 2004); Haedicke, *Organizing Organic*.

60. Goodman et al., *Alternative Food Networks*; Michaela DeSoucey and Isabelle Téchoueyres, "Virtue and Valorization: 'Local Food' in the United States and France," in *The Globalization of Food*, edited by David Inglis and Debra Gimlin (Oxford: Berg, 2009), 81–95.

61. Lisa F. Clark, *The Changing Politics of Organic Food in North America* (Cheltenham, UK: Edward Elger, 2015); Chad Lavin, "The Year of Eating Politically," *Theory and Event* 12, no. 2 (2009), doi:10.1353/tae.0.0074.

62. "Fast Food That's Straight from the Farm," *New York Times*, April 28, 2004. "Local" is not the only alternative to conventional food that has become a marketing ploy. Harriet Friedmann notes that other critiques of the food system have also been turned into lucrative market niches. Harriet Friedmann, "From Colonialism to Green Capitalism: Social Movements and Emergence of Food Regimes," *Research in Rural Sociology and Development* 11 (2005): 227–264. To her examples of "green" products one might add humane meat and GMO-free salt.

63. Neva Hassanein, "Practicing Food Democracy: A Pragmatic Politics of Transformation," *Journal of Rural Studies* 19, no. 1 (January 2003): 77–86; Gottlieb and Joshi, *Food Justice*; Alison Hope Alkon and Kari Marie Norgaard, "Breaking the Food Chains: An Investigation of Food Justice Activism," *Sociological Inquiry* 79, no. 3 (August 2009): 289–305.

64. Gerda R. Wekerle, "Food Justice Movements: Policy, Planning, and Networks," *Journal of Planning Education and Research* 23, no. 4 (June 2004): 378–386; Clancy et al., "Food Policy Councils"; Mooney et al., "Food Policy Council Movement in North America."

65. Margaret Gray, *Labor and the Locavore: The Making of a Comprehensive Food Ethic* (Berkeley: University of California Press, 2013).

References

Acres, USA. 1971–present. Raytown, MO.

Alcott, William A. 1859. *Forty Years in the Wilderness of Pills and Powders; or, The Cogitations and Confessions of an Aged Physician.* Boston: J. P. Jewett.

———, ed. 1837–1842. *The Library of Health and Teacher on the Human Constitution.* Boston: George W. Light.

———, ed. 1835–1836. *The Moral Reformer and Teacher on the Human Constitution.* Boston: Light and Horton.

Alkon, Alison Hope. 2013. "Food Justice." In *Routledge International Handbook of Food Studies,* edited by Ken Albala, 295–305. London: Taylor and Francis.

Alkon, Alison Hope, and Julian Agyeman, eds. 2011. *Cultivating Food Justice: Race, Class, and Sustainability.* Cambridge, MA: MIT Press.

Alkon, Alison Hope, and Julie Guthman, eds. 2017. *The New Food Activism: Opposition, Cooperation, and Collective Action.* Berkeley: University of California Press.

Alkon, Alison Hope, and Kari Marie Norgaard. 2009. "Breaking the Food Chains: An Investigation of Food Justice Activism." *Sociological Inquiry* 79, no. 3 (August): 289–305.

Allen, Patricia. 2004. *Together at the Table: Sustainability and Sustenance in the American Agrifood System.* University Park: Pennsylvania State University Press.

Allen, Patricia, Margaret FitzSimmons, Michael Goodman, and Keith Warner. 2003. "Shifting Plates in the Agrifood Landscape: The Tectonics of Alternative Agrifood Initiatives in California." *Journal of Rural Studies* 19, no. 1 (January): 61–75.

Allen, Patricia, and Clare Hinrichs. 2007. "Buying into 'Buy Local': Engagements of United States Local Food Initiatives." In *Alternative Food Geographies: Representation and Practice,* edited by Damian Maye, Lewis Holloway, and Moya Kneafsey, 255–272. Oxford: Elsevier.

Alternative Features Service. 1971–?. Berkeley, CA.

American City. 1909–1975. Pittsfield, MA.

American Kitchen. 1896–1903. Boston: Home Science Publishing.

American Physiological Society. 1837. *Constitution of the American Physiological Society.* Boston: Marsh.

Anderson, Oscar Edward. 1958. *The Health of a Nation: Harvey W. Wiley and the Fight for Pure Food.* Chicago: University of Chicago Press.

Ann Arbor Sun. 1971–1975. Ann Arbor, MI.

Ansell, Christopher, and David Vogel, eds. 2006. *What's the Beef? The Contested Governance of European Food Safety.* Cambridge, MA: MIT Press.

Archer, Melanie, and Judith R. Blau. 1993. "Class Formation in Nineteenth-Century America: The Case of the Middle Class." *Annual Review of Sociology* 19: 17–41.

Armstrong, Elizabeth A., and Mary Bernstein. 2008. "Culture, Power, and Institutions: A Multi-institutional Politics Approach to Social Movements." *Sociological Theory* 26, no. 1 (March): 74–99.

Atwater, Wilbur O. 1887. "The Chemistry of Food and Nutrition." *The Century* 34, no. 1 (May): 59–74.

———. 1895. "Food and Diet." In *Yearbook of the United States Department of Agriculture, 1894*, 357–388. Washington, DC: U.S. Government Printing Office.

Baics, Gergely. 2009. "Feeding Gotham: A Social History of Urban Provisioning, 1780–1860." Ph.D. diss., Northwestern University, Evanston, IL.

Balsiger, Philip. 2010. "Making Political Consumers: The Tactical Action Repertoire of a Campaign for Clean Clothes." *Social Movement Studies* 9, no. 3 (August): 311–329.

Barkan, Ilyse D. 1985. "Industry Invites Regulation: The Passage of the Pure Food and Drug Act of 1906." *American Journal of Public Health* 75, no. 1 (January): 18–26.

Beckert, Sven. 2001. "Propertied of a Different Kind: Bourgeoisie and Lower Middle Class in the Nineteenth-Century United States." In *The Middling Sorts: Explorations in the History of the American Middle Class*, edited by Burton J. Bledstein and Robert D. Johnston, 285–295. New York: Routledge.

Bedford, Riiko. 2015. "Heredity as Ideology: Ideas of the Woman's Christian Temperance Union of the United States and Ontario on Heredity and Social Reform, 1880–1910." *Canadian Bulletin of Medical History* 32, no. 1 (Spring): 77–100.

Beeman, Randal S., and James A. Pritchard. 2001. *A Green and Permanent Land: Ecology and Agriculture in the Twentieth Century.* Lawrence: University Press of Kansas.

Beisel, Nicola. 1997. *Imperiled Innocents: Anthony Comstock and Family Reproduction in Victorian America.* Princeton, NJ: Princeton University Press.

Belasco, Warren J. 2007. *Appetite for Change: How the Counterculture Took on the Food Industry, 1966–1988*, 2d ed. New York: Pantheon.

———. 1997. "Food, Morality and Social Reform." In *Morality and Health*, edited by Allan Brandt and Paul Rozin, 185–200. New York: Routledge.

Bendix, Reinhard. 1974. *Work and Authority in Industry: Ideologies of Management in the Course of Industrialization.* Berkeley: University of California Press.

Bennett, W. Lance. 2004. "Branded Political Communication: Lifestyle Politics, Logo Campaigns, and the Rise of Global Citizenship." In *Politics, Products, and Markets: Exploring Political Consumerism Past and Present*, edited by Michele Micheletti, Andreas Føllesdal, and Dietlind Stolle, 101–125. New Brunswick, NJ: Transaction.

Berkeley Barb. 1965–1980. Berkeley, CA.

Biddle, Brenda. 2009. "Food Sovereignty and Protest." In *The International Encyclopedia of Revolution and Protest*, vol. 3, edited by Immanuel Ness, 1210–1212. Chichester, UK: Wiley-Blackwell.

Bildtgård, Torbjörn. 2008. "Trust in Food in Modern and Late-Modern Societies." *Social Science Information* 47, no. 1 (March): 99–128.

Biltekoff, Charlotte. 2013. *Eating Right in America: The Cultural Politics of Food and Health.* Durham, NC: Duke University Press.

Bledstein, Burton J., and Robert D. Johnston, eds. 2001. *The Middling Sorts: Explorations in the History of the American Middle Class.* New York: Routledge.

Block, Daniel R. 2002. "Protecting and Connecting: Separation, Connection, and the U.S. Dairy Economy 1840–2002." *Journal for the Study of Food and Society* 6, no. 1 (Winter): 22–30.

Blumin, Stuart M. 1989. *The Emergence of the Middle Class: Social Experience in the American City, 1760–1900.* Cambridge: Cambridge University Press.

Bobrow-Strain, Aaron. 2012. *White Bread: A Social History of the Store-Bought Loaf.* Boston: Beacon.

Bordin, Ruth. 1981. *Woman and Temperance: The Quest for Power and Liberty, 1873–1900.* Philadelphia: Temple University Press.

Boyer, Paul. 1978. *Urban Masses and Moral Order in America, 1820–1920.* Cambridge, MA: Harvard University Press.

Boyle, T. Coraghessan. 1993. *The Road to Wellville.* New York: Viking.

Braunstein, Peter, and Michael William Doyle, eds. 2002. *Imagine Nation: The American Counterculture of the 1960s and '70s.* New York: Routledge.

Brent, Z. W., C. M. Schiavoni, and A. Fradejas. 2015. "Contextualising Food Sovereignty: The Politics of Convergence among Movements in the USA." *Third World Quarterly* 36, no. 3: 618–635.

Buenker, John D., John C. Burnham, and Robert M. Crunden. 1976. *Progressivism.* Cambridge, MA: Schenkman.

Burnham, Robert A. 2001. "The Boss Becomes a Manager: Executive Authority and City Charter Reform, 1880–1929." In *Making Sense of the City: Local Government, Civic Culture, and Community Life in Urban America*, edited by Robert B. Fairbanks and Patricia Mooney-Melvin, 75–94. Columbus: Ohio State University Press.

Bushman, Richard L. 1992. *The Refinement of America: Persons, Houses, Cities.* New York: Vintage.

Buttel, Frederick H. 2005. "The Environmental and Post-environmental Politics of Genetically Modified Crops and Foods." *Environmental Politics* 14, no. 3 (June): 309–323.

———. 2003. "The Global Politics of GEOs: The Achilles' Heel of the Globalization Regime?" In *Engineering Trouble: Biotechnology and Its Discontents*, edited by Rachel A. Schurman and Dennis Doyle Takahashi Kelso, 152–173. Berkeley: University of California Press.

Cairns, Kate, Josée Johnston, and Shyon Bauman. 2010. "Caring about Food: Doing Gender in the Foodie Kitchen." *Gender and Society* 24, no. 5 (October): 591–615.

Carpenter, K. J. 1994. "The Life and Times of W. O. Atwater (1844–1907)." *Journal of Nutrition* 124: 1707S–1714S.

Carson, Gerald. 1976. *Cornflake Crusade.* New York: Arno.

Case, John, and Rosemary C. R. Taylor, eds. 1979. *Co-ops, Communes and Collectives: Experiments in Social Change in the 1960s and 1970s.* New York: Pantheon.

Castells, Manuel. 1997. *The Power of Identity.* Malden, MA: Blackwell.

Charles, Daniel. 2001. *Lords of the Harvest: Biotech, Big Money, and the Future of Food.* Cambridge, MA: Perseus.

Cherry, Elizabeth. 2006. "Veganism as a Cultural Movement: A Relational Approach." *Social Movement Studies* 5, no. 2 (September): 155–170.

Chicago Seed. 1967–1971.

Clancy, Kate, Janet Hammer, and Debra Lippoldt. 2007. "Food Policy Councils." In *Remaking the North American Food System: Strategies for Sustainability*, edited by C. Clare Hinrichs and Thomas A. Lyson, 121–143. Lincoln: University of Nebraska Press.

Clark, Lisa F. 2015. *The Changing Politics of Organic Food in North America.* Cheltenham, UK: Edward Elger.

Clemens, Elisabeth S. 1997. *The People's Lobby: Organizational Innovation and the Rise of Interest Group Politics in the United States, 1890–1925.* Chicago: University of Chicago Press.

Cole, Edith Walters. 1975. "Sylvester Graham, Lecturer on the Science of Human Life: The Rhetoric of a Dietary Reformer." Ph.D. diss., Indiana University, Bloomington.

Coles, Anthony James. 1978. "The Moral Economy of the Crowd: Some Twentieth-Century Food Riots." *Journal of British Studies* 18, no. 1 (Autumn): 157–176.

Cone, Cynthia A., and A. Kakaliouras. 1995. "Community-Supported Agriculture: Building Moral Community or an Alternative Consumer Choice." *Culture and Agriculture* 15, no. 51–52 (March): 28–31.

Cone, Cynthia A., and Andrea Myhre. 2000. "Community-Supported Agriculture: A Sustainable Alternative to Industrial Agriculture?" *Human Organization* 59, no. 2 (Summer): 187–197.

Conford, Philip. 2001. *The Origins of the Organic Movement.* Edinburgh: Floris.

Cook, Sharon Anne. 1997. "'Do not . . . Do Anything That You Cannot Unblushingly Tell Your Mother': Gender and Social Purity in Canada." *Social History* 30, no. 60 (November): 215–238.

Cornucopia Project. 1981. *Empty Breadbasket? The Coming Challenge to America's Food Supply and What We Can Do about It.* Emmaus, PA: Rodale.

Cott, Nancy F. 1977. *The Bonds of Womanhood: "Woman's Sphere" in New England, 1780–1835.* New Haven, CT: Yale University Press.

Counihan, Carole, and Valeria Siniscalchi, eds. 2014. *Food Activism: Agency, Democracy and Economy.* London: Bloomsbury.

Cox, Craig. 1994. *Storefront Revolution: Food Co-ops and the Counterculture.* New Brunswick, NJ: Rutgers University Press.

Cravens, Hamilton. 1991. "Establishing the Science of Nutrition at the USDA: Ellen Swallow Richards and Her Allies." In *The United States Department of Agriculture in Historical Perspective*, edited by Alan I. Marcus and Richard Lowitt, 122–133. Washington, DC: Agricultural History Society.

Crawford, Alan Pell. 2002. "Richmond's Bread Riot." *American History* 37, no. 2 (June): 20–26.

Cronon, William. 1991. *Nature's Metropolis: Chicago and the Great West.* New York: W. W. Norton.

Danhof, Clarence H. 1969. *Change in Agriculture: The Northern United States, 1820–1870.* Cambridge, MA: Harvard University Press.

Dawley, Alan. 1991. *Struggles for Justice: Social Responsibility and the Liberal State.* Cambridge, MA: Harvard University Press.

DeLind, Laura B., and Anne E. Ferguson. 1999. "Is This a Women's Movement? The Relationship of Gender to Community-Supported Agriculture in Michigan." *Human Organization* 58, no. 2 (Summer): 190–200.

della Porta, Donatella, and Alice Mattoni, eds. 2014. *Spreading Protest: Social Movements in Times of Crisis.* Colchester, UK: ECPR.

della Porta, Donatella, and Lorenzo Mosca. 2007. "In Movimento: 'Contamination' in Action and the Italian Global Justice Movement." *Global Networks* 7, no. 1 (January): 1–27.

DeSoucey, Michaela, and Isabelle Téchoueyres. 2009. "Virtue and Valorization: 'Local Food' in the United States and France." In *The Globalization of Food,* edited by David Inglis and Debra Gimlin, 81–95. Oxford: Berg.

Deutsch, Tracey. 2010. *Building a Housewife's Paradise: Gender, Politics, and American Grocery Stores in the Twentieth Century.* Chapel Hill: University of North Carolina Press.

Dimitri, Carolyn, Anne Effland, and Neilson Conklin. 2005. *The 20th Century Transformation of U.S. Agriculture and Farm Policy.* Economic Information Bulletin no. 3. Washington, DC: USDA Economic Research Service.

Dirks, Robert. 2016. *Food in the Gilded Age: What Ordinary Americans Ate.* Lanham, MD: Rowman and Littlefield.

Donati, Kelly. 2005. "The Pleasure of Diversity in Slow Food's Ethics of Taste." *Food, Culture and Society* 8, no. 2 (Fall): 227–242.

Douglas, Ann. 1977. *The Feminization of American Culture.* New York: Knopf.

Douglas, Mary. 1966. *Purity and Danger: An Analysis of Concepts of Pollution and Taboo.* London: Routledge and Kegan Paul.

Dubofsky, Melvyn. 1975. *Industrialism and the American Worker, 1865–1920.* Arlington Heights, IL: AHM.

DuPuis, E. Melanie. 2007. "Angels and Vegetables: A Brief History of Food Advice in America." *Gastronomica* 7, no. 2 (Summer): 34–44.

———. 2015. *Dangerous Digestion: The Politics of American Dietary Advice.* Berkeley: University of California Press.

DuPuis, E. Melanie, Jill Lindsey Harrison, and David Goodman. 2011. "Just Food?" In *Cultivating Food Justice: Race, Class, and Sustainability,* edited by Alison Hope Alkon and Julian Agyeman, 283–307. Cambridge, MA: MIT Press.

East Village Other. 1965–1972. New York.

Edgington, Ryan H. 2008. "'Be Receptive to the Good Earth': Health, Nature, and Labor in Countercultural Back-to-the-Land Settlements." *Agricultural History* 82, no. 3 (Summer): 279–308.

Edwards, Gemma. 2014. "Infectious Innovations? The Diffusion of Tactical Innovation in Social Movement Networks, the Case of Suffragette Militancy." *Social Movement Studies* 13, no. 1: 48–69.

Egan, Michael. 2005. "Organizing Protest in the Changing City: Swill Milk and Social Activism in New York City, 1842–1864." *New York History* 86, no. 3 (Summer): 205–225.

Elias, Megan J. 2008. *Stir It Up: Home Economics in American Culture.* Philadelphia: University of Pennsylvania Press.

Engs, Ruth Clifford. 2001. *Clean Living Movements: American Cycles of Health Reform.* Westport, CT: Praeger.

Environment Action Bulletin and Organic Gardening and Farming. 1973. *The Organic Guide to Colleges and Universities.* Emmaus, PA: Rodale.

Equality. Geneva, Switzerland.

Ethington, Philip J. 1992. "Recasting Urban Political History: Gender, the Public, the Household, and Political Participation in Boston and San Francisco During the Progressive Era." *Social Science History* 16, no. 2 (Summer): 301–333.

Faler, Paul. 1974. "Cultural Aspects of the Industrial Revolution: Lynn, Massachusetts Shoemakers and Industrial Morality, 1826–1860." *Labor History* 15, no. 3 (Summer): 367–394.

Faulkner, Carol. 2007. "The Root of the Evil: Free Produce and Radical Antislavery, 1820–1860." *Journal of the Early Republic* 27, no. 3 (Fall): 377–405.

Feenstra, G. W. 1997. "Local Food Systems and Sustainable Communities." *American Journal of Alternative Agriculture* 12, no. 1 (March): 28–36.

Ferrières, Madeleine. 2006. *Sacred Cow, Mad Cow: A History of Food Fears.* New York: Columbia University Press.

Finegold, Kenneth. 1995. *Experts and Politicians: Reform Challenges to Machine Politics in New York, Cleveland, and Chicago.* Princeton, NJ: Princeton University Press.

Finn, S. Margot. 2017. *Discriminating Taste: How Class Anxiety Created the American Food Revolution.* New Brunswick, NJ: Rutgers University Press.

Fitzgerald, Deborah. 2003. *Every Farm a Factory: The Industrial Ideal in American Agriculture.* New Haven, CT: Yale University Press.

FitzGerald, Frances. 2017. *The Evangelicals: The Struggle to Shape America.* New York: Simon and Schuster.

FitzSimmons, Margaret. 1986. "The New Industrial Agriculture: The Regional Integration of Specialty Crop Production." *Economic Geography* 62, no. 4 (October): 334–353.

Flanagan, Maureen A. 2007. *America Reformed: Progressives and Progressivisms, 1890s–1920s.* New York: Oxford University Press.

Flandrin, Jean-Louis, and Massimo Montanari. 1999. *Food: A Culinary History from Antiquity to the Present.* New York: Columbia University Press.

Fletcher, Holly Berkley. 2008. *Gender and the American Temperance Movement of the Nineteenth Century.* New York: Routledge.

Fletcher, Horace. 1903. *The A.B.–Z. of Our Own Nutrition.* New York: Frederick A. Stokes.

Foote, Arthur, ed. 1835. *A Defence of the Graham System of Living, or, Remarks on Diet and Regimen: Dedicated to the Rising Generation.* New York: W. Applegate.

Frank, Dana. 1985. "Housewives, Socialists, and the Politics of Food: The 1917 New York Cost-of-Living Protests." *Feminist Studies* 11, no. 2 (Summer): 255–285.

Frank, Thomas. 1997. *The Conquest of Cool: Business Culture, Counterculture, and the Rise of Hip Consumerism.* Chicago: University of Chicago Press.

Freedman, Paul. 2019. *American Cuisine: And How It Got This Way.* New York: Liveright.

Frieburger, William. 1984. "War Prosperity and Hunger: The New York Food Riots of 1917." *Labor History* 25, no. 2 (Spring): 217–239.

Friedmann, Harriet. 2005. "From Colonialism to Green Capitalism: Social Movements and Emergence of Food Regimes." *Research in Rural Sociology and Development* 11: 227–264.

Fullilove, Courtney. 2014. "The Price of Bread: The New York City Flour Riot and the Paradox of Capitalist Food Systems." *Radical History Review*, no. 118 (Winter): 15–41.

Futrell, Robert, and Pete Simi. 2004. "Free Spaces, Collective Identity, and the Persistence of U.S. White Power Activism." *Social Problems* 51, no. 1 (February): 16–42.

Ganz, Marshall. 2009. *Why David Sometimes Wins: Leadership, Organization, and Strategy in the California Farm Worker Movement.* New York: Oxford University Press.

Garvey, Ellen Gruber. 1996. *The Adman in the Parlor: Magazines and the Gendering of Consumer Culture, 1880s to 1910s.* New York: Oxford University Press.

Gendzel, Glen. 2011. "What the Progressives Had in Common." *Journal of the Gilded Age and Progressive Era* 10, no. 3 (July): 331–339.

General Federation of Women's Clubs. 1897–1904. *Club Woman.* New York.

———. 1905–1911. *Federation Bulletin*. New York.

———. Various years. *Proceedings of the Biennial Meetings*.

Gershuny, Grace. 2016. *Organic Revolutionary: A Memoir of the Movement for Real Food, Planetary Healing, and Human Liberation*. Middletown, DE: Joes Brook.

Getz, Christy, Sandy Brown, and Aimee Shreck. 2008. "Class Politics and Agricultural Exceptionalism in California's Organic Agriculture Movement." *Politics and Society* 36, no. 4 (December): 478–507.

Gilkeson, John S., Jr. 1986. *Middle-Class Providence, 1820–1940*. Princeton, NJ: Princeton University Press.

Gillan, Kevin. 2020. "Temporality in Social Movement Theory: Vectors and Events in the Neoliberal Timescape." *Social Movement Studies* 19, no. 5–6: 516–536.

Givan, Rebecca Kolins, Kenneth M. Roberts, and Sarah A. Soule, eds. 2010. *The Diffusion of Social Movements: Actors, Mechanisms, and Political Effects*. Cambridge: Cambridge University Press.

Glickman, Lawrence B. 2004. "'Buy for the Sake of the Slave': Abolitionism and the Origins of American Consumer Activism." *American Quarterly* 56, no. 4 (December): 889–912.

———. 2009. *Buying Power: A History of Consumer Activism in America*. Chicago: University of Chicago Press.

Goldberg, Chad Alan. 2007. *Citizens and Paupers: Relief, Rights, and Race, from the Freedmen's Bureau to Workfare*. Chicago: University of Chicago Press.

Goldman, Barbara, and Katherine L. Clancy. 1991. "A Survey of Organic Produce Purchases and Related Attitudes of Food Cooperative Shoppers." *American Journal of Alternative Agriculture* 6, no. 2 (June): 89–96.

Goldstein, Carolyn M. 1994. "Mediating Consumption: Home Economics and American Consumers, 1900–1940." Ph.D. diss., University of Delaware, Newark.

Goldstein, Jerome, ed. 1973. *The New Food Chain: An Organic Link between Farm and City*. Emmaus, PA: Rodale.

Goode, Erich, and Nachman Ben-Yehuda. 1994. *Moral Panics: The Social Construction of Deviance*. Cambridge, MA: Blackwell.

Good Health. 1866–1922. Battle Creek, MI: Good Health Publishing.

Good Housekeeping. 1885–present. New York.

Goodman, David. 2003. "The Quality 'Turn' and Alternative Food Practices: Reflections and Agenda." *Journal of Rural Studies* 19, no. 1 (January): 1–7.

Goodman, David, E. Melanie DuPuis, and Michael K. Goodman. 2012. *Alternative Food Networks: Knowledge, Place and Politics*. New York: Routledge.

Goodman, David, and Michael Goodman. 2007. "Localism, Livelihoods, and the 'Post-Organic': Changing Perspectives on Alternative Food Networks in the United States." In *Alternative Food Geographies: Representation and Practice*, edited by Damien Maye, Lewis Holloway, and Moya Kneafsey, 23–38. Oxford: Elsevier.

Goodman, David, and Michael Redclift. 1991. *Refashioning Nature: Food, Ecology, and Culture*. London: Routledge.

Goodman, Michael K., and Colin Sage, eds. 2014. *Food Transgressions: Making Sense of Contemporary Food Politics*. Farnham, UK: Ashgate.

Good Times. 1969–?. San Francisco.

Goodwin, Lorine Swainston. 1999. *The Pure Food, Drink, and Drug Crusaders, 1879–1914*. Jefferson, NC: McFarland.

Goody, Jack. 1982. *Cooking, Cuisine, and Class: A Study in Comparative Sociology*. Cambridge: Cambridge University Press.

Gordon, Linda. 1995. "Putting Children First: Women, Maternalism, and Welfare in the Early Twentieth Century." In *United States History as Women's History*, edited by Linda Kerber, Alice Kessler-Harris, and Kathryn Kish Sklar, 63–86. Chapel Hill: University of North Carolina Press.

Gottlieb, Robert, and Anupama Joshi. 2010. *Food Justice*. Cambridge, MA: MIT Press.

Graham, Sylvester. 1834. *The Aesculapian Tablets of the Nineteenth Century*. Providence, RI: Weeden and Cory.

———. 1839. *Lectures on the Science of Human Life*, 2 vols. Boston: Marsh, Capen, Lyon and Webb.

———. 1838. *A Lecture to Young Men on Chastity*. Boston: Light and Stearns, Crocker and Brewster.

Graham Journal of Health and Longevity. 1837–1839. Boston.

Gray, Margaret. 2013. *Labor and the Locavore: The Making of a Comprehensive Food Ethic*. Berkeley, CA: University of California Press.

Great Speckled Bird. 1968–1985. Atlanta.

Guillén, Mauro F. 1994. *Models of Management: Work, Authority, and Organization in a Comparative Perspective*. Chicago: University of Chicago Press.

Gusfield, Joseph R. 1992. "Nature's Body and the Metaphors of Food." In *Cultivating Differences: Symbolic Boundaries and the Making of Inequality*, edited by Michèle Lamont and Marcel Fournier, 75–103. Chicago: University of Chicago Press.

———. 1981. "Social Movements and Social Change: Perspectives of Linearity and Fluidity." *Research in Social Movements, Conflicts and Change* 4: 317–339.

———. 1963. *Symbolic Crusade: Status Politics and the American Temperance Movement*. Urbana: University of Illinois Press.

Guthman, Julie. 2004. *Agrarian Dreams: The Paradox of Organic Farming in California*. Berkeley: University of California Press.

———. 2007. "From the Ground Up: California Organics and the Making of 'Yuppie Chow.'" In *Alternative Food Geographies: Representation and Practice*, edited by Damian Maye, Lewis Holloway, and Moya Kneafsey, 241–54. Oxford: Elsevier.

Guthman, Julie, and E. Melanie DuPuis. 2006. "Embodying Neoliberalism: Economy, Culture, and the Politics of Fat." *Environment and Planning. D, Society and Space* 24, no. 3 (June): 427–448.

Haber, Samuel. 1964. *Efficiency and Uplift: Scientific Management in the Progressive Era, 1890–1920*. Chicago: University of Chicago Press.

Haedicke, Michael A. 2012. "'Keeping Our Mission, Changing Our System': Translation and Organizational Change in Natural Foods Co-ops." *Sociological Quarterly* 53, no. 1: 44–67.

———. 2016. *Organizing Organic: Conflict and Compromise in an Emerging Market*. Stanford, CA: Stanford University Press.

Haenfler, Ross. 2004. "Collective Identity in the Straight Edge Movement: How Diffuse Movements Foster Commitment, Encourage Individualized Participation, and Promote Cultural Change." *Sociological Quarterly* 45, no. 4 (Autumn): 785–805.

Halttunen, Karen. 1982. *Confidence Men and Painted Women: A Study of Middle-Class Culture in America, 1830–1870*. New Haven, CT: Yale University Press.

Hamilton, Shane. 2003. "The Economies and Conveniences of Modern-Day Living: Frozen Foods and Mass Marketing, 1945–1965." *Business History Review* 77, no. 1 (Spring): 33–60.

Harper, Alethea, Annie Shattuck, Eric Holt-Giménez, Alison Alkon, and Frances Lambrick. 2009. *Food Policy Councils: Lessons Learned*. Institute for Food and Development Policy. Accessed February 7, 2021. http://foodfirst.org/publication/food-policy-councils-lessons-learned.

Hartford, William F. 2001. *Money, Morals, and Politics: Massachusetts in the Age of the Boston Associates*. Boston, MA: Northeastern University Press.

Hartman, Stephanie. 2003. "The Political Palate: Reading Commune Cookbooks." *Gastronomica* 3, no. 2 (Spring): 29–40.

Hassanein, Neva. 1999. *Changing the Way America Farms: Knowledge and Community in the Sustainable Agriculture Movement*. Lincoln: University of Nebraska Press.

———. 2003. "Practicing Food Democracy: A Pragmatic Politics of Transformation." *Journal of Rural Studies* 19, no. 1 (January): 77–86.

Hatch, Nathan O. 1989. *The Democratization of American Christianity*. New Haven, CT: Yale University Press.

Haydu, Jeffrey. 2008. *Citizen Employers: Business Communities and Labor in Cincinnati and San Francisco, 1870–1916*. Ithaca, NY: Cornell University Press.

———. 2012. "Frame Brokerage in the Pure Food Movement, 1879–1906." *Social Movement Studies* 11, no. 1 (January): 1–17.

Haydu, Jeffrey, and David Kadanoff. 2010. "Casing Political Consumerism." *Mobilization* 15, no. 2 (June): 159–177.

Hays, Samuel P. 1964. "The Politics of Reform in Municipal Government in the Progressive Era." *Pacific Northwest Quarterly* 55, no. 4 (October): 157–169.

Health Reformer. 1866–1879. Battle Creek, MI: Health Reform Institute.

Heldman, Caroline. 2017. *Protest Politics in the Marketplace: Consumer Activism in the Corporate Age*. Ithaca, NY: Cornell University Press.

Henderson, Elizabeth. 2000. "Rebuilding Local Food Systems from the Grassroots Up." In *Hungry for Profit: The Agribusiness Threat to Farmers, Food, and the Environment*, edited by Fred Magdoff, John Bellamy Foster, and Frederick H. Buttel, 175–188. New York: Monthly Review.

Hessinger, Rodney. 2005. *Seduced, Abandoned, and Reborn: Visions of Youth in Middle-Class America, 1780–1850*. Philadelphia: University of Pennsylvania Press.

Hilton, Matthew. 2007. "Social Activism in an Age of Consumption: The Organized Consumer Movement." *Social History* 32, no. 2 (May): 121–143.

Hinrichs, C. Clare. 2000. "Embeddedness and Local Food Systems: Notes on Two Types of Direct Agricultural Market." *Journal of Rural Studies* 16, no. 3 (July): 295–303.

———. 2003. "The Practice and Politics of Food System Localization." *Journal of Rural Studies* 19, no. 1 (January): 33–45.

Hinrichs, C. Clare, and Patricia Allen. 2008. "Selective Patronage and Social Justice: Local Food Consumer Campaigns in Historical Context." *Journal of Agricultural and Environmental Ethics* 21, no. 4 (August): 329–352.

Hofstadter, Richard. 1955. *The Age of Reform*. New York: Vintage.

Holt-Giménez, Eric, ed. 2011. *Food Movements Unite: Strategies to Transform Our Food System*. Oakland, CA: Food First.

———. 2011. "Food Security, Food Justice, or Food Sovereignty? Crises, Food Movements, and Regime Change." In *Cultivating Food Justice: Race, Class, and Sustainability*, edited by Alison Hope Alkon and Julian Agyeman, 309–330. Cambridge, MA: MIT Press.

Holt-Giménez, Eric, and Yi Wang. 2011. "Reform or Transformation? The Pivotal Role of Food Justice in the U.S. Food Movement." *Race/Ethnicity* 5, no. 1 (Autumn): 83–102.

Holzer, Boris. 2006. "Political Consumerism between Individual Choice and Collective Action: Social Movements, Role Mobilization and Signalling." *International Journal of Consumer Studies* 30, no. 5 (September): 405–415.

Horowitz, Roger. 2008. "The Politics of Meat Shopping in Antebellum New York City." In *Meat, Modernity, and the Rise of the Slaughterhouse*, edited by Paula Young Lee, 167–177. Durham: University of New Hampshire Press.

———. 2006. *Putting Meat on the American Table: Taste, Technology, Transformation.* Baltimore: Johns Hopkins University Press.

Howard, Philip H. 2009. "Consolidation in the North American Organic Food Processing Sector, 1997 to 2007." *International Journal of Sociology of Agriculture and Food* 16, no. 1 (April): 13–30.

"How Pure Is Your Food?" 1959. *U.S. News and World Report*, December 7, 86–90.

Hunt, Caroline L. 1912. *The Life of Ellen H. Richards.* Boston, MA: Whitcomb and Barrows.

Hurt, R. Douglas. 2002. *American Agriculture: A Brief History.* West Lafayette, IN: Purdue University Press.

Imhoff, Daniel. 2012. *Food Fight! The Citizen's Guide to the Next Food and Farm Bill.* Healdsburg, CA: Watershed Media.

Inglehart, Ronald. 1977. *The Silent Revolution: Changing Values and Political Styles among Western Publics.* Princeton, NJ: Princeton University Press.

Ingram, Mrill, and Helen Ingram. 2005. "Creating Credible Edibles: The Organic Agriculture Movement and the Emergence of U.S. Federal Organic Standards." In *Routing the Opposition: Social Movements, Public Policy, and Democracy*, edited by David S. Meyer, Valerie Jenness, and Helen Ingram, 121–148. Minneapolis: University of Minnesota Press.

Jackson, Peter. 2015. *Anxious Appetites: Food and Consumer Culture.* London: Bloomsbury Academic.

Jacob, Jeffrey. 1997. *New Pioneers: The Back-to-the-Land Movement and the Search for a Sustainable Future.* University Park: Pennsylvania State University Press.

Jaffee, Daniel, and Philip H. Howard. 2010. "Corporate Cooptation of Organic and Fair Trade Standards." *Agriculture and Human Values* 27, no. 4 (December): 387–399.

Jampel, Sarah. "Is Cool Whip Food?" In *Food52*, April 8, 2016, accessed April 21, 2020. https://food52.com/blog/16524-is-cool-whip-food-looking-back-on-50-years.

Jansen, Robert S. 2007. "Resurrection and Appropriation: Reputational Trajectories, Memory Work, and the Political Use of Historical Figures." *American Journal of Sociology* 112, no. 4 (January): 953–1007.

Johnson, Paul E. 1986. "Drinking, Temperance and the Construction of Identity in Nineteenth-Century America." *Social Science Information* 25, no. 2 (June): 521–530.

———. 1978. *A Shopkeeper's Millennium: Society and Revivals in Rochester, New York, 1815–1837.* New York: Hill and Wang.

Johnston, Josée. 2008. "The Citizen-Consumer Hybrid: Ideological Tensions and the Case of Whole Foods Market." *Theory and Society* 37, no. 3 (June): 229–70.

Johnston, Josée, and Shyon Baumann. 2010. *Foodies: Democracy and Distinction in the Gourmet Foodscape.* New York: Routledge.

Johnston, Josée, Michelle Szabo, and Alexandra Rodney. 2011. "Good Food, Good People: Understanding the Cultural Repertoire of Ethical Eating." *Journal of Consumer Culture* 11, no. 3 (November): 293–318.

Jolly, Desmond A. 1991. "Differences between Buyers and Nonbuyers of Organic Produce and Willingness to Pay Organic Price Premiums." *Journal of Agribusiness* 9, no. 1 (Spring): 97–111.

Josephson, Paul. 2008. "The Ocean's Hot Dog: The Development of the Fish Stick." *Technology and Culture* 49, no. 1 (January): 41–61.

Junod, Suzanne White. 2000. "Food Standards in the United States: The Case of the Peanut Butter and Jelly Sandwich." In *Food, Science, Policy, and Regulation in the Twentieth Century: International and Comparative Perspectives*, edited by David F. Smith and Jim Phillips, 167–188. London: Routledge.

Kamp, David. 2006. *The United States of Arugula: The Sun-Dried, Cold-Pressed, Dark-Roasted, Extra Virgin Story of the American Food Revolution*. New York: Broadway.

Kane, R. James. 1964. "Populism, Progressivism, and Pure Food." *Agricultural History* 38, no. 3 (July): 161–166.

Kansteiner, Wulf. 2002. "Finding Meaning in Memory: A Methodological Critique of Collective Memory Studies." *History and Theory* 41, no. 2 (May): 179–197.

Kasson, John F. 1990. *Rudeness and Civility: Manners in Nineteenth-Century Urban America*. New York: Hill and Wang.

Kauffman, Jonathan. 2018. *Hippie Food: How Back-to-the-Landers, Longhairs, and Revolutionaries Changed the Way We Eat*. New York: William Morrow.

Kauffman, L. 1976. *South San Francisco: A History*. San Francisco: Self-published.

Kellogg, John Harvey. 1882. *Plain Facts for Young and Old*. Burlington, IA: I. F. Segner.

Kellogg, John Harvey, and Ella E. Kellogg. 1889. *Social Purity: An Address and a Talk to Girls: An Address on the Social Purity Pledge*. Battle Creek, MI: Good Health.

Kennedy, Emily Huddart, John R. Parkins, and Josée Johnston. 2018. "Food Activists, Consumer Strategies, and the Democratic Imagination: Insights from Eat-Local Movements." *Journal of Consumer Culture* 18, no. 1 (February): 149–168.

Kirk, Andrew G. 2007. *Counterculture Green: The Whole Earth Catalog and American Environmentalism*. Lawrence: University Press of Kansas.

Kjaernes, Unni. 2013. "Risk and Trust in the Food Supply." In *The Handbook of Food Research*, edited by Anne Murcott, Warren Belasco, and Peter Jackson, 410–424. London: Bloomsbury.

Kjaernes, Unni, Mark Harvey, and Alan Warde. 2007. *Trust in Food: A Comparative and Institutional Analysis*. Basingstoke, UK: Palgrave Macmillan.

Kloppenburg, Jack R., Jr., Sharon Lezberg, Kathryn De Master, George W. Stevenson, and John Hendrickson. 2000. "Tasting Food, Tasting Sustainability: Defining the Attributes of an Alternative Food System with Competent, Ordinary People." *Human Organization* 59, no. 2 (Summer): 177–186.

Knupfer, Anne Meis. 2013. *Food Co-ops in America: Communities, Consumption, and Economic Democracy*. Ithaca, NY: Cornell University Press.

Koehn, Nancy F. 1999. "Henry Heinz and Brand Creation in the Late Nineteenth Century: Making Markets for Processed Food." *Business History Review* 73, no. 3 (Autumn): 349–393.

Kolko, Gabriel. 1967. *The Triumph of Conservatism: A Reinterpretation of American History, 1900–1916*. Chicago: Quadrangle.

Kraig, Bruce. 2017. *A Rich and Fertile Land: A History of Food in America*. London: Reaktion.

Krimsky, Sheldon, and Roger P. Wrubel. 1996. *Agricultural Biotechnology and the Environment: Science, Policy, and Social Issues*. Urbana: University of Illinois Press.

Krinsky, John. 2013. "Marxism and the Politics of Possibility: Beyond Academic Boundaries." In *Marxism and Social Movements*, edited by Colin Barker, Laurence Cox, John Krinsky, and Alf Gunvald, 103–121. Leiden: Brill.

———. 2011. "Neoliberal Times: Intersecting Temporalities and the Neoliberalization of New York City's Public-Sector Labor Relations." *Social Science History* 35, no. 3 (Fall): 381–422.

Larchet, Nicolas. 2012. "Food Reform Movements." In *The Oxford Encyclopedia of Food and Drink in America*, edited by Andrew F. Smith, 796–805. New York: Oxford University Press.

Laurie, Bruce. 1980. *Working People of Philadelphia, 1800–1850*. Philadelphia: Temple University Press.

Lavin, Chad. 2013. *Eating Anxiety: The Perils of Food Politics*. Minneapolis: University of Minnesota Press.

———. 2009. "The Year of Eating Politically." *Theory and Event* 12, no. 2. doi:10.1353 /tae.0.0074.

Lebsock, Suzanne. 1990. "Women and American Politics, 1880–1920." In *Women, Politics, and Change*, edited by Louise Tilly and Patricia Gurin, 35–62. New York: Russell Sage Foundation.

LeDuc, Thomas H. 1939. "Grahamites and Garrisonites." *New York History* 20, no. 2 (April): 189–191.

Lee, Paul A. 2013. *There Is a Garden in the Mind: A Memoir of Alan Chadwick and the Organic Movement in California*. Berkeley, CA: North Atlantic.

Lesy, Michael, and Lisa Stoffer. 2013. *Repast: Dining Out at the Dawn of the New American Century, 1900–1910*. New York: W. W. Norton.

Levenstein, Harvey. 2003. *Paradox of Plenty: A Social History of Eating in Modern America*. Berkeley: University of California Press.

———. 2003. *Revolution at the Table: The Transformation of the American Diet*. Berkeley, CA: University of California Press.

Levine, Deborah I. 2008. "Managing American Bodies: Diet, Nutrition, and Obesity in America, 1840–1920." Ph.D. diss., Harvard University, Cambridge, MA.

Lobel, Cindy R. 2003. "Consuming Classes: Changing Food Consumption Patterns in New York City, 1790–1860." Ph.D. diss., City University of New York.

Los Angeles Free Press. 1964–1978.

Loughridge, Kenneth Brandon Lang. 2002. "Community Supported Agriculture (CSA) in the Mid-Atlantic United States: A Sociological Analysis." Ph.D. diss., University of Wisconsin, Madison.

Lyson, Thomas A. 2007. "Civic Agriculture and the North American Food System." In *Remaking the North American Food System: Strategies for Sustainability*, edited by C. Clare Hinrichs and Thomas A. Lyson, 19–32. Lincoln: University of Nebraska Press.

Mahoney, Timothy R. 1999. *Provincial Lives: Middle-Class Experience in the Antebellum Middle West*. Cambridge: Cambridge University Press.

Marcus, Alan I. 1987. "Setting the Standard: Fertilizers, State Chemists, and Early National Commercial Regulation, 1880–1887." *Agricultural History* 61, no. 1 (Winter): 47–73.

Markel, Howard. 2017. *The Kelloggs: The Battling Brothers of Battle Creek*. New York: Pantheon.

Martin, Scott C. 2008. *Devil of the Domestic Sphere: Temperance, Gender, and Middle-Class Ideology, 1800–1860*. DeKalb: Northern Illinois University Press.

Masonic Mirror. 1824–1828. Boston.

Mayer, Robert N. 1989. *The Consumer Movement: Guardians of the Marketplace*. Boston: Twayne.

McAdam, Doug. 1982. *Political Process and the Development of Black Insurgency, 1930–1970*. Chicago: University of Chicago Press.

McAdam, Doug, John D. McCarthy, and Mayer N. Zald, eds. 1996. *Comparative Perspectives on Social Movements: Political Opportunities, Mobilizing Structures, and Cultural Framings*. Cambridge: Cambridge University Press.

McAdam, Doug, and Dieter Rucht. 1993. "The Cross-National Diffusion of Movement Ideas." *Annals of the American Academy of Political and Social Science* 528, no. 1 (July): 56–74.

McAdam, Doug, Robert J. Sampson, Simon Weffer, and Heather MacIndoe. 2005. "'There Will Be Fighting in the Streets': The Distorting Lens of Social Movement Theory." *Mobilization* 10, no. 1 (February): 1–18.

McAdam, Doug, Sidney Tarrow, and Charles Tilly. 2001. *Dynamics of Contention*. New York: Cambridge University Press.

McCarthy, Kathleen D. 2003. *American Creed: Philanthropy and the Rise of Civil Society, 1700–1865*. Chicago: University of Chicago Press.

McClintock, Nathan, and Michael Simpson. 2018. "Stacking Functions: Identifying Motivational Frames Guiding Urban Agriculture Organizations and Businesses in the United States and Canada." *Agriculture and Human Values* 35, no. 1 (March): 19–39.

McGerr, Michael. 2003. *A Fierce Discontent: The Rise and Fall of the Progressive Movement in America, 1870–1920*. New York: Free Press.

McGrath, Maria. 2019. *Food for Dissent: Natural Foods and the Consumer Counterculture since the 1960s*. Amherst: University of Massachusetts Press.

———. 2006. "Recipes for a New World: Utopianism and Alternative Eating in Vegetarian Natural-Foods Cookbooks, 1970–84." In *Eating in Eden: Food and American Utopias*, edited by Etta M. Madden and Martha L. Finch, 162–183. Lincoln: University of Nebraska Press.

———. 2004. "'That's Capitalism, Not a Co-op': Countercultural Idealism and Business Realism in 1970s U.S. Food Co-ops." *Business and Economic History On-Line* 2: 1–14.

McMahon, Sarah F. 1985. "A Comfortable Subsistence: The Changing Composition of Diet in Rural New England, 1620–1840." *William and Mary Quarterly* 42, no. 1 (January): 25–65.

McMichael, Philip. 2009. "A Food Regime Genealogy." *Journal of Peasant Studies* 36, no. 1 (January): 139–169.

McWilliams, Carey. 1939. *Factories in the Field: The Story of Migratory Farm Labor in California*. Boston: Little, Brown.

Melucci, Alberto. 1996. *Challenging Codes: Collective Action in the Information Age*. Cambridge: Cambridge University Press.

———. 1989. *Nomads of the Present: Social Movements and Individual Needs in Contemporary Society*. Philadelphia: Temple University Press.

Meneley, Anne. 2004. "Extra Virgin Olive Oil and Slow Food." *Anthropologica* 46, no. 2: 165–176.

Mennell, Stephen. 1996. *All Manners of Food: Eating and Taste in England and France from the Middle Ages to the Present*. Urbana: University of Illinois Press.

Mertig, Angela G., Riley E. Dunlap, and Denton E. Morrison. 2000. "The Environmental Movement in the United States." In *Handbook of Environmental Sociology*, edited by Riley E. Dunlap and William Michelson, 448–481. Westport, CT: Greenwood.

Meyers, Marvin. 1960. *The Jacksonian Persuasion: Politics and Belief*. Stanford, CA: Stanford University Press.

Micheletti, Michele. 2003. *Political Virtue and Shopping: Individuals, Consumerism, and Collective Action*. New York: Palgrave Macmillan.

Miller, Laura J. 2017. *Building Nature's Market: The Business and Politics of Natural Foods*. Chicago: University of Chicago Press.

Minkoff, Debra C. 1997. "The Sequencing of Social Movements." *American Sociological Review* 62, no. 5 (October): 779–799.

Möllering, Guido. 2001. "The Nature of Trust: From Georg Simmel to a Theory of Expectation, Interpretation and Suspension." *Sociology* 35, no. 2 (May): 403–420.

Mooney, Patrick H., and Theodore J. Majka. 1995. *Farmers' and Farm Workers' Movements: Social Protest in American Agriculture*. New York: Twayne.

Mooney, Patrick H., Keiko Tanaka, and Gabriele Ciciurkaite. 2014. "Food Policy Council Movement in North America: A Convergence of Alternative Local Agrifood Interests?" *Research in Rural Sociology and Development* 21: 229–255.

Morris, Aldon D. 1984. *The Origins of the Civil Rights Movement: Black Communities Organizing for Change*. New York: Free Press.

Mother Earth News. 1970–present. Arden, NC.

Mudry, Jessica J. 2009. *Measured Meals: Nutrition in America*. Albany: State University of New York Press.

Murray, David. 2008. "The American Counterculture." *Journal of American Studies* 42, no. 1 (April): 155.

Natenburg, Maurice. 1957. *The Legacy of Doctor Wiley*. Chicago: Regent House.

National Consumers League. *Annual Reports*. New York: National Consumers League.

National Provisioner. 1889–present. New York: Food Trade Publishing.

National Pure Food and Drug Congress. 1898. *Journal of Proceedings of the National Pure Food and Drug Congress Held in Columbian University Hall, Washington, D.C., March 2, 3, 4, and 5, 1898*. Washington, DC: N.p.

———. 1899. *Report of Proceedings of the Second Annual Convention of the National Pure Food and Drug Congress Held in Columbia University Hall, Washington, D. C., January 18, 19, 20 and 21, 1899*. Hightstown, NJ: Barr.

National Resources Defense Council. 1989. *Intolerable Risk: Pesticides in Our Children's Food*. New York: The Council.

Nestle, Marion. 2013. *Eat Drink Vote: An Illustrated Guide to Food Politics*. New York: Rodale.

———. "Latest Court Ruling: Pringles Are Potato Chips (Sort Of)." *Food Politics*, May 26, 2009. Accessed April 21, 2020. https://www.foodpolitics.com/2009/05/latest-court-ruling-pringles-are-potato-chips-sort-of.

New England Kitchen. 1894–1895. New England Kitchen Publishing, Boston.

New York Evangelist. 1830–1902. New York.

New York Times. New York, NY.

Nissenbaum, Stephen. 1980. *Sex, Diet, and Debility in Jacksonian America: Sylvester Graham and Health Reform*. Westport, CT: Greenwood.

Noble, David. 1977. *America by Design: Science, Technology, and the Rise of Corporate Capitalism*. New York: Alfred A. Knopf.

Noll, Mark A. 2002. *America's God: From Jonathan Edwards to Abraham Lincoln*. New York: Oxford University Press.

Nowacek, David. 1997. "The Organic Foods System from 1969–1996: A Defense of Associative Order and Democratic Control Over a Market." M.A. diss.. University of
Wisconsin, Madison.

Numbers, Ronald L. 1992. *Prophetess of Health: Ellen G. White and the Origins of Seventh-
Day Adventist Health Reform.* Knoxville: University of Tennessee Press.

Obach, Brian K. 2015. *Organic Struggle: The Movement for Sustainable Agriculture in the
United States.* Cambridge, MA: MIT Press.

Okun, Mitchell. 1986. *Fair Play in the Marketplace: The First Battle for Pure Food and
Drugs.* Dekalb: Northern Illinois University Press.

Olick, Jeffrey K., and Joyce Robbins. 1998. "Social Memory Studies: From 'Collective
Memory' to the Historical Sociology of Mnemonic Practices." *Annual Review of
Sociology* 24: 105–140.

Oliver, Pamela E., and Daniel J. Myers. 2003. "Networks, Diffusion, and Cycles of Collective Action." In *Social Movements and Networks: Relational Approaches to Collective Action,* edited by Mario Diani and Doug McAdam, 173–203. New York: Oxford
University Press.

Orenstein, Peggy. 2010. "The Femivore's Dilemma." *New York Times,* March 11.

Organic Gardening and Farming. 1954–1978. Emmaus, PA: Rodale.

Ostrom, Marcia R. 1997. "Toward a Community Supported Agriculture: A Case Study
of Resistance and Change in the Modern Food System." Ph.D. diss., University of
Wisconsin, Madison.

Paddock, Jessica. 2016. "Positioning Food Cultures: 'Alternative' Food as Distinctive
Consumer Practice." *Sociology* 50, no. 6 (December): 1039–1055.

Parker, Alison M. 1997. *Purifying America: Women, Cultural Reform, and Pro-censorship
Activism, 1873–1933.* Urbana: University of Illinois Press.

Patel, Raj. 2011. "Survival Pending Revolution: What the Black Panthers Can Teach the
U.S. Food Movement." In *Food Movements Unite! Strategies to Transform Our Food
Systems,* edited by Eric Holt-Giménez, 115–135. Oakland, CA: Food First.

Peace, Adrian. 2006. "Barossa Slow: The Representation and Rhetoric of Slow Food's
Regional Cooking." *Gastronomica* 6, no. 1 (February): 51–59.

The Peacemaker. 1965–1980. Cincinnati.

Pellow, David Naguib, and Robert J. Brulle, eds. 2005. *Power, Justice, and the Environment: A Critical Appraisal of the Environmental Justice Movement.* Cambridge, MA:
MIT Press.

Perry, Elisabeth Israels. 2002. "Men Are from the Gilded Age, Women Are from the Progressive Era." *Journal of the Gilded Age and Progressive Era* 1, no. 1 (January): 25–48.

Peters, Suzanne. 1979. "The Land in Trust." Ph.D. diss., McGill University, Montreal.

Petrick, Gabriella M. 2006. "The Arbiters of Taste: Producers, Consumers and the Industrialization of Taste in America, 1900–1960." Ph.D. diss., University of Delaware,
Newark.

———. 2011. "'Purity as Life': H. J. Heinz, Religious Sentiment, and the Beginning of the
Industrial Diet." *History and Technology* 27, no. 1 (March): 37–64.

Phillips, Sarah T., Dale Potts, Adrienne Petty, Mark Schultz, Sam Stalcup, and Anne Effland. 2013. *Reflections on One Hundred and Fifty Years of the United States Department of Agriculture.* Hanover, PA: Agricultural History Society.

Pivar, David J. 2002. *Purity and Hygiene: Women, Prostitution, and the "American Plan,"
1900–1930.* Westport, CT: Greenwood.

———. 1973. *Purity Crusade: Sexual Morality and Social Control, 1868–1900.* Westport, CT: Greenwood.

Pollan, Michael. 2008. *In Defense of Food: An Eater's Manifesto.* New York: Penguin.

———. 2006. *The Omnivore's Dilemma: A Natural History of Four Meals.* New York: Penguin.

———. 2009. "Out of the Kitchen, Onto the Couch." *New York Times,* July 29.

Poughkeepsie Casket. 1836–1841. Poughkeepsie, NY.

Pratt, Jeff. 2007. "Food Values: The Local and the Authentic." *Critique of Anthropology* 27, no. 3 (September): 285–300.

Pringle, Peter. 2003. *Food, Inc.: Mendel to Monsanto—The Promises and Perils of the Biotech Harvest.* New York: Simon and Schuster.

Proceedings of the Annual Conference. 1899–1908. Lake Placid Conference on Home Economics, Lake Placid, NY.

Providence Patriot. 1809–1934. Providence, RI.

Ramparts. 1962–1974. San Francisco.

Reed, Matthew. 2010. *Rebels for the Soil: The Rise of the Global Organic Food and Farming Movement.* London: Earthscan.

Regional History Project, University of California, Santa Cruz. "Cultivating a Movement: Organic and Sustainable Farming." https://library.ucsc.edu/reg-hist/cultiv/home.

Rhomberg, Chris. 2012. *The Broken Table: The Detroit Newspaper Strike and the State of American Labor.* New York: Russell Sage Foundation.

———. 2004. *No There There: Race, Class, and Political Community in Oakland.* Berkeley: University of California Press.

Rice, Stephen P. 2004. *Minding the Machine: Languages of Class in Early Industrial America.* Berkeley, CA: University of California Press.

Richards, Ellen H. 1898. *Food Materials and Their Adulterations.* Boston: Home Science.

Robinson, Jennifer Meta, and James R. Farmer. 2017. *Selling Local: Why Local Food Movements Matter.* Bloomington: Indiana University Press.

Rodale, J. I. 1945. *Pay Dirt: Farming and Gardening with Composts.* New York: Rodale.

Rodgers, Daniel T. 1998. *Atlantic Crossings: Social Politics in a Progressive Age.* Cambridge, MA: Harvard University Press.

———. 2014. "Capitalism and Politics in the Progressive Era and in Ours." *Journal of the Gilded Age and Progressive Era* 13, no. 3 (July): 379–386.

Rolston, Bill. 2010. "'Trying to Reach the Future through the Past': Murals and Memory in Northern Ireland." *Crime, Media, and Culture* 6, no. 3 (December): 285–307.

Rome, Adam. 2003. "'Give Earth a Chance': The Environmental Movement and the Sixties." *Journal of American History* 90, no. 2 (September): 525–554.

Root, Waverly, and Richard de Rochemont. 1981. *Eating in America: A History.* New York: Ecco.

Rosenberg, Nathan A., and Bryce Wilson Stucki. 2017. "The Butz Stops Here: Why the Food Movement Needs to Rethink Agricultural History." *Journal of Food Law and Policy* 13, no. 1 (Spring): 12–25.

Rose-Smith, Imogen. 2015. "Institutional, Impact Investing Find Common Ground in Agriculture." *Institutional Investor,* January.

Ross, Steven J. 1985. *Workers on the Edge: Work, Leisure, and Politics in Industrializing Cincinnati, 1788–1890.* New York: Columbia University Press.

Rossinow, Doug. 1997. "The New Left in the Counterculture: Hypotheses and Evidence." *Radical History Review* 67 (Winter): 79–120.

Ryan, Mary P. 1981. *Cradle of the Middle Class: The Family in Oneida County, New York 1790-1865*. New York: Cambridge University Press.

Sack, Daniel. 2000. *Whitebread Protestants: Food and Religion in American Culture*. New York: St. Martin's.

Saito, Hiro. 2006. "Reiterated Commemoration: Hiroshima as National Trauma." *Sociological Theory* 24, no. 4 (December): 353–376.

San Francisco Chronicle. San Francisco, CA.

San Jose Free University. 1968–?. San Jose, CA.

San Jose Red Eye. 1969–1972. San Jose, CA.

Sassatelli, Roberta, and Alan Scott. 2001. "Novel Food, New Markets and Trust Regimes: Responses to the Erosion of Consumers' Confidence in Austria, Italy and the UK." *European Societies* 3, no. 2 (June): 213–244.

Sayre, Laura. 2011. "The Politics of Organic Farming: Populists, Evangelicals and the Agriculture of the Middle." *Gastronomica* 11, no. 2 (May): 38–47.

Sbicca, Joshua. 2018. *Food Justice Now! Deepening the Roots of Social Struggle*. Minneapolis: University of Minnesota Press.

Schiesl, Martin J. 1977. *The Politics of Efficiency: Municipal Administration and Reform in America, 1800–1920*. Berkeley: University of California Press.

Schrank, Zachary, and Katrina Running. 2018. "Individualist and Collectivist Consumer Motivations in Local Organic Food Markets." *Journal of Consumer Culture* 18, no. 1 (February): 184–201.

Schurman, Rachel A., and William A. Munro. 2010. *Fighting for the Future of Food: Activists versus Agribusiness in the Struggle over Biotechnology*. Minneapolis: University of Minnesota Press.

Schwarz, Richard W. 1970. *John Harvey Kellogg, M.D.* Nashville, TN: Southern Publishing Association.

Sedition. 1971–1976. San Jose, CA.

Selfa, Theresa, and Joan Qazi. 2005. "Place, Taste, or Face-to-Face: Understanding Producer-Consumer Networks in 'Local' Food Systems in Washington State." *Agriculture and Human Values* 22, no. 4 (December): 451–464.

Sellers, Charles. 1991. *The Market Revolution: Jacksonian America, 1815–1846*. New York: Oxford University Press.

Sellers, Christopher C. 2012. *Crabgrass Crucible: Suburban Nature and the Rise of Environmentalism in Twentieth-Century America*. Chapel Hill: University of North Carolina Press.

Sewell, William H., Jr. 1980. *Work and Revolution in France: The Language of Labor from the Old Regime to 1848*. Cambridge: Cambridge University Press.

Shah, Dhavan V., Lewis A. Friedland, Chris Wells, Young Mie Kim, and Hernando Rojas. 2012. "Communication, Consumers, and Citizens: Revisiting the Politics of Consumption." *Annals of the American Academy of Political and Social Science* 644, no. 1 (November): 6–19.

Shah, Dhavan V., Douglas M. McLeod, Lewis Friedland, and Michelle R. Nelson. 2007. "The Politics of Consumption/The Consumption of Politics." *Annals of the American Academy of Political and Social Science* 611, no. 1 (May): 6–15.

Shah, Dhavan V., Douglas M. McLeod, Eunkyung Kim, Sun Young Lee, Melissa R. Gotlieb, Shirley S. Ho, and Hilde Breivik. 2007. "Political Consumerism: How Communication and Consumption Orientations Drive 'Lifestyle Politics.'" *Annals of the American Academy of Political and Social Science* 611, no. 1 (May): 217–235.

Shapin, Steven. 2006. "Paradise Sold: What Are You Buying When You Buy Organic?" *New Yorker*, vol. 82, no. 13 (May 15): 84–88.

———. 2014. "'You Are What You Eat': Historical Changes in Ideas about Food and Identity." *Historical Research* 87, no. 237 (August): 377–392.

Shapiro, Laura. 1986. *Perfection Salad: Women and Cooking at the Turn of the Century.* Berkeley, CA: University of California Press.

Shawki, Noha. 2012. "The 2008 Food Crisis as a Critical Event for the Food Sovereignty and Food Justice Movements." *International Journal of Sociology of Agriculture and Food* 19, no. 3 (October): 423–444.

Shenhav, Yehouda. 1999. *Manufacturing Rationality: The Engineering Foundations of the Managerial Revolution.* New York: Oxford University Press.

Shome, Siddhartha. 2015. "The Social Vision of the Alternative Food Movement." In *The Oxford Handbook of Food, Politics, and Society*, edited by Ronald J. Herring, 523–542. Oxford: Oxford University Press.

Shprintzen, Adam D. 2012. "Looks like Meat, Smells like Meat, Tastes like Meat: Battle Creek, Protose and the Making of Modern American Vegetarianism." *Food, Culture and Society* 15, no. 1 (March): 113–128.

Silver, Beverly J., and Sahan Savas Karatasli. 2015. "Historical Dynamics of Capitalism and Labor Movements." In *The Oxford Handbook of Social Movements*, edited by Donatella della Porta and Mario Diani, 133–145. Oxford: Oxford University Press.

Sklar, Kathryn Kish. 1998. "The Consumers' White Label Campaign of the National Consumers' League 1898–1919." In *Getting and Spending: European and American Consumer Societies in the Twentieth Century*, edited by Susan Strasser, Charles McGovern, and Matthias Judt, 17–35. New York: Cambridge University Press.

———. 1995. "Two Political Cultures in the Progressive Era: The National Consumers' League and the American Association for Labor Legislation." In *United States History as Women's History*, edited by Linda Kerber, Alice Kessler-Harris, and Kathryn Kish Sklar, 36–62. Chapel Hill: University of North Carolina Press.

Skocpol, Theda. 1992. *Protecting Soldiers and Mothers: The Political Origins of Social Policy in the United States.* Cambridge, MA: Harvard University Press.

Smith, Andrew F. 2009. *Eating History: 30 Turning Points in the Making of American Cuisine.* New York: Columbia University Press.

———. 2012. *Fast Food and Junk Food: An Encyclopedia of What We Love to Eat.* Santa Barbara, CA: Greenwood.

Smith, Barbara Clark. 1994. "Food Rioters and the American Revolution." *William and Mary Quarterly* 51, no. 1 (January): 3–38.

Smith, David F., and Jim Phillips, eds. 2000. *Food, Science, Policy, and Regulation in the Twentieth Century: International and Comparative Perspectives.* London: Routledge.

Smith, Kimberly K. 2003. *Wendell Berry and the Agrarian Tradition: A Common Grace.* Lawrence: University Press of Kansas.

Sokolow, Jayme A. 1983. *Eros and Modernization: Sylvester Graham, Health Reform, and the Origins of Victorian Sexuality in America.* Rutherford, NJ: Fairleigh Dickinson University Press.

Sommer, Robert. 1984. "More Than Cheap Cheese: The Food Co-op Movement in the United States." *Research in Social Movements, Conflicts and Change* 7: 71–94.

Soule, Sarah A. 2004. "Diffusion Processes within and across Movements." In *The Blackwell Companion to Social Movements*, edited by David Snow, Sarah A. Soule, and Hanspeter Kriesi, 294–310. Malden, MA: Blackwell.

Soule, Sarah A., and Jennifer Earl. 2005. "A Movement Society Evaluated: Collective Protest in the United States, 1960–1986." *Mobilization* 10, no. 3 (October): 345–364.

Spiekermann, Uwe. 2011. "Redefining Food: The Standardization of Products and Production in Europe and the United States, 1880–1914." *History and Technology* 27, no. 1 (March): 11–36.

Sproat, John G. 1968. *"The Best Men": Liberal Reformers in the Gilded Age.* New York: Oxford University Press.

Stage, Sarah, and Virginia B. Vincenti, eds. 1997. *Rethinking Home Economics: Women and the History of a Profession.* Ithaca, NY: Cornell University Press.

Starr, Amory. 2010. "Local Food: A Social Movement?" *Cultural Studies—Critical Methodologies* 10, no. 6 (December): 479–490.

Steel, Ronald. 1981. *Walter Lippmann and the American Century.* New York: Vintage.

Steinberg, Marc W. 1999. *Fighting Words: Working-Class Formation, Collective Action, and Discourse in Early Nineteenth-Century England.* Ithaca, NY: Cornell University Press.

Stevenson, J. 1974. "Food Riots in England, 1792–1818." In *Popular Protest and Public Order: Six Studies in British History 1790–1920*, edited by R. Quinault and J. Stevenson, 33–74. New York: St. Martin's.

Stokes, Melvyn, and Stephen Conway, eds. 1996. *The Market Revolution in America: Social, Political, and Religious Expressions, 1800–1880.* Charlottesville: University Press of Virginia.

Stolle, Dietlind, Marc Hooghe, and Michele Micheletti. 2005. "Politics in the Supermarket: Political Consumption as a Form of Political Participation." *International Political Science Review* 26, no. 3 (July): 245–269.

Strang, David, and Sarah A. Soule. 1998. "Diffusion in Organizations and Social Movements: From Hybrid Corn to Poison Pills." *Annual Review of Sociology* 24: 265–290.

Strasser, Susan. 1982. *Never Done: A History of American Housework.* New York: Pantheon.

———. 1989. *Satisfaction Guaranteed: The Making of the American Mass Market.* New York: Pantheon.

Stromquist, Shelton. 2006. *Reinventing "The People": The Progressive Movement, the Class Problem, and the Origins of Modern Liberalism.* Urbana: University of Illinois Press.

Suri, Jeremi. 2009. "The Rise and Fall of an International Counterculture, 1960–1975." *American Historical Review* 114, no. 1 (February): 61–68.

Szczygiel, Bonj. 2003. "'City Beautiful' Revisited: An Analysis of Nineteenth-Century Civic Improvement Efforts." *Journal of Urban History* 29, no. 2 (December): 107–132.

Table Talk. 1885–1920. Philadelphia.

Tangires, Helen. 2003. *Public Markets and Civic Culture in Nineteenth-Century America.* Baltimore: Johns Hopkins University Press.

Tarr, Joel A., and Mark Tebeau. 1996. "Managing Danger in the Home Environment, 1900–1940." *Journal of Social History* 29, no. 4 (Summer): 797–816.

Tarrow, Sidney. 2013. *The Language of Contention: Revolutions in Words, 1688–2012.* New York: Cambridge University Press.

———. 1998. *Power in Movement: Social Movements and Contentious Politics.* Cambridge: Cambridge University Press.

Tarrow, Sidney, and Doug McAdam. 2005. "Scale Shift in Transnational Contention." In *Transnational Protest and Global Activism*, edited by Donatella della Porta and Sidney Tarrow, 121–147. Lanham, MD: Rowman and Littlefield.

Taupin, Sidonia C. 1963. "Christianity in the Kitchen, or a Moral Guide for Gourmets." *American Quarterly* 15, no. 1 (Spring): 85–89.

Taylor, Frederick Winslow. 1911. *The Principles of Scientific Management*. New York: Harper and Row.

Taylor, Verta. 1989. "Social Movement Continuity: The Women's Movement in Abeyance." *American Sociological Review* 54, no. 5 (October): 761–775.

Thompson, E. P. 1971. "The Moral Economy of the English Crowd in the Eighteenth Century." *Past and Present* 50, no. 1 (February): 76–136.

Thorsøe, Martin, and Chris Kjeldsen. 2016. "The Constitution of Trust: Function, Configuration and Generation of Trust in Alternative Food Networks." *Sociologia Ruralis* 56, no. 2 (April): 157–175.

Tilly, Charles. 2008. *Contentious Performances*. New York: Cambridge University Press.

———. 1995. *Popular Contention in Great Britain 1758–1834*. Cambridge, MA: Harvard University Press.

Tilly, Charles, and Sidney Tarrow. 2007. *Contentious Politics*. Boulder, CO: Paradigm.

Tomes, Nancy. 1998. *The Gospel of Germs: Men, Women, and the Microbe in American Life*. Cambridge, MA: Harvard University Press.

Traugott, Mark. 2010. *The Insurgent Barricade*. Berkeley, CA: University of California Press.

Turner, Katherine Leonard. 2006. "Buying, Not Cooking." *Food, Culture and Society* 9, no. 1 (Spring): 13–39.

———. 2014. *How the Other Half Ate: A History of Working-Class Meals at the Turn of the Century*. Berkeley: University of California Press.

Upright, Craig B. 2020. *Grocery Activism: The Radical History of Food Cooperatives in Minnesota*. Minneapolis: University of Minnesota Press.

U.S. Census Bureau. 1975. *Historical Statistics of the United States, Colonial Times to 1970*. Washington, DC: U.S. Department of Commerce, Bureau of the Census.

U.S. Department of Agriculture, Agricultural Marketing Service. 2000. "National Organic Program: Final Rule." *Federal Register* 65, no. 246 (December 21): 80548–80684.

U.S. House of Representatives. 1950. *Hearings before the House Select Committee to Investigate the Use of Chemicals in Food Products*. Washington, DC: U.S. Government Printing Office.

U.S. Senate. 1898. *Memorial from the National Pure Food and Drug Congress*. Doc. no. 233, 55th Cong., 2d sess. Washington, DC: U.S. Government Printing Office.

U.S. Senate, Committee on Agriculture and Forestry. 1908. *Bureau of Domestic Science*. Washington, DC: U.S. Government Printing Office.

Van Buren, Martin Cornelius. 1977. "The Indispensable God of Health: A Study of Republican Hygiene and the Ideology of William Alcott." Ph.D. diss., University of California, Los Angeles.

van Waarden, Frans. 2006. "Taste, Traditions, and Transactions: The Public and Private Regulation of Food." In *What's the Beef? The Contested Governance of European Food Safety*, edited by Christopher Ansell and David Vogel, 35–59. Cambridge, MA: MIT Press.

Vileisis, Ann. 2008. *Kitchen Literacy: How We Lost Knowledge of Where Food Comes from and Why We Need to Get It Back*. Washington, DC: Island Press/Shearwater.

Visser, Margaret. 1991. *The Rituals of Dinner: The Origins, Evolution, Eccentricities, and Meaning of Table Manners*. New York: Grove Weidenfeld.

Vos, Timothy. 2000. "Visions of the Middle Landscape: Organic Farming and the Politics of Nature." *Agriculture and Human Values* 17, no. 3 (September): 245–256.

Walker, William B. 1955. "The Health Reform Movement in the United States, 1830–1870." Ph.D. diss., Johns Hopkins University, Baltimore.

Wallace, Anthony F. C. 1972. *Rockdale: The Growth of an American Village in the Early Industrial Revolution.* New York: W. W. Norton.

Walters, Ronald G. 1997. *American Reformers, 1815–1860.* Rev. ed. New York: Hill and Wang.

Walton, John. 1992. *Western Times and Water Wars: State, Culture, and Rebellion in California.* Berkeley: University of California Press.

Wang, Dan, and Sarah Soule. 2012. "Social Movement Organizational Collaboration: Networks of Learning and the Diffusion of Protest Tactics, 1960–1995." *American Journal of Sociology* 117, no. 6 (December): 1674–1722.

Warner, Melanie. 2013. *Pandora's Lunchbox: How Processed Food Took Over the American Meal.* New York: Scribner.

Weinstein, James. 1968. *The Corporate Ideal in the Liberal State: 1900–1918.* Boston: Beacon.

Wekerle, Gerda R. 2004. "Food Justice Movements: Policy, Planning, and Networks." *Journal of Planning Education and Research* 23, no. 4 (June): 378–386.

Wermuth, Thomas S. 2003. "'The Women! in This Place Have Risen in a Mob': Women Rioters and the American Revolution in the Hudson River Valley." *Hudson River Valley Review* 20, no. 1 (Summer): 65–71.

What to Eat. 1896–1908. Minneapolis.

Whittier, Nancy. 2004. "The Consequences of Social Movements for Each Other." In *The Blackwell Companion to Social Movements,* edited by David Snow, Sarah A. Soule, and Hanspeter Kriesi, 531–551. Malden, MA: Blackwell.

———. 1995. *Feminist Generations: The Persistence of the Radical Women's Movement.* Philadelphia: Temple University Press.

Whorton, James C. 1982. *Crusaders for Fitness: The History of American Health Reformers.* Princeton, NJ: Princeton University Press.

Wiebe, Robert H. 1967. *The Search for Order, 1877–1920.* New York: Hill and Wang.

Wilde, Mark William. 1988. "Industrialization of Food Processing in the United States, 1860–1960." Ph.D. diss., University of Delaware, Newark.

Wilentz, Sean. 1984. *Chants Democratic: New York City and the Rise of the American Working Class, 1788–1850.* New York: Oxford University Press.

Wiley, Harvey Washington. 1930. *Harvey W. Wiley: An Autobiography.* Indianapolis: Bobbs-Merrill.

Williams, Stacy J. 2017. "Personal Prefigurative Politics: Cooking up an Ideal Society in the Woman's Temperance and Woman's Suffrage Movements, 1870–1920." *Sociological Quarterly* 58, no. 1 (November): 72–90.

———. 2017. "Recipes for Resistance: Feminist Political Discourse About Cooking, 1870–1985." Ph.D. diss., University of California, San Diego.

Winne, Mark. 2008. *Closing the Food Gap: Resetting the Table in the Land of Plenty.* Boston: Beacon.

Winter, Michael. 2003. "Embeddedness, the New Food Economy and Defensive Localism." *Journal of Rural Studies* 19, no. 1 (January): 23–32.

Wirtschafter, Jonathan Dine. 1958. "The Genesis and Impact of the Medical Lobby: 1898–1906." *Journal of the History of Medicine and Allied Sciences* 13, no. 1 (January): 15–49.

Wood, Donna J. 1985. "The Strategic Use of Public Policy: Business Support for the 1906 Food and Drug Act." *Business History Review* 59, no. 3 (Autumn): 403–432.

Woodhouse, Keith M. 2008. "The Politics of Ecology: Environmentalism and Liberalism in the 1960s." *Journal for the Study of Radicalism* 2, no. 2 (Fall): 53–84.

Young, James Harvey. 1989. *Pure Food: Securing the Federal Food and Drugs Act of 1906.* Princeton, NJ: Princeton University Press.

Young, Linda. 2003. *Middle-Class Culture in the Nineteenth Century: America, Australia, and Britain.* Houndmills, UK: Palgrave.

Young, Michael P. 2006. *Bearing Witness against Sin: The Evangelical Birth of the American Social Movement.* Chicago: University of Chicago Press.

Youngberg, Garth. 1978. "Alternative Agriculturalists: Ideology, Politics, and Prospects." In *The New Politics of Food*, edited by Don F. Hadwiger and William P. Browne, 227–246. Lexington, MA: Lexington Books.

Youngberg, Garth, and Suzanne P. DeMuth. 2013. "Organic Agriculture in the United States: A 30-Year Retrospective." *Renewable Agriculture and Food Systems* 28, no. 4 (December): 294–328.

Zavestoski, Stephen, Stuart Shulman, and David Schlosberg. 2006. "Democracy and the Environment on the Internet: Electronic Citizen Participation in Regulatory Rulemaking." *Science, Technology, and Human Values* 31, no. 4 (July): 383–408.

Zeide, Anna. 2018. *Canned: The Rise and Fall of Consumer Confidence in the American Food Industry.* Berkeley: University of California Press.

Zion's Herald. 1833–1841. Boston.

Index